If you want to stretch your imagination and explore alternative origins for humanity, Mike Brenner's book will help you out. *Evolution Diverted* is based on ancient Sumerian tablets telling of colonists from outer space who redirected our species' evolution, not necessarily for the better...tales of invaders who, if they actually existed, left a legacy of trauma that is being played out before our eyes in civil wars, environmental destruction, aggressive devastation, and mass psychosis. Mike provides avenues of redemption for our fallen species, many of which make sense whether one accepts the alien hypothesis or not.

Perhaps those old Sumerians wrote their accounts just as present day men and women write tales of science fiction. This author, however, joins the company of Zecharia Sitchin, Christine Hardy, and other erudite scholars, who see the ancient accounts as more than metaphors.

Yet even as metaphor, *Evolution Diverted* reminds readers of humanity's perilous status and of the steps that need to be taken to prevent the disaster currently envisioned in novels, films, comics and other mainstream media. Read this account with an open mind; you might accept its thesis, reject it, or remain agnostic, but you will not be bored!

Stanley Krippner, Ph.D.

Professor, Department of Psychology, Saybrook University
Fellow, American Psychological Association

After reading *Evolution Diverted*, you will not see the world as you did before...or yourself, either. The book strips away much that is misguided, getting to the core of the human condition. Having known both Immanuel Velikovsky and Zecharia Sitchin, I am confident that if they were alive today, they'd be among the first to commend and endorse Mike Brenner's work, since it confirms and magnifies the validity of their contributions.

As a life-long student of Judaism, I admire the way Mike uses the Hebrew Bible as a lens with which, in one direction, we can appreciate the full reality of the Mesopotamians, and in the other, appreciate how the Jewish tradition developed out of Mesopotamian culture.

Rabbi Dr. Reeve Robert Brenner (No family connection to author)

Author of *While the Skies Were Falling: The Exodus and the Cosmos*
Senior Staff Chaplain, NIH Clinical Center, ret.

Mainstream thinking is neither solving the problems we face nor containing the cascade of facts coming our way that clash violently with conventional belief. The question addressed by Mike Brenner is what could have caused our species to become so out of harmony with the natural world that, along with the many maladaptive behaviors we display, we are recklessly injuring and depleting our environment.

The answer, he contends, lies in our remarkable genesis, the story of which has been hidden in plain sight for over a century. It can be read in the most ancient of written records, the Sumerian clay tablets, tens of thousands of which are available in museums all over the world.

The first person to consider the elaborate stories on those tablets about the gods on Earth to be actual history and not fantasy was named Zecharia Sitchin. Mike has combined the initial insights of Sitchin with information from more recent studies, and with his own understanding of psychopathology, to come to a startling conclusion: that we are a species both amnestic and traumatized, and that recognizing the truth about our state is the first step toward transformation and entry into a larger world.

The narrative contained in the Mesopotamian tablets is that the species Homo sapiens is the product of genetic manipulation performed by beings from elsewhere who crafted us as slaves for their purposes. Those beings also determined the conditions of our early existence, circumstances that continue to haunt every one of us, in the form of shame and trauma passed down from generation to generation unto the present day.

The challenge presented to the reader by *Evolution Diverted* is to try on for size a new reality; to explore its implications and possibilities without a priori claiming it to have veracity; and to find out for oneself if accepting that our species' original challenges are a factor in our personal difficulties can actually be of help in overcoming one's own. Given the chaotic state of our world, I believe that such an exploration is worthy of the reader's investment.

Linda Gooding, Ph.D.

Professor *Emerita*, Emory University
Department of Microbiology & Immunology

A remarkable piece of work.

Milton Glaser

Co-founder, *New York Magazine*
Faculty *Emeritus*, School of Visual Arts

Evolution Diverted takes up several threads of inquiry into early human origins. As an educated polymath, I've followed these since graduate school. Back then, catastrophes chronicled in cultural mythologies got dismissed out of hand by hardline geological gradualism. Now, however, evidence for massive cosmic impact flooding only 12,000 years ago is irrefutable. So were the destroyed, clearly advanced, pre-diluvian civilizations now obvious in ruins originally seeded by extraterrestrials? Or were they purely human? Why are the individual and geopolitical collective behaviors of our species so destructive — to ourselves and to the planet itself? Velikovsky, Sitchin, von Däniken, Hancock, Carlson – I've tracked them all. As a seasoned researcher, and now therapist in the areas of personal and inherited trauma, I had come to feel our species as a whole must have been deeply, perhaps fatally wounded. But how? When? In all that long quest, there was no credible source for the damage.

Evolution Diverted offers one. Whether correct in all details or not, here is a credible explanation. Brenner has critically reorganized Sitchin's rendering of the Sumerian tablets. Suppose the Solar System IS only periodically stable? What if we are the genetically modified, initially enslaved product of a technologically advanced, extraterrestrial species? Not "aliens" at all, but humanoid relatives themselves badly traumatized earlier on under the same sun? Where does the evidence for that lie?

Find it for yourself in the richly documented later chapters of *Evolution Diverted*. For they do something new. They point out in detail how such a traumatic origin makes perfect sense of so many disastrous human cultures, religions, and historical turning points. On that basis, I'm willing to say Mike Brenner has created a powerful, important, entirely readable book. It shifted me into a different paradigm. One in which a route towards healing glimmers in the darkness. You might want to read it ...

Michael Reddy, Ph.D.

Author of *Health, Happiness, and Family Constellations: How Ancestors, Family Systems, and Hidden Loyalties Shape Your Life — and What YOU Can do About It*.

Former Assistant Professor, Columbia University, Departments of Linguistics and English

Evolution Diverted thrills us as it merges nature, nurture, and history to describe the development of we human beings. Readers will find powerful themes in this courageous work. If we ever thought, *We're complicated creatures*, Mike Brenner's tale demonstrates, *And how!* This well organized, provocative book guides us to seeing ourselves and the world freshly by its updated account of our extraordinary biological development. Readers will find stimulating riches throughout that reward their attention.

James Silverthorne, AB, MFA

Independent researcher in Ecological Agriculture

As a spiritual carnivore, I like meaty ribs and I enjoy every aspect of a tasty offering. *Evolution Diverted* satisfies my taste…a meaty masterpiece. Before I had a chance to read it in sequence, I would pick up the book and randomly choose a page to savor. Not only is Mike's work well written, it is well researched, and includes wonderful illustrations. He does not merely talk about the jeopardy we are in as a culture; he offers hope based on our history and on choices we can now make. Read it.

Jonathan Cohen, Ph.D.

Clinical psychologist
International leader emeritus, *The Mankind Project*

At the beginning of this amazing work, Mike Brenner challenges the skeptical reader to ask, "What if…?" What if the ills that have beset humanity since the inception of our species really do stem from our misuse and abuse at the hands of aliens who called themselves gods and whose presence is evidenced in ancient Mesopotamian stone carvings and writings? What if an awareness of this historical origin could begin to heal our broken world through re-integrated spiritual life, reoriented therapy, re-framed politics? As a skeptical reader, I found the fascinating wealth and depth of evidence adduced from many different fields at times actually leading me to wonder, "What if…?" A stimulating read!

Peter Luborsky, Ph.D.

Assistant Professor, Department of Modern Languages, Ursinus College

As a teen growing up during the race to the moon, I read stories of earlier space travelers and inter-planetary escapades, such as Von Däniken's *Chariots of the Gods* and Velikovsky's *Worlds in Collision*. While those authors advanced their claims by citing accounts in ancient sources, the explanations were difficult to reconcile with what I was learning in physics class, and so I moved on into the future of space exploration.

However, with *Evolution Diverted*, Mike Brenner brought me back to that early fascination by providing a careful study and more complete review of the ancient texts — informed by recent scholarship on Mesopotamian history during the last fifty years. He poses the question "what if the Sumerian accounts of *Lofty Ones* — the gods, were real and not fiction?" To me, if they were fiction, why would the narrative — written by many different authors over thousands of years — continue to evolve and develop if there were no on-going relationship between humans and these *AN.UN.NA.KI*? Moreover, the accounts describe the home planet of the Lofty Ones, as *NI.BI.RU* — Planet Of The Crossing, with an orbit of some 3,600 years, and recent astronomical observations support the existence of a 'Planet X' [*SciAm*, v.314, n.2, Feb 2016]

This account of the vast Mesopotamian literature pulls together many loose threads and puts forward a consistent theory that addresses many of the criticisms against those earlier authors. It asks honest questions about how our human race might have been affected by our interaction with alien visitors over a time span far longer than our written history accounts. I highly recommend *Evolution Diverted* as a worthwhile read that asks, and sometimes answers, important questions about our pre-history, our shared values, and our pathological behaviors.

Stephen Loughin, Ph.D.

Department of Physics, Saint Joseph's University

Evolution Diverted

How a Forgotten Intrusion Is Driving Humanity To Self-Destruct

Revised Edition

Mike Brenner

Copyright © 2021 by Mike Brenner

All rights reserved. This book may not be reproduced in whole or in part, or transmitted in any form, without written permission from the publisher except by a reviewer who may quote brief passages in a review; nor may any part of this book be reproduced, stored in a retrieval system or transmitted in any form or by any means electronic, mechanical, photocopying, recording or any other without written permission from the publisher.

Earlier version published 2018 under the title **Finding Our Long Way Home**
First edition published 2019 as **Evolution Diverted**

ISBN: 978-0-578-61691-9

Intentions Books
239 Main Street
Reisterstown, MD
21136

Illustrations by Author
Production Services by Clark Thomas Riley
Cover by Sandy Carlsen-Rougeux
Printing and Distribution by IngramSpark

Dedication

For my children

Jane and Daniel

Acknowledgment

The primary thesis of this book is that the words and images unearthed from the ruins of the cities of Mesopotamia concerning the divinities who ruled those cultures are for the most part factual records, not fantasies. The first person to propose this radical idea was Zecharia Sitchin. He relentlessly pursued the history contained in the ancient artifacts, producing the books that were my first points of contact with a great deal of what this book conveys. I never had a chance to meet the man, though I once did hear him give a public lecture.

As an immigrant child in Palestine between the two world wars, young Zecharia was learning the Hebrew language through a time-honored practice: translating from the Bible. In class one day he raised his hand. A passage concerning the age before the Flood included a phrase that has always been rendered *giants in the Earth*. But an accurate translation of the word said to mean *giants* is actually *those who came down*. His teacher dismissed his earnest question about the mistranslation, but did not squelch his curiosity, which propelled a long lifetime of inquiry.

Beyond Sitchin, I confess that I'm unable to acknowledge the many people whose learning and support has smoothed and illuminated the path leading to the writing and publicaton of *Evolution Diverted*. If I attempted to do so, my effort would feel utterly inadequate. Could I possibly recall every one of the guides, friends, and helpers who have provided me with direction, support, encouragement, and love at points on a lifelong adventure that's largely, without my knowledge, been directed toward this life's work? Could I sufficiently thank those who generously offered assistance these last few years as ideas kept flowing through me? For all who've shared with me their wisdom, skills, and hope, my feelings are deep and complex and my gratitude is beyond the reach of words. Blessings to all of them and to the memories of those who've passed on.

And yet there is one whom I must cite. Without her companionship these last few years, the writing would have been more difficult, the result not so well-balanced, and myself less well-suited to present this vision to the world ... Delia.

Forward

The premise of *Evolution Diverted* is bold. It has come to sit within me with the heft of truth. I feel a lift as I journey with Mike's ideas, feeling inspired by the hopes they unravel…hopes that resonate with my own desire for a world that works well for all human beings. I derive confidence from the promise of the book that humanity will succeed in the great work of individual self-determination and collective harmonious integration.

Evolution Diverted gives us a fresh look in our "known" historical facts and resounds with a deeper and alternative truth to the global party line of human and planetary history. We have all participated in a conspiracy of limited view of self and species. Ultimately, I take this work into a resolve to become evermore personally self-determined and to promote that principle in my community and the world. We can overcome individual enslavement by the past and by false beliefs; racial enslavement by dominating cultures that have held us down and given us distorted perspectives of ourselves; and a global shackling of consciousness that threatens to doom our civilization to a smallness of spirit.

This book's expansive perspective on planetary history and human purpose helps us achieve a broader context for our lives and for modern society by lifting our minds out of a constricted sense of reality. Mike's work adds fuel to the freeing fire of mental and spiritual liberation. In looking back upon an expanded sense of origin, we are empowered to gaze forward and conceive new and different possible futures than we could have otherwise hoped for.

I appreciate that this book is grounded in psychology, spirituality, and science. It is an intriguing, fascinating, and absorbing work of scholarship on the one hand, and depth-interpretation on the other. A stirring is underway in human consciousness. *Evolution Diverted* can inspire and contribute to the various currents of our awakening.

Xavier Eikerenkoetter

Co-founder, Rhythm Arts Alliance, Los Angeles, CA
Spiritual Director Emeritus, United Palace House of Inspiration, NY, NY

Preface

Why read *Evolution Diverted*? Well...

Why the rise of Trump?
Why autocrats gaining control?
Why wealth and power concentrated in so few?
Why light-skinned people suppressing dark-skinned people?
Why the mindless exploitation of resources?
Why so much pain around sexuality?
Why religious hatred?
Why endless war?

What if there's a single path leading to answers for all those questions?
What if the answers lie in things we once knew but have forgotten?
What if they're hiding in plain sight in museums and libraries?

This book proposes that astounding truths long buried in mass amnesia, ones we could put to use to escape the global fate that's looming, are contained in texts and carvings recovered from the ruins of Mesopotamia. As you're about to learn, those ancient relics reveal that ...

• We were born into confusion about our identity and purpose, crafted by tall, fair, humanoids from another planet who used their own genes to modify the creature that was then Earth's most evolved homonin.

• The first human beings were slaves ... small and dark-skinned ... a circumstance that imposed on humanity an exquisite and costly sensitivity to shame, and a cruel legacy of racism.

• Intermarriage of the first humans with the alien race resulted in an elite breed, smarter and lighter-skinned than the mass of humanity...yet because of the identity of lowly servant within, they were deeply insecure about their privilege. Ever since, the elite have been internally driven to dominate and exploit those who are less fortunate than they are.

- Civilized humanity became locked in trauma through service in the endless wars of their revered rulers, and caught up in a love of war itself.

- Our violence-prone lords taught civilized humanity to worship them as deities, thus interfering with our innate connection with Source. That has led to hatred for people devoted to deities other than our own.

The tales of the *gods* of Mesopotamia, the basis for the conclusions stated above, cannot at the moment be proven beyond all reasonable doubt to be historically accurate accounts. *Evolution Diverted* aims instead to show how plausible they are, and to explain the causal connections between forgotten early realities and the plight of humanity, and to use those insights to light the way toward the kind of world for which we yearn.

Mike Brenner
Ardmore, Pennsylvania
November, 2020

Table of Contents

Part One: Preliminaries   Page

1.1	Our Journey	3
1.2	Life or Death	5
1.3	The Missing Key	7
1.4	Overview	15
1.5	Author's Note	19

Part Two: The Mesopotamian Tale

2.0	Preface	23
2.1	Proposed Chronology	25
2.2	The Mesopotamian Tale	29

Part Three: The Mesopotamian Tale Explored

3.0	Preface	37
3.1	Another Planet	39
3.2	Collision	43
3.3	Crisis on Nibiru	47
3.4	Settling on Earth	51
3.5	Crisis on Earth	61
3.6	Giants in the Earth	75
3.7	Deluge	85
3.8	Rebuilding	103
3.9	Conflict and Catastrophe	119
3.10	Finale	135

Part Four: Unanswered Questions

4.0	Preface	147
4.1	Burials in Ur	149
4.2	Desert Lines	157
4.3	Great Stones	161
4.4	Impossible Skill and Knowledge	169
4.5	The Origin of Civilization	175
4.6	The Origin of Our Species	181
4.7	The Human Condition	185

4.8	Words of the Bible	197
4.9	The Gods of Greece	201
4.10	The Cross	207
4.11	Planetary Anomalies	219
4.12	The Aquatic Ape	225

Part Five: The Rest of the Picture

5.0	Preface	233
5.1	Sexuality	235
5.2	Brother Against Brother	237
5.3	Jerusalem	241
5.4	God, Savior, Prophet	247
5.5	How We Are Ruled	253
5.6	Civil War in America	261
5.7	A Few Other Things	267

Part Six: Conclusion

6.0	Preface	273
6.1	What Now?	275
6.2	More Questions	289
6.3	May it Come to Pass	295

Part Seven: Appendices

7.1	The Psychologies of Trauma & Emotion	299
7.2	The Field	309
7.3	Endless Conflict	315
7.4	The Movies	325

Part Eight: Coda

8.1	Summary	331
8.2	Bibliography	333
8.3	Author's Parting Note	347

Part One

Preliminaries

Our Journey

We thrill to the glory of Nature. We make music. We dance. We create beauty with color and form. We write stories and compose poems. We touch one another in tenderness and ecstasy. We visit worlds of dream and mystery. We take pride in our labors. We embrace divine light. In these and other ways our lives are enriched, energized, and informed.

And all the while human life is plagued by destruction, waste, and violence. Our dysfunction is likely to be our undoing. Many of the realities of our existence are so awful that we are tempted to ignore them in order to keep going. For an update, though, we need only to read the international and national news in *The New York Times* for a few days.

Ameliorating the horrors that plague human existence will take more than incremental problem-solving and more than fostering kindness and love, as necessary as those activities and attitudes may be. It will require learning the origin of our tragic condition. *Evolution Diverted* goes to the dark beginnings of the story of humanity. Only by finding how we got into our trap will we be able to grasp the key that can let us out.

Our challenging journey begins with a mystery. How could Nature work everywhere with such magnificent perfection and yet produce as its most advanced life form a creature like us: destructive of ourselves, other species, and the physical world? The mystery deepens when we examine our problematic behavior, as we do in this book, and find that it is rooted in malfunctioning neurologic systems that evolved to enhance our survival. What could have turned brain functions meant to protect us into engines of disruption? Did something derail the process of our evolution? Were early injuries that we've been unable to heal inflicted upon us?

Life or Death

When we open our awareness fully to the splendor of life on this planet, we reach the limits of our understanding. We sense the fullness and glory of the living world and are profoundly moved. Our souls resonate with what we behold. We find a unity of form and function, a balance of need with ability, an economy in material and energy, and a breathtaking ingenuity. We are spellbound when we try to grasp the wonder of it all.

Yet there is one glaring exception: *Homo sapiens*. While our species is capable of perfection that matches the works of nature, we can also be utterly out of harmony with our selves and with our planet. It's encouraging to know that devoted people are striving to bring our species out of our collective madness, but by any objective measure they are not succeeding. Despite all that's done to have sanity rule us, not a single destructive trend has been fully and permanently reversed. Naturally, we must maintain the hope that we'll be able to rescue ourselves, yet it's clear that our gifts, our grit, and our luck will not be enough to save us if we remain on our path — the only one we've ever known.

The list of our aberrant ways is long: pollution in the atmosphere, in bodies of water, and in living things as a result of emissions, spillage, the promiscuous use of unsafe chemicals, and overdependence on plastics; deforestation; depletion of soil and groundwater; devastation of coral beds; record levels of extinction; exhaustion of nonrenewable resources; greenhouse gases; accumulation of radioactive waste; unsafe construction; overpopulation; slums; racism; poverty; economic exploitation; famine; abuse of children and elders; addictions; epidemic obesity; prostitution; human trafficking; pornography; child labor; genocide; terrorism; mass murder; and the epitome of human dysfunction — organized warfare.

A collection of nouns can only hint at the horrors they label. We injure and kill each other in ghastly ways and in great numbers. We compromise our health through ignorance, laziness, greed, and gluttony. We tolerate mismanagement and recklessness by those who have power and responsibility in industry, trade, and government. We elect destructive leaders. We surround ourselves with soul-crushing ugliness. We foster poisonous levels of economic stratification within and between societies. We choke in bureaucracy. We rend the web of life on which we depend. We foul our nest in revolting ways. We fail to consider the long-term results of our actions. In sum, *Homo sapiens*, Man Who Knows, all too often acts like *Homo demens*, Man Who Is Demented.

We are driving species to extinction at a rate that matches the mass die-offs of past ages.[1] While those sudden contractions of life on Earth were the results of asteroid impacts and super-volcano eruptions, the global biological disaster unfolding now is of our own making. There is no precedent for this. Of course, an evolutionary line can come to a dead end when environmental conditions rapidly change. But nothing in the fossil record suggests that any species ever wreaked havoc on its environment. Our understanding of the balance of nature and our grasp of the harmony of life tell us that evolution does not lead to the kind of mistake we seem to be. With nature as skillful as it clearly is in fitting each evolving organism into an evolving environment, how are we to explain that any life form, let alone the planet's most advanced, evolved into an agent of chaos?

There's no logical way to explain the disparity, yet that's exactly what we're obliged to do if we accept the scientific consensus that natural evolution was the sole process leading to the emergence of our species. In order to preserve the authority of its theories, orthodox science ignores this conundrum. The other way our culture has to explain humankind's origin, the one favored by religious orthodoxy, posits supernatural events. That constitutes another means of evading the quandary.

If we do not learn how we got into this trap and do not use that knowledge to find a way to escape it, conditions on Earth will continue to deteriorate, eventually reaching a point where the catastrophic collapse of life cannot be prevented.[2] We get a warning that this is coming when we watch one of our apocalyptic movies; then we soothe ourselves by saying, *it's only a movie*. The tipping point is not in the distant future; it is one or two centuries away–perhaps a bit more if our stopgap measures work.

We have truly come to a time of *life or death* decisions. The pages that follow propose that the information we need to save our species and our green-blue jewel of a planet is within reach.

---

[1] Scientists' predictions of extinctions to come are chilling. Compared with the numbers of living species at the start of 21st century–assuming no major change in current trends–by mid-century the die-offs in numbers of species will be: mammals 25%, reptiles 20%, birds 15%. These losses will be in addition to those of the 19th and 20th centuries. This rate of extinction is approximately 1,000 times the rate that naturally occurs during ordinary, non-catastrophic periods. In a 2017 article in the Proceedings of the National Academy of Science in the United States, what's taking place was termed *Earth's sixth mass extinction event*.

[2] In 2015 we got a glimpse into the future. Authorities in India acknowledged that the air pollution in New Delhi had gotten so severe that most of the millions of children who were growing up there would have seriously compromised health their entire lives. Westerners stationed in New Delhi quickly started moving their families back home. In 2017 the World Health Organization reported that ambient air pollution was causing the deaths of 3,000,000 children a year worldwide.

The Missing Key

We once believed that the arts, sciences, and religions of western civilization had their original sources in Greece, Rome, and Judea in the first millennium BCE. Then we learned that those societies received what they knew from Assyria and Babylonia in the second millennium, and from Egypt in the third millennium BCE. Now we know that the skills that constitute western culture first appeared in the fourth millennium in the land we call Sumer, in what is now southern Iraq. (Figures 1.4.1 and 1.4.2)

In the Sumerian tongue their land was *KI.EN.GI, Land of the Earth Lords*. In Akkadian, the next language to develop in the region, it was *SHU.MER, Land of the Watchers*. As we shall see, these two names were laden with meaning. In the Hebrew Bible the land was *SHINAR*, a derivative of the Akkadian name. We'll refer to the land as Šumer, rendering the Middle Eastern consonant SH as Š.

In the cities of Šumer in the fourth millennium BCE, scribes began to represent language in writing, something humans had never before done. The first symbols were pictographs cut into stone tablets. In the next phase of writing, those characters were turned on their sides. Then a script of strokes we call *cuneiform* was abstracted from the pictographs, c. 3,500 BCE. (Figure 1.4.3) The strokes were incised on small tablets of moist clay, a few inches on a side. (Figure 1.4.4) The tablets, when dried and hardened, were stored in temples, palaces, and merchants' quarters. Though the buildings of Šumer, made of soft clay bricks and unbaked mud, melted into the Earth long ago, the hard clay tablets remained intact in the ground, as did those produced by the later cultures of the region. Tens of thousands of them, written over the course of four millennia in Mesopotamia, the land of the rivers Tigris and Euphrates, are now held in museums and libraries.[1] They've been studied since the mid 19th century.[2]

The scribes of Mesopotamia wrote in rich, sophisticated languages.[3] The range of subjects was wide: records of royal dynasties and wars; legal codes and court proceedings, criminal and civil; matters of marriage and inheritance; love songs; memoirs; recipes for foods and beverages; treatises on mathematics and chemistry; astronomical tables; medical formulas and surgical manuals; works of philosophy; commercial transactions, systems of finance, and shipping manifests.

There is another category of tablets on which we will focus. In the same vocabulary and voice they used for all the subjects above, the scribes told of tall extraterrestrial beings in human form living among them and worshipped as divinities. (Figure 1.4.5) They wrote of the personalities, roles, powers, and families of those revered *gods*. Calling them *lofty ones*, the

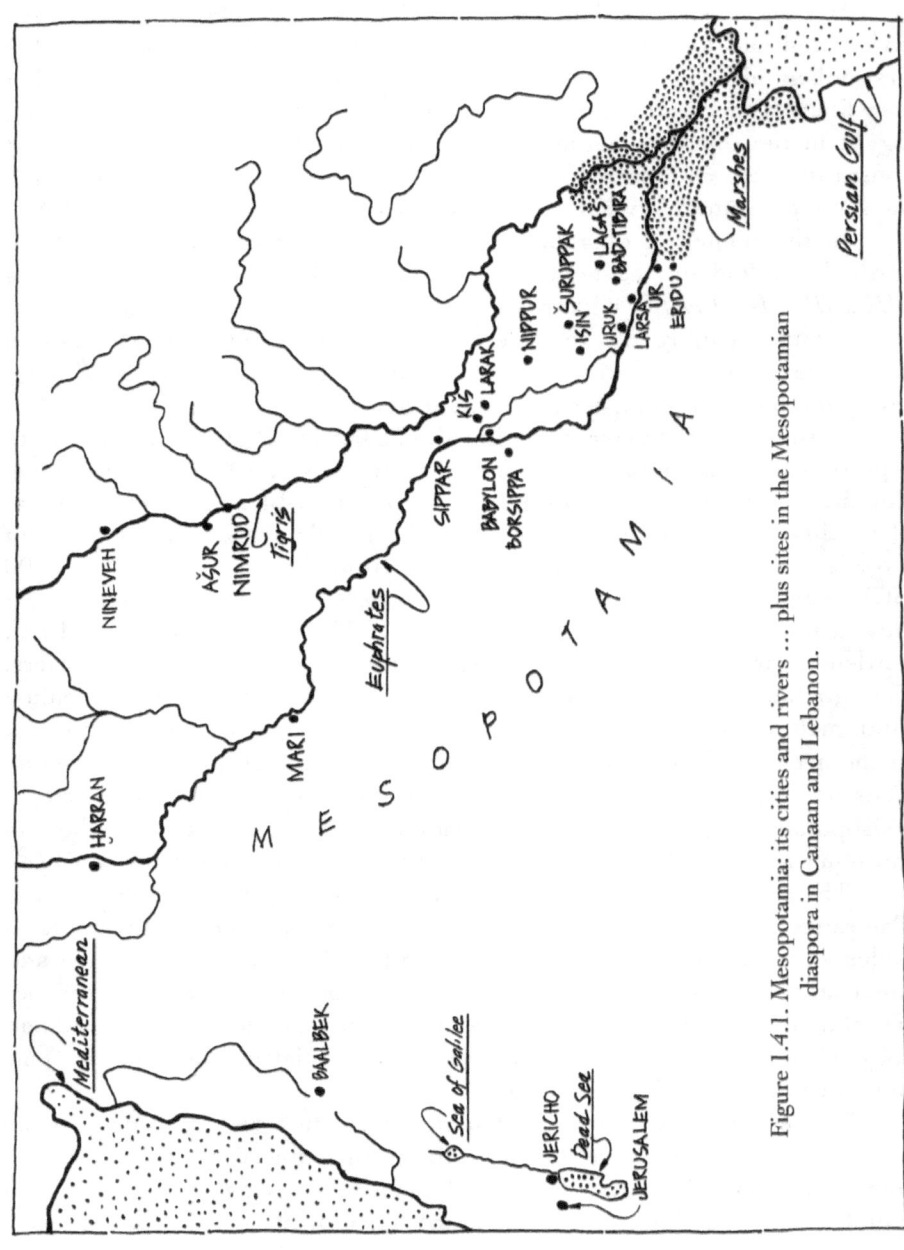

Figure 1.4.1. Mesopotamia: its cities and rivers ... plus sites in the Mesopotamian diaspora in Canaan and Lebanon.

1.3 The Missing Key

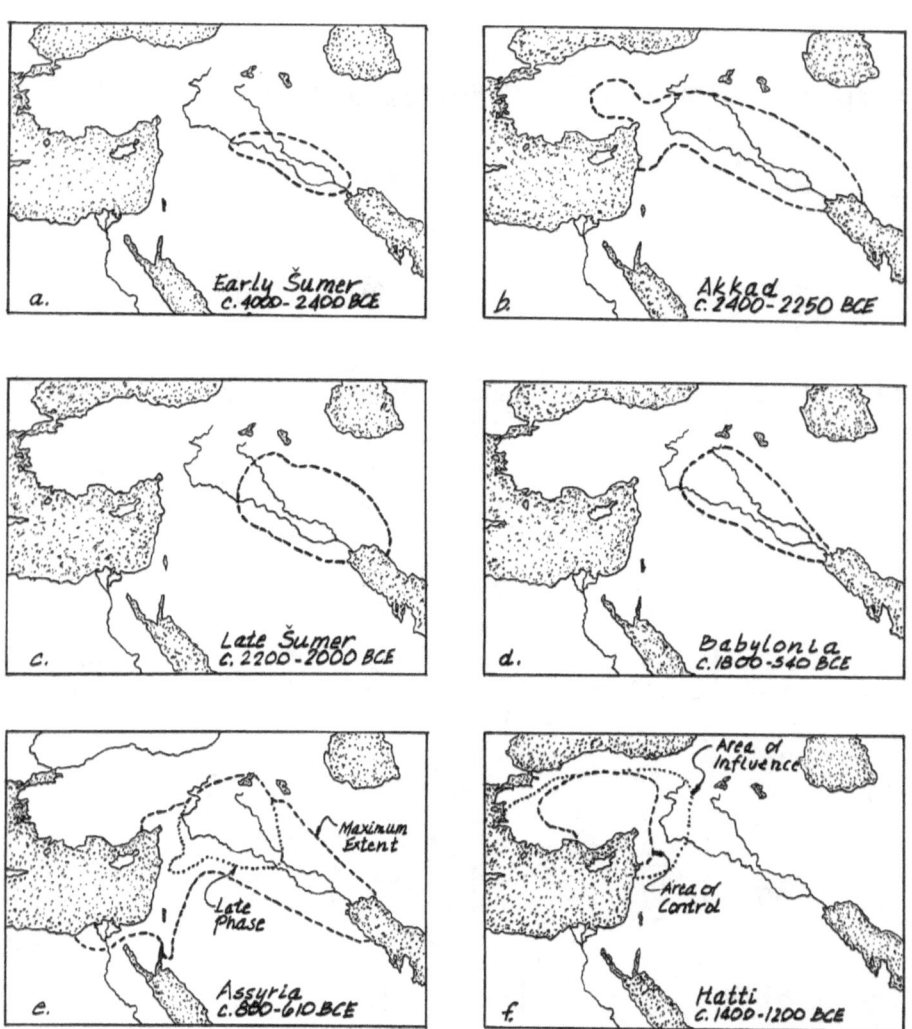

Figure 1.4.2. The Mesopotamian Cultures — at the peaks of their influence. Boundaries and dates are approximate.

		PICTOGRAPH		CUNEIFORM		
WORD	MEANING	ORIGINAL	ROTATED	ARCHAIC	MIDDLE	LATE
SAG	HEAD					
A	WATER					
NAG	DRINK					
KI	EARTH					
KUR	MOUNTAIN					
ḪA	FISH					
GUD	OX					
DU	GO					
SAL	WOMAN					

Figure 1.4.3. Examples of the development of Šumerian script, from earliest pictographs to mature cuneiform.

1.3 The Missing Key

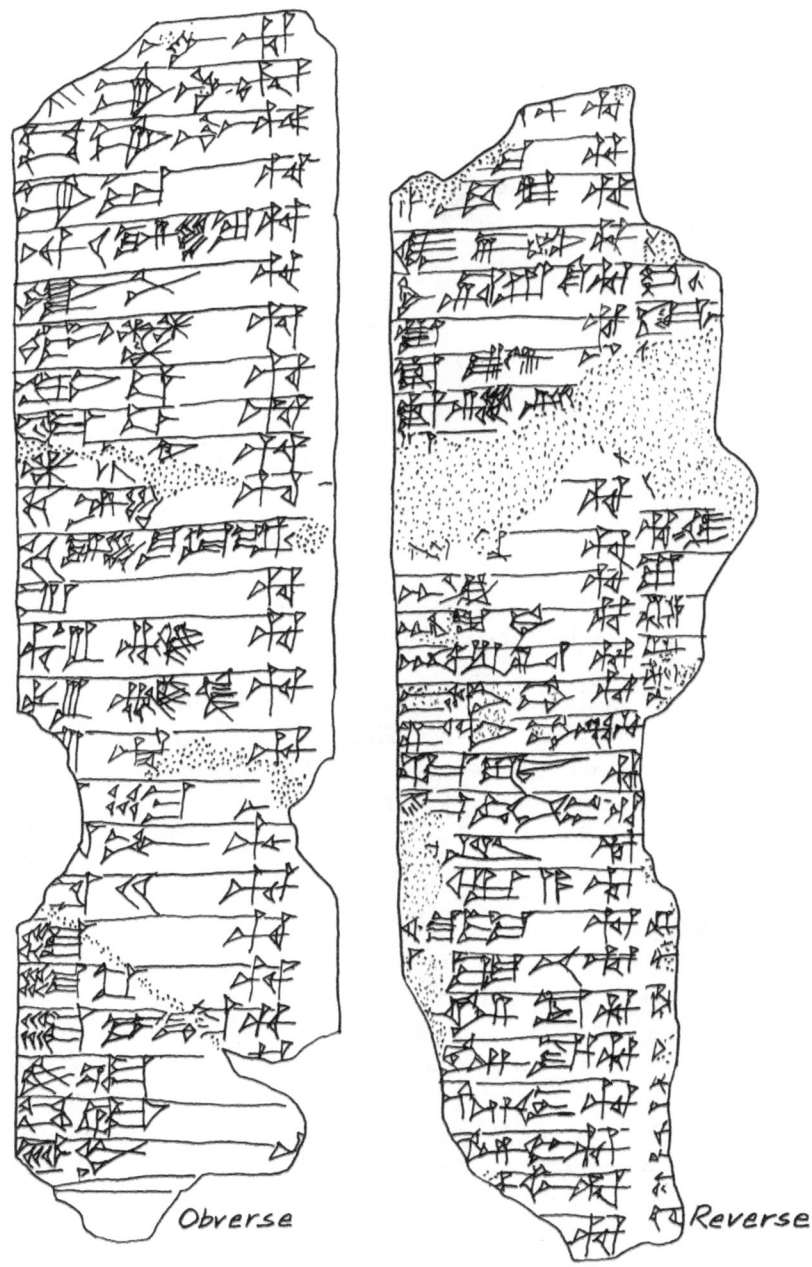

Figure 1.4.4. A typical clay tablet, with some portions intact, some damaged, and some lost. (The writing on many tablets was denser than in this example.)

Figure 1.4.5. The upper part of a statuette of a priest in devotion to his *god*. From the city of Uruk (Éreḫ in the Hebrew Bible).

scribes recorded what these *gods* told them about the planet they came from and what had brought them to Earth. The *lofty ones* also revealed how they combined their *essence* with that of a primitive terrestrial primate, creating a new hybrid species to be their workers and servants — humankind.

The belief systems of the archaeologists and linguists who first worked with the tablets kept them from thinking that the texts concerning the *gods* might be factual accounts. Humanoids from another planet could not possibly have dwelt on Earth and created mankind. Yet the scholars relied without hesitation on the tablets' overlapping accounts of dynasties and wars to establish a chronology of events spanning several millennia. The scholars sensed the solidity of what the Mesopotamians wrote about law, science, commerce, and warfare, but held that when it came to the early history of humankind and the presence of *gods*, they had slipped into a completely imaginary mode. After all, the Greeks and Romans had divinities who clearly were creations of the human mind, and the *lofty ones* of Mesopotamia were similar to those later deities. The scientific consensus was that the *gods* of Šumer were mythical figures without basis in reality. And so it remains in scholarship, theology, and popular opinion.

But that conclusion is problematic. Among other things, it implies a fundamental difference between the Šumerians and ourselves, yet the lives described in their tablets are much like our own. Their concerns were a great deal like ours. Their poetry moves us. Many of our interests (like

1.3 The Missing Key

meticulous record-keeping) are similar to theirs. The tablets establish a kinship of feeling across the ages. Are we justified in believing that the peoples of Mesopotamia simply invented godlike beings who were deeply involved in the affairs of mankind? Could they really have woven totally fictional narratives all through their factual histories?

Taking the ancient accounts of the *lofty ones* as intriguing fancy may have been necessary when the tales from Mesopotamia were first encountered. If, however, we give our ancestors the honor they deserve, reflect with open minds on what they left behind, and tentatively accept that what they wrote is essentially the truth, as we shall do in the pages to follow, the way opens to make sense of our massive dysfunction.

Figure 1.4.6. Carving in honor of King Ašurbanipal showing him making a water offering to his *god*.

Figure 1.4.7. Carving of horses and attendants in the north palace of King Ašurbanipal.

---

[1] One of the first troves unearthed was that of Ašurbanipal, king of Assyria, with more than 25,000 tablets excavated from the mound covering Nineveh, the city he ruled. Collecting and studying texts in languages and scripts, some of which were then archaic, he was the first archaeologist we know of. (Figures 1.4.6 & 1.4.7) Toward the end of the 19th century 10,000 tablets were found in the buried royal library of Lagaš, and 30,000 more in the mound covering the ruins of Nippur.

[2] The first cities were located near the head of the Persian Gulf. Later settlements were established in a northwesterly progression as civilization moved inland, first on the alluvial plain of the two rivers, then onto the piedmont through which they run. The discoveries of the cities of Mesopotamia began in the mid-19th century on the piedmont, where a mound covered the ruins of Nimrud. Archaeologists uncovered a succession of other cities as they ventured back in time, moving southeast, onto the broad plain below Babylon, toward the head of the Gulf.

[3] Akkadian, the tongue that evolved directly from Šumerian, exemplifies the fullness of the languages of Mesopotamia. The scholars at the Oriental Institute of the University of Chicago published the definitive dictionary of Akkadian in 2011. It had taken 90 years to complete and filled 21 volumes.

Overview

The main thesis of *Evolution Diverted* is that the tales written and illustrated by the Šumerians about humanity's origin and earliest times are truthful histories. This is more than just a challenge for scientists and scholars who think of them as fictions, and more than a rallying call for *ancient alien* enthusiasts. If a race of humanoid giants came to Earth and, to craft a servant species, combined their genes with those of the most advanced terrestrial primate of the time, the implications are staggering.

This book's secondary thesis is that the human condition re-enacts the confusing, humiliating, and traumatizing circumstances of our earliest life, transmitted over the ages through contagion, mass amnesia, and the collective unconscious. Here is how we shall proceed.

- The accounts left by our ancestors will be presented in a unified narrative called The Mesopotamian Tale.
- Then for each chapter of The Mesopotamian Tale we will consider its sources in text and image, and examine its correlations with scientific fact.
- Next, we'll show how The Mesopotamian Tale provides solutions to puzzles that conventional thinking is unable to resolve.
- Then we will use The Mesopotamian Tale to explain several aspects of human nature and experience more fully than we've ever been able to.
- Finally, we'll explore how The Mesopotamian Tale could open the way to the harmonious culture we dream about.

At this point, we ought to consider how personal processes could cause real discomfort to some readers of *Evolution Diverted*. We like to think that in intellectual matters we're guided by our intellect. When we feel distress, irritation, or even disgust in encountering an idea with which we disagree, we imagine that our emotions result from the disagreement. When a favored idea is opposed, however, the relationship between intellect and emotion is the reverse: feelings lead and thoughts follow.[1]

One's state of mind is pleasant when the basic facts he accepts fit together well, his understanding of things seems satisfactory, and his world generally makes sense. But if ideas one holds to be important and well-founded are seriously challenged, he instantly experiences a particular negative emotional state. Our nervous system is programmed to produce specific aversive feelings when an interruption of positive feeling suddenly occurs. Those aversive feelings then lead to cognitions that oppose the challenging one. (This process will be discussed in sections 4.7 and 7.1.)[2]

Another feeling process that can cause distress in the reader is connected with the phenomena of traumatic amnesia. After overwhelming events, one of the ways a person has of maintaining mental stability is by repressing his memory for what happened. But if repressed memories are suddenly brought into awareness, they can produce emotional upheaval. The Mesopotamian Tale begins to undo our mass amnesia for the eons during which we killed and died for the *gods*. Some readers will respond to the distress they feel as they begin to encounter the source of our species' traumatization by rejecting the idea that The Mesopotamian Tale conveys our true history. (To be discussed in sections 4.7 and 7.1.)

The thesis that The Mesopotamian Tale is largely true progressively gains plausibility as we use it to resolve one after another logical quandary that conventional thinking has been unable to address, and as we discover that it clarifies many puzzling human situations. But that is far from establishing proof. In fact, there's no logical process that can provide proof at this time. Confirming the validity of the thesis will require extensive scientific, scholarly, and spiritual examination. Too many facts in too many disciplines have to be confirmed and correlated for that to be achieved.

The only kind of acceptance that's possible now for our hypothesis is one that is felt more than reasoned, one based more on internal rather than external factors. It's the type of knowing the Greeks of classical times called *gnosis*, an immediate, deep understanding, distinct from the more concrete kind of knowing derived from observable fact, which they called *episteme*. But here we enter upon difficult ground, for humanity's desire to know things in a deep way can be high-jacked. People have at times behaved abominably because of what they've been led to believe.

While it's good to realize that there are limits to knowledge based in *episteme* that *gnosis* can bypass, it's important to also realize that *gnosis* cannot be relied upon when contradicted by *episteme*. What feels like solid intuitive knowing can merely be impassioned belief.

The Germanic root of the word *belief* is *lieb*, *love*. A *belief*, then, is just something one *loves to think*. How are we to distinguish truly knowing something from simply liking to think that way? Deeply knowing doesn't do to you the things that believing tends to. It doesn't drive you. It doesn't feel urgent. It doesn't claim to be necessary. It doesn't force you to defend it. Deep knowing seems to rise spontaneously, as if it's a part of your being that's always been within you. It fosters tolerance for opposing ideas.[3]

As you reflect on this book's account of the texts and images left by our ancestors in Mesopotamia, perhaps you'll feel that kind of knowing developing within you concerning their tales of the *gods*. I hope that if you find yourself struggling because an idea precious to you is being challenged by what you are reading, you'll consider that you're being asked to confront one of humanity's unfounded beliefs that you've accept as true. Indeed, if one day the tales from Mesopotamia are accepted as basically factual, a great deal of what is now thought to be truth will be demoted to the realm of long-held yet mistaken belief.

To avoid repetitive qualifiers[4], I've presented the world of the *lofty ones* with a tone that conveys, *This is the way it was.* The reader who's not convinced about the validity of my theses hopefully, instead of rejecting them, will ask, *What if this is the way it was?* [5]

---

[1] The 2015 animated film *Inside Out* illustrated how that's the way it generally works — feelings shaping thinking (and memory, too). That's what the 17th century philosopher Blaise Pascal seems to have suggested when he said, *The heart has more reasons than reason is aware of.*

[2] Leo Tolstoy was commenting on how new information is resisted when he wrote, *… the simplest thing cannot be made clear to the most intelligent man if he is firmly persuaded that he knows already, without a shadow of a doubt, [the opposite of] what is laid before him.* The physicist Max Planck addressed the issue in more pithy terms when he said, *Science advances, one funeral at a time.*

[3] In the ancient Toltec tradition in Mexico, *belief* was considered to be one of the four curses of mankind, along with *lying to oneself*, *pretense*, and *laziness*. Belief was to them a curse because of the harm that can come about when something false is held to be true. In some spiritual traditions, *deep knowing* comes from a resonance between the person's soul and the Oversoul.

[4] That is, phrases that quickly become annoying, such as "Could it be that…" and "It seems reasonable that…" and "It appears likely that…"

[5] In this *thought experiments*, Albert Einstein would ask, *What if this hypothesis is true?* He would then pursue the logical consequences of the hypothesis, as one means of evaluating it. The skeptical reader could do much the same with the whole of *Evolution Diverted*.

Author's Note

Not long after the searing events of September 11, 2001, I delved into the psychology and treatment of trauma in a specialized training program, fittingly, in New York City. I was amazed to realize that as a species we behave very much like a traumatized person. We're violent, self-destructive, both numb and over-reactive, out of touch with our surroundings, and challenged to learn from our mistakes, ... just like many people who live in the grip of overwhelming events. Humankind has always had a strong tendency to function this way. I reasoned that if we behave as if traumatized, we must actually have been, en masse. Since traumatized individuals often reenact the events that wounded them, our violent destructiveness suggested that whatever had traumatized our species must have involved violence. What could that have been?

A few years later, as I was looking more deeply than I had before into the psychology of emotion, I was taken with another realization: as a species we also act like a person who's trying to escape the emotions produced by the core experience of shame. We are prone to behaviors that defend us against shame-based emotions. Though the connection to feelings based in shame may not be immediately obvious, these behaviors include addiction, raging, suicide, and hostility toward other groups. I reasoned that the circumstances that produced so much dysfunction must have involved widespread shame. What could *those* have been?

It struck me that the tablets and carvings from Mesopotamia whose stories I was learning depicted two realms of experience that, if they actually characterized early civilized life, would have been profoundly humiliating and traumatizing: de facto slavery for the entire population, and service in endless warfare. Could the ancient tales be the key to understanding the sources of humanity's blatant disturbance?

I realized that my circuitous life path had led me to a unique place, one that gave me obligation. I'll explain. Early on, I'd had a pretty good grounding in the hard sciences. I'd been a young astronomy buff and on entering college I was headed for a career in applied physics. Later, my medical education oriented me in slightly softer sciences, like genetics and evolution. My experience as a psychiatrist schooled me in the dynamics of human dysfunction. My early years as an architect equipped me to evaluate matters concerning ancient structures. My encounter with the work of Wilhelm Reich, radical psychiatrist and scientist, woke me to the fact that generally accepted scientific ideas can be quite wrong. Sensing the truth in Zecharia Sitchin's take on Mesopotamian texts and carvings, it felt as if I had in my hands all the pieces of an enormously complex puzzle, and that I was obligated to put it together.

As I pondered all of this, *Evolution Diverted* started to take form. When for the very first time I mentioned I had a book project to someone I encountered, she asked if I was writing fiction or nonfiction. I surprised myself by saying that it would be a work of *anti-fiction*. I was thinking that if the Mesopotamian tablets and carvings revealed our true story, as I'd come to believe they did, a great deal of what we consider to be our biological and social history is widely accepted fiction, not fact

My witticism had come easily. It reflected what, as a psychiatrist, I'd done for many years: confront fictions that are thought to be facts. When we're young, we create stories about what we're living through, both to soften the memories we are laying down, and to make sense of the world as best we can, given our childish understanding of things. Those stories are preserved, and as a result the mind of an adult operates with memories of early life that mix fact with fiction. Actually, that's true not only for a grownup's memories of the past, but also for his perceptions of the present, since one's world gets interpreted through the frame of the stories laid down in childhood. I'd found that success in psychotherapy resulted to a great extent from liberating the reality of what occurred in the past (as well as the reality of what's going on in the present) from the invented scripts that conflate with historical truth and color reality.

I'd witnessed how the liberation of truth could bring healing to a motivated person. I began to envision such a process on a vast scale. What I was starting to write might have a role to play in a transformation of that sort. I imagined humanity making good use of a mass *anti-fiction* campaign.

There was something besides my personality making it easy for me to challenge generally accepted ideas in the way that my book was going to do: the knowledge I'd gathered from the works of serious nonconventional scientists. On my shelves were books whose authors developed theses using facts ignored or trivialized by the authorities in their fields. For anyone able to approach those authors' works without preconception, what they proposed often upended conventional laws and principles. They had labored in many fields: astronomy, cosmology, nuclear physics, virology, cellular biology, medicine, psychology, and anthropology.

I learned thanks to those neglected and denigrated thinkers that some of the basic beliefs scientists hold dear are simply wrong and that in consensus scientific thinking, valid principles and theories with bases in sound logic and methodology are interwoven with totally invalid concepts. The errors embedded in widely accepted ideas have several sources: obedience to dogma, professional jealousy, intellectual laziness, fear of nonconformity, personal ambition, and egoism ... aided and abetted by poor statistical analysis, shoddy logic, and fraud. In other words, the

1.5 Author's Note

practice of science is flawed, as any human enterprise can be, and as a group scientists are more resistant to self-correction than they claim to be.

Though *Evolution Diverted* is based on the efforts of scholars and scientists, it was never meant to be a scholarly or scientific work. Even if I could have mustered the patience to make it one, which is doubtful, I came to this task too late in life to have had the opportunity. If this book has the inherent authority I think it has, there's no need to add the look of authority that extensive referencing would afford. I realized early in the writing that I ought to be directed to inspiring, not to convincing.[1]

This is a visionary work meant to energize labors in a number of disciplines, to open the way to a more truthful world view than our present one…and thus to give the human race a better chance at achieving a long and healthy future. Under the most favorable of circumstances, it will take time for this book's theses to be substantiated, for its message to gain broad acceptance, and for effective action to be the result. I pray that the work has been well enough conceived and executed that eventually those who are inspired by it will accomplish its mission.

---

[1] Had I wished to cite original sources, I would have faced an insurmountable obstacle. Zechariah Sitchin, on whose work this book heavily relies, learned the languages of Mesopotamia – Šumerian, Akkadian, Assyrian, and Babylonian – and pored over original texts and translations. Over the course of his life he visited ancient sites and studied artifacts in person. Born into a scholarly family, he had a professional journalist's dedication to accuracy. Those who knew him considered his research impeccable. But his publisher, aiming for a mass market, concerned that extensive referencing would hurt sales, had him delete almost all his citations. Alas.

Part Two

The Mesopotamian Tale

The term *Mesopotamia* refers to the cultures that rose and fell in the plains and uplands of the rivers Tigris and Euphrates, in present day Iraq, and in the immediately adjacent areas. (See Figs. 1.4.1 and 1.4.2) The clay tablets, seals, and sculptures that are the sources of the narrative to follow were created by those cultures over a period of more than 3,000 years. The tales they relate begin with events that took place 454,000 years ago and end with things that happened in the mid-6th century BCE. Though each ancient text covers only a limited span of time or a limited thematic range, there is enough overlap between tablets and so much copying went on, that scholars, with monumental effort, have been able to delineate relationships among the cultures and construct a firm time line for important events.

Crafting the narrative of The Mesopotamian Tale involved taking the artifacts' accounts of the *gods* to be as factual as their accounts of the kings and kingdoms and as authentic as their legal codes. Piecing together information from texts separated from each other by time and distance to assemble a unified tale is somewhat subjective, as much art as science. Hopefully, experts in the literature of Mesopotamia will in time confirm that what you are about to read is a representative, accurate extract of the immensity of the source material. I have done my best to make it so.[1]

The red thread running through this fabric of tales is the presence of the beings the tablets referred to as *gods*. The texts and images reveal how we loved and worshipped them, labored for them, fed them sumptuous foods, attended their comings and goings, obeyed their laws, fought their wars, and learned from them all manner of things. Though the thoughts and feelings of the peoples of Mesopotamia come through between the lines of text and in the images, human interests and experiences were overshadowed by those of the magnificent *gods* who graced humanity with their presence. (Figure 2.0.1)

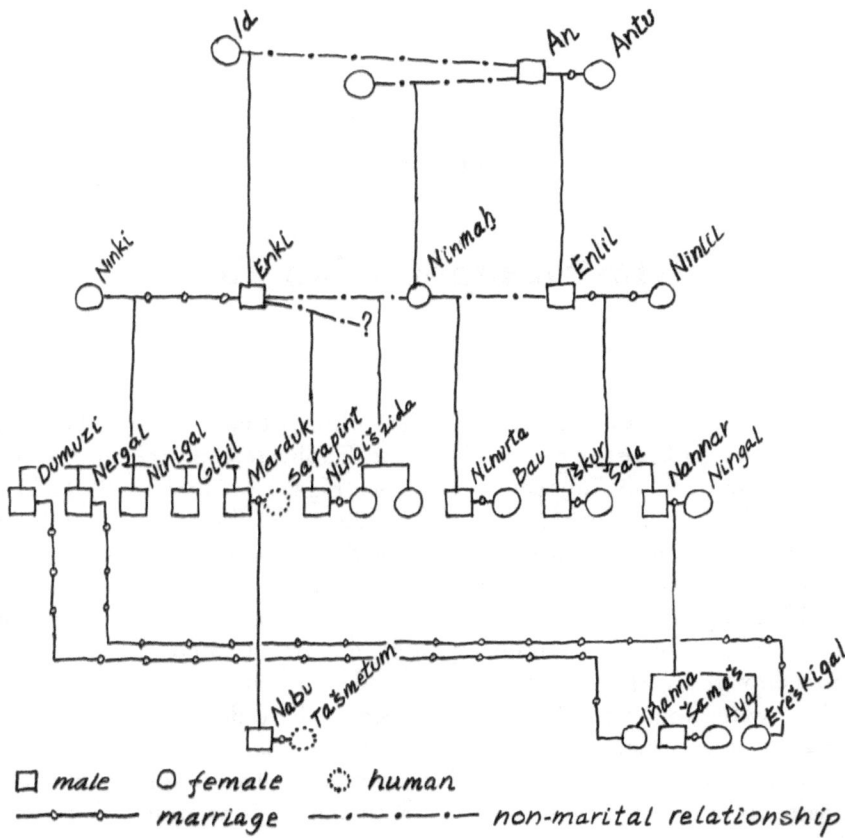

Figure 2.0.1 The Anunnaki Lords.

---

[1] *Evolution Diverted* endeavors to reveal how critical early events, obscured by mass amnesia, have shaped the human condition, and how we might use knowledge of those events to help ourselves. The facts and the story about the facts — that is, the actual events and the most accurate history we can construct — are intertwined. Acknowledging forgotten facts has beneficial effects, even if our access to them is through accounts somewhat flawed by exaggeration and elaboration, and by errors and gaps in the chronology. At this point in time it would be unrealistic to expect sharp definition in the reconstruction of humanity's early history.

Proposed Chronology

Date BCE	Event
14,000,000	The homonin line appears. Earth's temperature is cooling.
6,000,000	The genus *Homo* appears. Earth cools further.
1,800,000	*Homo erectus* appears.
1,600,000	A period of glaciation begins.
480,000	Another period of glaciation begins.
451,356	The *anunnaki* arrive and establish their first settlement.
433,356	Enlil arrives (while a period of glaciation is ending).
420,000	First findings of the enigmatic Denisovan homonin.
409,000	The first inland city is founded.
400,000	Sippar, Nippur, Badtibira, and Šuruppak are founded.
380,000	Battle on Earth between An and Alalu, his predecessor.
310,000	The miners mutiny. Crafting of *H. sapiens* authorized.
250,000	Earliest findings of *Homo sapiens neandertaliensis* fossils.[1]
200,000	Glaciation begins. *Homo erectus* dies out in Africa.[2]
150,000	Earliest findings of *Homo sapiens sapiens* fossils.[3]
120,000	The atmosphere becomes significantly warmer.[4]
100,000	Glaciation ends. Humans and *anunnaki* interbreed.
75,000	A period of glaciation begins.
65,000	Earliest findings of cave ritual (in Botswana).
52,000	*H. sapiens sapiens* and *H. sapiens neandertaliensis* interbreed.

50,000	Enlil campaigns to eliminate mankind.
45,000	Hunter-gatherers of African origin populate Europe.
40,000	Earliest findings of cave art in Europe and Indonesia.
30,000	Last findings of *Homo sapiens neandertaliensis*.
20,000	The period of glaciation reaches its peak.
13,000	The period of glaciation ends.
11,356	Nibiru crosses the Solar System. The global deluge.
8,500	Jericho and nearby cities are founded.
6,500	Farmers from the Middle East populate Europe.
4,000	Eridu, Uruk, and Nippur are reconstructed.
3,760	An visits, grants kingship to mankind, and initiates the calendar in Nippur.[5] Kiš becomes the post-deluge capital.
3,500	Marduk stages a coup in Babylon.
3,100	Cities in Egypt begin reconstruction.
3,000	The reconstruction of Ur begins.
2,900	Uruk is made capital. Indus Valley cities are founded.
2,600	Ur is made capital. A period of turmoil begins.
2,400	The Akkadian empire is founded by Šarrukin I.
2,255	Akkad is overrun. Ninurta is made Enlil's successor.
2,220	A ziggurat is built for Ninurta in a resurgent Lagaš.
2,130	Inanna attempts to gain rule of Uruk.
2,110	Ur, resurgent, becomes the new capital.

2.1 Proposed Chronology

2,100	Turmoil in Ur follows the death in battle of its king.
2,050	Forces loyal to Marduk make a thrust into the Sinai.
2,040	War of 5 kings loyal to Marduk with 4 loyal to Enlil.
2,024	Attack on the Sinai base. Šumer is devastated.
1,792	Hammurabi ascends to the throne of Babylon.
722	The ten northern tribes of Israel are dispersed.
612	Nineveh is sacked.
610	Nannar leaves Earth.
556	Nibiru appears.
555	Nannar returns. Nabunaid is crowned king of Babylon.
550	Nabunaid leaves Mesopotamia for Arabia.
539	Cyrus enters Babylon with his army.

---

[1] In widely separated locations in Africa, skulls have been found dating around the time of the authorization to craft *H. sapiens*. They differ so much from each other that their place in the hominin line is unclear. Furthermore, the 60,000 year gap between the authorization and the earliest findings of fossils of *H. sapiens neandertaliensis* needs explaining.

[2] A *Homo erectus* skull found in Java has recently been dated to 106,000 BCE, showing that groups far from Africa survived longer. Furthermore, a thigh bone found in China, dated to 14,000 BCE, appears to be that of *H. erectus*. Isolated, remote populations may have survived for a considerable time.

[3] Also the approximate date of the appearance of the modern Y chromosome, and of the origin of the species as determined by mitochondrial DNA conformity.

[4] Recently learned by studying layers of salt deposits on the floor of the Dead Sea.

[5] The Latin word for year, *annum*, derives from the connection of this calendar with An, who blessed its promulgation and authorized its maintenance.

The Mesopotamian Tale

Another Planet

In the cold darkness of deep space, far, far from the Sun, dwells a forgotten member of our family of planets. Once every 3,600 years, like a comet, it comes near. This planet was famous in Mesopotamia for the fateful way it crossed the inner Solar System. In fact, one of its many names was The Planet of the Crossing, NI.BI.RU (in the first language of Mesopotamia). It was riveting when it approached, for NI.BI.RU appeared as a great golden orb, its brilliance rivaling the Sun.

To the Mesopotamians the planets were great bodies of consciousness, celestial deities. With its majestic orbit and its brilliance, NI.BI.RU was deemed ruler of them all. As it passed by, if The Planet of the Crossing didn't come close, there could be drama in the heavens, but nothing more. Yet if NI.BI.RU came too near it would disturb Earth's atmosphere, crust, and ocean. This was a god to be reckoned with.

Collision

The Mesopotamians knew that in the distant past a water-rich, life-supporting planet had existed, circling the Sun between Mars and Jupiter. Their name for that world was TI.AM.AT, Maiden Who Gives Life. When NI.BI.RU made its transits of the Solar System, it crossed the ecliptic, the plane in which all the other planets spin, in the same way every time: it always transected the path of TI.AM.AT. On one fateful crossing, it came so close to TI.AM.AT that one of its moons crashed into her, tearing off a portion of her crust. The impact moved TI.AM.AT into an orbit closer to the Sun. Wounded and relocated, TI.AM.AT earned a new epithet: KI, Hollowed Out. In the orbit that had been TI.AM.AT's, the debris from the collision spread out, forming a ring of rocky bodies.

Crisis on Nibiru

The Planet of the Crossing is home to an advanced humanoid race, tall beings living immensely long lives. The surface of their sunless world was made habitable by a reflective golden shell high in the atmosphere. An environmental crisis loomed: the golden shell was failing, but the planet's gold supplies were depleted. An explorer had earlier found gold on Earth. An expedition was organized. If enough of the mineral could be mined on Earth and sent back home, the crisis would be averted.

Settling on Earth

The king of NI.BI.RU, AN, meaning Heavenly One, chose as leader of the mining colony the eldest of his sons, a prince born to his concubine. A gifted scientist and engineer, he would be called EN.KI, meaning Lord of Earth. This took place about four hundred fifty thousand years ago ... long before the age of man.

EN.KI's epithets in time would include He Whose House is Water (as lord of the seas), He Who Makes Things (for his technical prowess), He Who Solves Secrets (for his scientific knowledge), Chief Decider of Luster (gold), and Lord of the Bright Seer (i.e., the Moon, ruler of the tides).

In Šumerian, the first language of Mesopotamia, the settlers were called the AN.UN.NA.KI, those of Heaven Who Are on Earth. In Akkadian, the region's next language and the first of the Semitic tongues, they were the I.LU, the Lofty Ones. The colonists named their first settlement E.RI.DU, meaning Home Faraway Built.

After some initial difficulties, EN.KI found that gold mining would be successful. AN sent more colonists, led by a son with his queen, a prince outranking EN.KI in prestige. He would be called EN.LIL, meaning Lord of the Command. Tensions developed. EN.KI, founder of the colony and AN's firstborn, was unwilling to yield leadership to EN.LIL as his father asked. AN, prepared to lead the colony himself and to make one of his sons viceroy on NI.BI.RU, travelled to Earth to see the fraternal dispute resolved. The three royals drew lots and the winner was EN.LIL. Authority over the colony was to be divided. EN.KI would be chief of all technical matters and lord of the oceans ... and subordinate to EN.LIL.

With later arrivals, the number of AN.UN.NA.KI on Earth grew to six hundred, while another three hundred lived off-planet, the I.GI.GI, those who observe. Using rocket-propelled craft to fly from place to place on Earth and to ascend into orbit, The Lofty Ones were also known to the Mesopotamians as DIN.GIR, The Righteous Ones of the Sky Chambers. The region around E.RI.DU was called E.DIN, meaning Home of the Righteous Ones.

Crisis, Again

Golden ingots were flown to NI.BI.RU every time the shining planet approached. The mines and smelters in southern and eastern Africa were in full production. The working conditions in the mines, however, were brutal. Suddenly, having borne a hard fate for a very long time, the ordinarily obedient commoners had had enough, and mutinied. NI.BI.RU was still in need of gold. EN.LIL left E.DIN to see for himself what was happening and was taken hostage. AN came to Earth and convened a council. EN.LIL said he'd resign and return to NI.BI.RU unless the leader of the mutiny was executed, but to AN the miners' case was compelling. He insisted that a solution be found. EN.KI envisioned a way to resolve the impasse. He'd observed hominin creatures in the nearby wilds, small and primitive, yet similar to their own race in many ways. He boldly proposed a solution: he would use AN.UN.NA.KI "essence" to modify the native creatures for service in the mines. His partner in the laboratory would be NIN.MAḤ, half-sister to himself and to EN.LIL, a scientist and royal midwife.

Gaining EN.LIL's grumpy consent, AN told EN.KI and NIN.MAḤ to proceed. NIN.MAḤ, meaning Great Lady, revered in Mesopotamia for her role in the origin of humankind, was also known as MAM.MU, meaning Mother Goddess, and as NIN.TI, meaning Lady Life. Her symbol was the umbilical cord cutter.

After a prolonged time of trial and error, the new race was born. EN.KI's wife was the first surrogate birth mother, attended by noble females. Next, fourteen female AN.UN.NA.KI served as surrogates. Finally, EN.KI was able to give the servant face fertility...but not the long lifespan of the Lofty Ones.

Giants in the Earth

The new Earthmen were distinct from the two species that had been blended to bring them into existence, the four-to-five-foot-tall, dark, hairy, forward leaning African hominin, and the fair, seven-foot-tall, smooth-skinned, erect being from NI.BI.RU. Intermediate in height between the two, the human beings had features of each ... a head of dark terrestrial hair and a smooth alien skin, for example.

The AN.UN.NA.KI commoners in Mesopotamia asked that humans be brought out of Africa so that they, too, could be relieved of labor. EN.KI objected, so EN.LIL assaulted his compound. The attack succeeded. EN.LIL then took "black headed ones" to E.DIN, where they became laborers, farmers, builders, and cooks.

While the noble AN.UN.NA.KI males had female partners, hardly any of the commoners did. The ordinary AN.UN.NA.KI began to take human women as wives ... resulting in a second round of hybridization of the terrestrial and celestial species. Many of the fruits of those unions had greater size, intelligence, and longevity than humans had ever known.

Cities were founded on the plains and uplands of the rivers Tigris and Euphrates, as settlement moved inland from E.RI.DU, which was near the head of the Persian Gulf. The overall authority for each city rested with one of the twelve highest AN.UN.NA.KI lords. He and EN.LIL together appointed a noble of lesser rank to administer the city as its king. Kingship had been granted to the colony by AN. On NI.BI.RU, AN's insignia were the tiara, for his royal stature; the scepter, for his power; and the staff, for the guidance he *provided. Replicas of AN's insignia were given to the kings on Earth.*

Enthralled with the tall, brilliant, skilled, beautifully clothed, fair Lofty Ones, the humans living in the cities, materially dependent, inferior physically as well as intellectually, short-lived, dark, and naked, did not need to be coerced into serving their superiors. In addition to being the laborers of the cities, humans were the foot soldiers in the armies of the Lofty Ones. For this role, too, no coercion was needed. To fight and die for one's beloved god and to kill the followers of his enemy were glorious deeds.

The AN.UN.NA.KI, flying from place to place and into the heavens in their "sky chambers" and bearing their "thunderbolt" weapons, claimed divinity for themselves. In fact, several of the most highly ranked of the Lofty Ones claimed to be the personifications on Earth of the celestial deities, the planets of the Solar System and the signs of the Zodiac.

Deluge

The AN.UN.NA.KI were thriving, supported in luxury by their enthralled human servants. But disaster loomed. The Lofty Ones learned that on its next passage NI.BI.RU would come close to Earth, wreak havoc, and cause a watery catastrophe. Before the deluge would strike, the Lofty Ones could take to their spacecraft...yet what of the humans? EN.LIL had long before then come to regard humanity as an abomination, out of disgust for the interbreeding between humans and AN.UN.NA.KI. He'd even tried to decimate civilized humanity, but EN.KI had blocked his cruel campaigns. Now a natural event was going to do the job for him...as long as the people were kept in the dark. EN.LIL directed the ruling circle to swear an oath not to disclose the approaching disaster, thus sealing the fate of the peoples of Mesopotamia. EN.KI initially refused the oath, but eventually gave in.

However, EN.KI couldn't really accept the total annihilation of his Mesopotamian children. He designed a vessel that could save a few souls from the city of Šuruppak so that the population of civilized humanity could in time be restored. The craft would also carry "seeds of life", genetic material from the culture's animals and plants. He gave instructions to an esteemed devotee, using a trick to avoid overtly breaking the oath. Keeping the craft's true purpose secret, the man enlisted help to build it.

This is the sequence of events in the flood epics of Mesopotamia: • The golden planet approaches • The AN.UN.NA.KI learn of the impending flood • A powerful gale blows from the south • A loud roar fills the air • Clouds darken the sky • The Lofty Ones ascend • After massive rains ... a wall of water.

As NI.BI.RU passed over, the AN.UN.NA.KI watched in horror and grief as all they'd built and nurtured in Mesopotamia was obliterated. As the water drained off, they spotted the vessel of salvation. EN.LIL was furious over the violation of the oath. He was urged to relent and did ... and pledged to never again harm humankind.

Rebuilding

If the AN.UN.NA.KI were to once again have the way of life they'd been enjoying, the tasks ahead were staggering. As EN.KI and EN.LIL contemplated rebuilding the cities, restoring agriculture, and resuming gold shipments, they came to a momentous decision. No longer would humans be restricted to relatively low-level tasks. As the population was rebuilt, promising humans would be endowed with the knowledge and skills needed to restore and maintain civilization. There would be human scribes, scientists, technicians, teachers, artists, musicians...and even kings, for AN decreed that kingship would again be granted to Earth. As before, each city would have its Lofty One and he, along with EN.LIL, would summon a king to the throne. Only now the sovereign would be a "man of renown", descended from high ranking AN.UN.NA.KI and humans distinguished by lineage.

Following the flood, the lands ruled by the AN.UN.NA.KI were divided into domains. Three were assigned to members of the clans of the two royal brothers. The one around TIL.MUN was not; it was awarded to NIN.MAH, who, as sister to both royal brothers, would keep it neutral.

It would take time for the mud left by the flood to dry so that the cities could be rebuilt, food production could rise, and the population could be restored ... about four thousand years. A new spaceport, though, was needed quickly, because the two in Mesopotamia had been deeply buried in mud. A new facility was built in the mountains immediately to the west of Mesopotamia. While a base serving the AN.UN.NA.KI ruling Egypt had survived in the central Sinai, it was too distant from the settlements being restored.

Conflict and Catastrophe

The AN.UN.NA.KI mining colony had not been long in existence when a great battle between nobles took place. From that moment on, warfare among the Lofty Ones was never long absent. If there was no war in progress among the noble AN.UN.NA.KI, one was surely brewing. The city of a ranking Lofty One would win dominance over the other centers; sooner or later its forces would suffer defeat and another city and its lord would come to rule supreme. Alliances were made and broken. Rivalries waxed and waned. The flood interrupted this brutal drama, yet as the populations recovered, the armies were rebuilt and the Lofty Ones returned to their bloody ways.

MAR.DUK, eldest son of EN.KI, made a startling announcement. His astrologic sign was Aries, the Ram, and since Earth was entering the Age of

Aries, he proclaimed that it was time for him to ascend and be acknowledged as the chief of all the Lofty Ones.

Meaning to undo what he saw as the original theft of his father's rights by his uncle, MAR.DUK began drives of conquest, rousing fresh hostility between the two clans. EN.LIL was shocked when he realized that MAR.DUK intended to attack the Sinai spaceport, and that his army was unstoppable.

The prospect of his belligerent nephew having control of one of the two launch facilities so alarmed EN.LIL that he resolved to deny MAR.DUK the base with the only means available to him: destroying it. Dismissing dire warnings from his brother EN.KI, he empowered two of MAR.DUK's rivals to use the colony's long-hidden weapons of terror, seven powerful bombs. He also authorized the simultaneous destruction of five small cities just north of the Sinai, with the aim of killing MAR.DUK's son. In his fear and rage EN.LIL didn't envision the cloud of death the assault would spawn. Killing vapors drifted east with the prevailing winds, devastating (but not destroying) the cities of southern and central Mesopotamia. The near total collapse of Šumerian culture followed, documented in many lamentation texts.

The unintended devastation utterly demoralized the AN.UN.NA.KI. They'd brought about horror beyond anything their warfare had ever before caused. And the AN.UN.NA.KI had another grave problem to deal with. It had become clear that the Lofty Ones who'd come to Earth were aging faster than their peers on NI.BI.RU, and that those born here were aging even faster. Why stay much longer?

Finale

Lying northwest of the devastated portions of Šumer, barely touched by the cloud of death, stood proud Babylon, city of MAR.DUK. He convinced the remaining nobles, reeling from the result of having opposed him, to proclaim him their supreme lord. He consolidated political power. He revised the assignments of planets, claiming and renaming NI.BI.RU for himself. He had a new creation epic written, with him as its focus.

Marduk predicted that his would be a glorious age, but it actually was a time of turmoil in the region, in part because of the earthquakes, volcanoes, and famines that struck the Middle East and the basin of the Mediterranean. The shift of power from AN.UN.NA.KI nobles to human kings, going on for some time, accelerated. Human rulers for the first time waged war, plundering and destroying totally on their own. There was one more round of warfare directed by the few remaining AN.UN.NA.KI lords, finally exhausting the last remaining cultures of Mesopotamia.

A monotheistic king from east of Mesopotamia, Cyrus, was welcomed with his army into Babylon. From then on the tablets of Mesopotamia would make no mention of the AN.UN.NA.KI.

And so ends The Mesopotamian Tale.

Part Three

The Mesopotamian Tale Explored

We are about to discuss The Mesopotamian Tale, each of its ten parts accompanied by textual and visual source material, supportive science, and this author's interpretations and speculations. The four categories of content involved will be presented in four different typefaces:

- *The Mesopotamian Tale*

- Quotations from Mesopotamian & biblical sources

- Paraphrases of Mesopotamian and biblical sources

- Author's commentary

Another Planet

In the cold of deep space, far, far from the Sun, dwells a now forgotten member of our family of planets. Once every 3,600 years, like a comet, it comes near. This planet was famous in Mesopotamia for the fateful way it crossed the inner Solar System. In fact, one of its many names was The Planet of the Crossing, NI.BI.RU (in the first language of Mesopotamia). It was riveting when it approached, for NI.BI.RU appeared as a great golden orb, its brilliance rivaling the Sun.

Revered in Mesopotamia, a large planet moves through the Solar System in a vast, elongated orbit. Trends in astronomy make it easier to accept the existence of an undiscovered major planet. (Figure 3.1.1)

- Astronomers concur that there's a large body in our system beyond the known planets. Its presence was first posited to explain perturbations in the orbits of Uranus and Neptune. It is also affecting the motions of small bodies in the distant Kuiper Belt. The consensus is that this planet is more massive than Earth and that it's moving in our direction.[1]
- It is now generally understood that the early Solar System was not stable and that significant rearrangements took place before the planets settled into their present orbits. The giants Uranus and Neptune, for example, must once have been located elsewhere. Planets form by the gravitational accretion of matter from their surroundings. There could not have been enough material available for those two bodies to have grown so massive if they had they drawn matter only from their current vicinities.[2]
- Scientists have recently worked out the math describing how a planet can be ejected from its system. Those calculations were done for systems with two stars, yet a conjunction of Jupiter and Saturn could have ejected a planet in the same way, since their combined mass is greater than that of many small stars. Furthermore, if a planet can be ejected from a system, it is logical that a planet can be *almost* ejected, that is, sent from its circular orbit into a highly elongated one. Some of the planets recently discovered orbiting nearby stars have eccentric paths, looping far from their suns, just as the tablets say Nibiru does. In the well-founded consensus about the development of sun systems, planets take form while in circular orbits relatively close to their stars. That implies that the newly found planets moving around nearby stars in greatly elongated ellipses first coalesced in circular orbits and were later ejected.

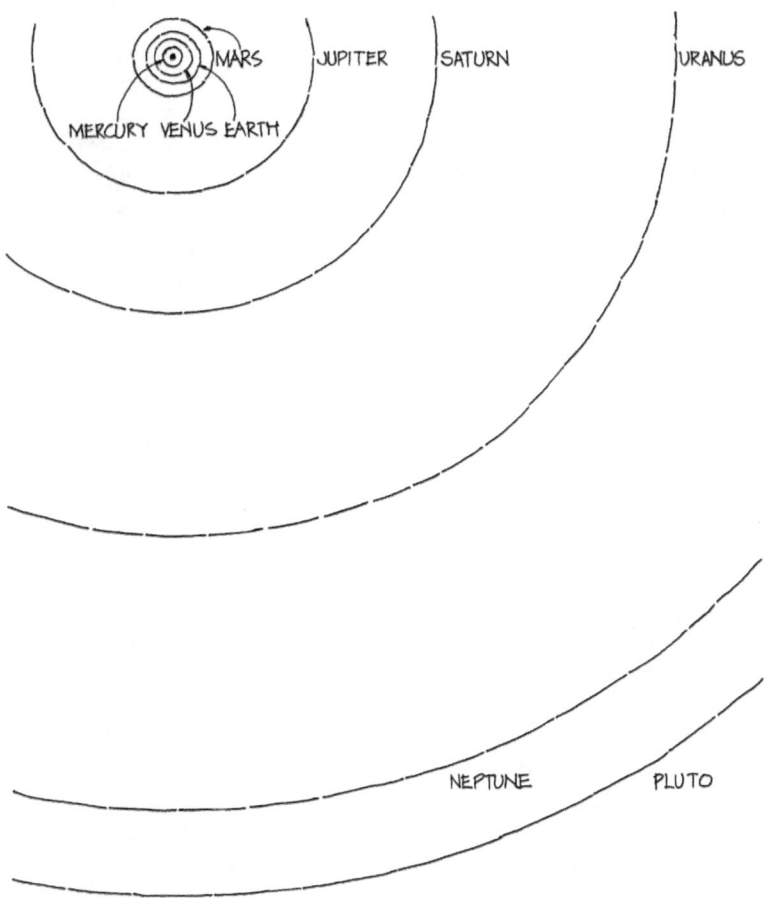

Figure 3.1.1. The orbits of the known planets, showing their relative distances from the sun. (Pluto's bizarre path cannot be accurately represented here.)

Nibiru is an exception in our Solar System, but its orbit may be a common type in our Galaxy. It appears that Nibiru developed in the same way as did the known planets in our system, gathering material in its vicinity while moving in a circle around the Sun ... and that with the Sun's radiant energy it became a platform for the development of life ... and that it later was flung into an elongated path by a gravitational slingshot created by other planets.[3]

3.1 Another Planet

To the Mesopotamians the planets were great bodies of consciousness, celestial deities. With its majestic orbit and its brilliance, NI.BI.RU was deemed ruler of them all. As it passed by, if The Planet of the Crossing didn't come close, there could be drama in the heavens, but nothing more. Yet if NI.BI.RU came too near, it would disrupt Earth's atmosphere, crust, and ocean. This was a god to be reckoned with.

When Nibiru is in deep space, where the Mesopotamian texts say it dwells, it lies below the ecliptic, the plane in which the known planets reside. When Nibiru approaches the Sun, it passes through that plane. After it loops around the Sun and begins its outbound journey, it transects the ecliptic again. It was called the *Planet of the Crossing* because one of its crossings of the plane was fateful, as we discuss in the next chapter.

---

[1] In January, 2016, a discussion about the undiscovered planet made the front page of The New York Times. One of the American astronomers leading the search for the planet was quoted expressing confidence that it would soon be spotted. Earlier, a Spanish astronomer, surely unaware that he was agreeing with the Šumerian creation epic, calculated that this planet has an elongated path that brings it through the Solar System at intervals of a few thousand years.

[2] Astronomers propose that they were pulled out of locations nearer the Sun by conjunctions of the two other giant planets, Saturn and Jupiter. In the 1950s Immanuel Velikovsky presented radical ideas about planetary rearrangement. From his study of Egyptian, Vedic, and late Mesopotamian texts, he concluded that quite recently there had been instability in the system. He proposed that Venus formerly had an eccentric path that involved periodic close encounters with Earth — including one that facilitated the Hebrews' escape from Egypt. An early Šumerian tablet lends support to his thesis; it tells that in a realignment of the planets Venus received a *glorious dwelling place*, a typically Šumerian way of describing a circular orbit.

[3] We use gravitational slingshots to accelerate space probes, sending them far out in the Solar System ... and beyond.

Collision

The Mesopotamians knew that in the distant past, a water-rich, life-supporting planet had existed, circling the Sun between Mars and Jupiter. Their name for that world was TI.AM.AT, meaning Maiden Who Gives Life. When NI.BI.RU made its transits of the Solar System, it crossed the ecliptic, the plane in which all the other planets spin, in the same way every time: it always transected the path of TI.AM.AT. On one fateful crossing, NI.BI.RU came so close to TI.AM.AT that one of its moons crashed into her, tearing off a portion of her crust. The impact drove TI.AM.AT into an orbit closer to the Sun. Wounded and relocated, TI.AM.AT earned a new epithet: KI, meaning Hollowed Out. In the orbit that had been TI.AM.AT's, the debris from the collision spread out, forming a ring of rocky bodies.

Tiamat was struck by one of Nibiru's moons. Part of the planet was torn away and reduced to fragments. The impact moved the wounded planet closer to the Sun; it found an orbit between Mars and Venus.[1] Over time it reshaped itself into a slightly smaller sphere, becoming Ki ... our Earth. The tablets say that Tiamat was watery. That fits. Seventy percent of Earth's surface is water. The debris from the collision spread out along Tiamat's original orbit, forming a band of rocks...the Asteroid Belt.

The interaction between the two planets is related as a battle between a pair of celestial *gods*, Tiamat, disruptive and rebellious, and Nibiru, righteous and corrective.[2] The Babylonian creation epic, known by its first words, *enuma elish*, *When in the Heights*, calls the ring of minor bodies resulting from the collision a *bracelet*. Speaking of the hero Planet of the Crossing and the miscreant Tiamat, the epic states:

the other half of her he set up as a screen for the skies
locking the pieces together as watchmen he stationed them ...
he bent Tiamat's [bottom part] to form the great band as a bracelet

Long before the first Mesopotamian tablets were recovered and translated, a highly modified version of many of the events they reported had been promulgated...in the Hebrew Bible. Its authors apparently revered the then ancient tales as treasures from the culture that had given birth to their own. Their attachment to the Mesopotamian creation epics led the Jewish scribes to fold the olden accounts of the collision between two planetary *gods* into their new story of the creation of the Universe by the Maker. As they put it at the opening of the entire edifice:

In the beginning God created the heaven and the earth ...
And God said let there be a firmament in the midst of the waters ...
And God called the firmament heaven

This is the most prominent of countless places where the authors of the Hebrew Bible incorporated Mesopotamian texts. The Hebrew word rendered as *firmament, raki'a*, really means *beaten surface* ... such as a goldsmith might hammer out, recalling the Babylonian reference cited above: *bracelet*. The word that is rendered as *heaven* is really a contraction meaning *where waters were*. Thus, a literal translation from the Hebrew would say that the Asteroid Belt, consisting of fragments arranged in a ring like a *bracelet*, and resulting from a *hammering* by Nibiru's moon, occupied the place *where waters were*, that is, where watery Tiamat once dwelled. Our planet's violent history, revealed to the Šumerians by the *gods*, still resonated and couldn't be ignored. Faithful to the past, the Hebrew scribes repurposed ancient terms as they composed the scriptures of the new belief system.

Other biblical tales of events in the heavens take on new meaning when understood as adaptations of the Šumerian account of Tiamat's encounter with Nibiru. Speaking about the *God of the Universe*, not the *ruling celestial planet* of the Šumerians, Isaiah says:

[the mighty Lord] carved the haughty one, made spin the watery monster, drained off the waters of the mighty TEHOM

Tehom is traditionally translated as *abyss*, and yet it really is a Hebrew rendition of Tiamat. Isaiah contains another passage that we are now in a position to read as an account of the collision with Nibiru's moon.

from a far away land they come,
from the end point of the Heaven
do the Lord and his weapons of wrath come to destroy ...
therefore will I agitate the Heaven
and Earth shall be shaken out its place
when the Lord of Hosts shall be crossing
the day of His burning wrath

3.2 Collision

There are actions of God in the Psalms that echo those of Nibiru in the Mesopotamian tablets:

The heavens bespeak the glory of the Lord
The hammered bracelet proclaims His handiwork ...
By thy might, the waters Thou didst disperse,
the leader of the watery monsters Thou didst break up

And in the Book of Job:

[the celestial Lord smote] the assistants of the haughty one ... the hammered canopy stretched out in the place of the watery deep, the Earth suspended in the void ... His energy the Holy One did cleave, His wind the hammered bracelet measured out in the place of TEHOM

The Jewish scribes evidently believed that the history recorded by their predecessors, the Mesopotamian scribes, should not be discarded; to them the olden tales must have had both the ring of truth and the feel of precious keepsakes. Yet they didn't use the texts they revered in other than fragmentary, esoteric ways. Perhaps it didn't seem fitting for more than a few among their people to know that the new scriptures glorifying the Creator of the Universe were drawing upon ancient accounts of the deified planet once thought to rule the Solar System. Thus, the scribes secretly embedded terms taken from then-ancient historically based accounts into the sacred myths of their evolving faith.

The biblical authors were composing their poetry in a time of enormous change: from the city-states of the olden gods, to the universe of the One God; from the only world civilized humanity had ever known, to one yet to be defined. It was natural for the written word to serve as a bridge joining the two worlds, creating a record of the transition from the one to the other.[3] When we study the Hebrew Bible we get to gaze across the bridge its words provide, glimpsing a much older world.

We next discuss what the Šumerians were told about Nibiru's society.

---

[1] The kinetic, gravitational, and electromagnetic interactions between Tiamat, Nibiru, and Nibiru's moon apparently reduced the orbital momentum of Tiamat so much that it had to relocate in an orbit much closer to the Sun.

[2] The intersection of the orbit of Nibiru with the orbit of Tiamat suggests that Tiamat had a role in Nibiru's ejection from the inner Solar System. That could be why Tiamat was characterized as a trouble-maker.

[3] In the Psalms, the bridge is quite solid. The Jewish psalmists adapted the poetic forms of Mesopotamian psalms and hymns, as well as much of their imagery...and occasionally, entire sequences of lines.

Crisis on Nibiru

The Planet of the Crossing is home to an advanced humanoid race, tall beings living immensely long lives. The surface of their sunless world was made habitable by a reflective golden shell high in its atmosphere.

For a planet in the frigid depths of space to house advanced native life, it must once have been close to its sun, since life cannot evolve very far without a star nearby. If the life-supporting energy of a planet's sun was to become unavailable, life might be maintained with artificially produced energy. This apparently was what happened on Nibiru. A humanoid species had evolved while their planet was in its original place in the inner Solar System. Eventually they developed a culture advanced enough for their scientists to know they were about to be flung far from the Sun, and for their engineers to know how to prepare for the crisis and survive.

The temperature on the exposed surface of a planet deep in space is not compatible with life. There were three options for Nibiru's population: excavate underground caverns, build protective domes over areas on the surface, or develop an enclosure for the entire atmosphere. Without giving details, the tablets imply that Nibiru chose the third option.[1]

Extrapolating from our knowledge of gold and of nanotechnology, we can imagine how the *lofty ones* responded to their new circumstances: they suspended tiny gold particles high in the atmosphere, forming a shell.[2] Through reflection, a golden globe around the planet would provide the heat retention needed to make its surface habitable.[3] The shell would also render the planet stunningly bright when it came nearer to the Sun. That is indeed how the Mesopotamian texts describe Nibiru as it passed through the inner Solar System.[4]

An environmental crisis loomed: the golden shell was failing, but the planet's gold supplies were depleted. An explorer had earlier found gold on Earth. An expedition was organized. If enough of the mineral could be mined on Earth and sent back home, the crisis would be averted.

A Šumerian epic tells of an earlier voyage to Earth by a high noble. On his return he had spoken positively about Earth's environment and had reported on the presence of gold. Actually, evidence has been found on Earth that long before his visit, our planet had been explored by others.[5]

The colonists traveled to Earth as Nibiru entered the inner Solar System; the diminishing distance between the two planets made the voyage feasible. Their aim was to evaluate the prospects for extracting gold. If that proved feasible, they'd transport the mineral to Nibiru on its passes through the inner planets. From the Šumerian king lists, we learn that the colony was begun almost half a million years ago.

The first abode of the original fifty settlers was in what is now southern Iraq, near present-day Basra, a location with many advantages: access to the sea for the transport of gold from distant locations; marshes thick with giant reeds (still growing there) ideal for crafting their first houses and boats; deposits of clay with which to make bricks and pottery; a broad plain to the north on which spacecraft could easily glide to land; and petroleum near the surface, a ready source of energy.[6]

In the next chapter we'll focus on the development of the colony.

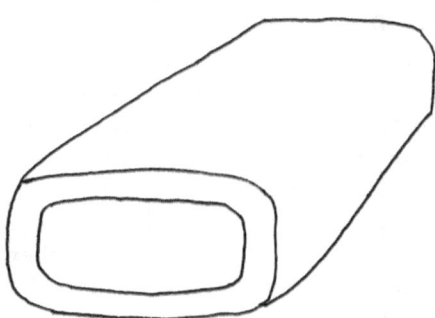

Figure 3.3.1. One of several metal tubes found in Cretaceous chalk 65 million years old near S. Jean de Livet, France in 1968, and submitted to the University of Caen.

Figure 3.3.2. One of hundreds of metal spheres found by miners in West Transvaal, South Africa, in Precambrian deposits 2 billion years old. Their surfaces are extraordinarily hard. This particular specimen has unusual equatorial grooves.

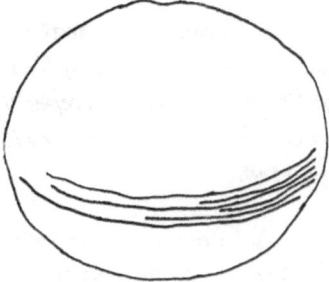

[1] Before Nibiru's cataclysmic ejection from its original orbit, the *lofty ones* probably took shelter in caverns until the planet's surface was made habitable.

[2] We are just beginning to explore the potential of manipulating gold nanoparticles with electromagnetic fields; we can barely glimpse the possibilities of what might be achieved using mono-atomic gold.

[3] A thin layer of gold reflects 99% of the heat energy falling on it. That's why gold foil is routinely used as a reflective shield on probes sent into space.

[4] Atop the steeple or dome on churches the world over, the penultimate ornament is a gilded sphere, a reminder of the awesome sight of Nibiru during one of its close passes.

[5] Geometrically-shaped metal artifacts were found by miners in coal formations in England and the United States in the 19th century and were reported in periodicals at the time. Manufactured objects found in coal implied that alien beings had been here millions of years ago, when the plants whose carbon eventually became coal were living. As with other anomalous findings, they were called hoaxes, and eventually the specimens were lost (Figures 3.3.1 and 3.3.2).

[6] The Šumerian language had names for more than a dozen different types of natural petroleum substances. Mesopotamia was a source of liquid and semiliquid fuels for distant societies through at least the time of the Roman Empire.

Part Three: The Mesopotamian Tale Explored

Settling on Earth

The king of NI.BI.RU, AN, meaning Heavenly One, chose as leader of the mining colony the eldest of his sons, a prince born to his concubine. A gifted scientist and engineer, he would be called EN.KI, meaning Lord of Earth. This took place about four hundred fifty thousand years ago ... long before the age of man. (Figures 3.4.1, 3.4.2, and 3.4.3)

Figure 3.4.1. Carvings on two stellae showing AN, King of Nibiru. On the left, his planet is represented by a radiating cross. On the right the image with twelve rays is probably the Solar System, which An's planet rules.

Figure 3.4.2. A copper figurine of Enki with two of his symbols: water and fish. The annunaki lords are always depicted wearing tall conical crowns or stylized representations them, as in the next figure.

Figure 3.4.3. Enki receiving three *gods*, on an Akkadian cylinder seal. Here he is shown with water and with another of his symbols, the Moon. We will discuss the significance of the *god* who faces Enki and also faces away from him.

In a poem called *Enki and the World Order*, the great *god* proclaims:

I am the leader of the [settlers]
engendered by fecund seed
firstborn son of divine An
the great brother of all the lofty ones

Enki goes on to say that he...

... made the rivers Tigris and Euphrates navigable and clear; built a canal between them; opened marshland waterways; taught the settlers metallurgy, brickmaking, building construction, and shipbuilding ...

EN.KI's epithets in time would include He Whose House is Water (as lord of the seas), He Who Makes Things (for his technical prowess), He Who Solves Secrets (for his scientific knowledge), Chief Decider of Luster (gold), and Lord of the Bright Seer (i.e., the Moon, ruler of the tides).

The marsh was vast, fed by the waters of the rivers (four, as we shall learn) that interlaced as they neared the Persian Gulf. The colony's first structures were built at the edge of these wetlands.

3.4 Settling on Earth

In *Šumerian, the first language of Mesopotamia,* the settlers were called the *AN.UN.NA.KI, Those of Heaven Who Are on Earth.* In Akkadian, the region's next language and the first of the Semitic tongues, they were the *I.LU, the Lofty Ones.* The colonists named their first settlement *E.RI.DU,* meaning *Home Faraway Built.*[1]

After some initial difficulties, *EN.KI* found that gold mining would be successful. *AN* sent more colonists, led by a son with his queen, a prince outranking *EN.KI* in prestige. He would be called *EN.LIL,* meaning *Lord of the Command.* Tensions developed. *EN.KI,* founder of the colony and *AN's* firstborn, was unwilling to yield leadership to *EN.LIL* as his father asked. *AN,* prepared to lead the colony himself and to make one of the brothers viceroy on *NI.BI.RU,* travelled to Earth to see the fraternal dispute resolved. The three royals drew lots and *EN.LIL* was the winner. Authority over the colony was to be divided. *EN.KI* would be chief of all technical matters and lord of the oceans ... and subordinate to *EN.LIL.*

A Babylonian epic, based on Šumerian originals, gives this account:

the gods clasped hands together
cast lots and divided
An went up to heaven
[to Enlil] Earth was made subject
the seas enclosed as with a loop
to Enki the prince were given [2]

A settlement, *Laarsa,* was built for Enlil. Later, the city of *Nibruki,* meaning *Earth Crossing Place* and also *Earth place of Nibiru,* the city we know as Nippur, was founded as Enlil's permanent seat of power. In keeping with his supremacy, the equipment for contacting Nibiru was located there: the *Duranki, Bond between Heaven and Earth,* installed atop the *Kiur, Place of the Earth Root,* placed within the *Ekur,* the *Lofty House.* The *Dirga,* the *Glowing Chamber,* also kept in the *Ekur,* contained:

the emblems of the stars...the tablets of [the orbits]...

In a devotional poem lauding the *Ekur:*

A lifted eye scans the land…a lifted beam searches the heart of all the land. A terrible weapon protects the settlement its sight is awesome fear dread. Within is a fast stepping bird whose hand the wicked and evil could not escape. A heavenward tall pillar reaching to the sky serves to pronounce his word

Enlil's rule would be undiminished for millenniums. When the empire of Akkad absorbed Šumer, Enlil became Akkad's supreme *lofty one*. When Babylon became the supreme city and the Code of Ḥammurabi was proclaimed, the king began the first tablet of the code saying:

AN and ENLIL named me to promote the welfare of the people…to cause justice to prevail in the land. (Figure 3.4.4)

Figure 3.4.4. On a stella, Enlil, radiating emanations, gives the Babylonian code of laws to King Ḥammurabi, whose right hand is raised in the gesture of reverence and awe.

With later arrivals, the number of AN.UN.NA.KI on Earth grew to six hundred, while another three hundred lived off-planet, the

3.4 Settling on Earth

I.GI.GI, Those Who Observe. Using rocket-propelled craft to fly from place to place on Earth and to ascend into orbit, The Lofty Ones were also known to the Mesopotamians as **DIN.GIR, The Righteous Ones of the Sky Chambers.** The region near E.RI.DU was E.DIN, meaning Home of the Righteous Ones.

Regarding the epithet *dingir*: the original ideogram *din* looks much like the body of a rocket, with one end shooting fire and on the other end, a connecting place for the ideogram *gir*, whose pointed shape makes it resemble the personnel capsules on our first space vehicles. Clearly, for the Šumerians, flying was central to the *anunnaki* identity. (Figure 3.4.5)

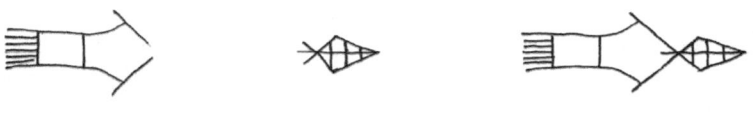

Figure 3.4.5. Early pictographs representing the *anunnaki*.

Edin, the area surrounding the first *anunnaki* settlement, is the source of the Hebrew name of God's garden in the Book of Genesis.[3] Šumer, the name for the broad area in which the later cities of the *anunnaki* were founded, meant *land of the watchers*. The colonists indeed were watchers: they could look down from the air and from orbit, and later they would oversee all human activity in their domain.[4] They had their *mu*, *sky chambers*, to go from place to place, and their *gir*, *rockets*, to reach the heavens.

Šumerian, linguistically unique, was followed by the language of Akkad, the first Semitic language. In Akkadian, the *anunnaki* were the *ilu*, meaning *lofty ones*.[5] In Hebrew, a later Semitic tongue, *ilu* became *el*.[6] Because *el* was used exclusively to refer to the *lofty ones*, and since they were considered divine, the term came to denote *god*. But *el* originally did not signify divinity, only height, physically and socially.[7]

Besides Enlil and Enki there were ten other *anunnaki* of exalted social rank. They constituted the council of twelve *gods of heaven and earth*, six male and six female. From time to time, the place of one of the *lofty ones* on the council was vacated and another *anunnaki* noble was appointed, so there were always twelve. The *anunnaki* believed that the number twelve ruled the Solar System. There were twelve major bodies by their reckoning: the nine planets we know (including Pluto), Nibiru, the Sun, and the Moon. The circle made by the projection of the plane of the ecliptic onto the stars is evenly divided among twelve constellations, the signs of the Zodiac (the same signs used by astrologers today). In addition, the bands of sky above and below the ecliptic are each divided among twelve other constellations. The *anunnaki* didn't reveal their spiritual beliefs to the scribes, yet clearly they thought it important to align their society with the heavenly bodies by maintaining a ruling circle of twelve.[8]

The divided leadership of Earth was usually not a problem. Though Enki at times defied Enlil's rulings, he eventually got over his jealousy; disagreements between the royal brothers usually were well managed. However, conflicts over power, prestige, and riches continually arose among their descendants. Enki's clan complained that their rights had been usurped when Enlil had been made supreme. Aristocrats came into fierce, jealous opposition with each other...often leading to war.

In truth, dynastic opposition was a way of life on Nibiru, so it was natural that it came to characterize the Earth colony. The Šumerian *god* lists tell of long-festering troubles surrounding the rule of Nibiru, such as the conflict between An and his predecessor, Alalu, who claimed that An had stolen his throne. It played out on Earth when the colony was still young, with a hand-to-hand fight between the rivals. Their dispute incited a rebellion by the *igigi* and led to an epic battle involving many nobles.[9] Later, in a bid for power, a young descendant of Alalu's, Zu, stole an information device from Enlil, one that controlled technical functions throughout the area of settlement. This wreaked havoc in Šumer:

Suspended was the issuance of commands...The hallowed inner chamber lost its brilliance ... Stillness spreads... Silence prevails

Recovery of the device was accomplished through a dramatic one-to-one aerial battle in which Ninurta, a son of Enlil, defeated Zu with a missile. These events were so important that Zu's trial and execution were incorporated in the New Year ceremonies of Šumer.

At first glance, the chronology developed from the Mesopotamian lists of *gods* and kings appears to present a huge obstacle to accepting the tales of the *gods* as factual. *Anunnaki* lifespans seem impossibly long. The most extreme example is the span of over 400,000 years between the arrivals on Earth of Enki and Enlil and a pivotal global event in which they were both involved. Could they possibly have lived that long? And there are many accounts of lives of lesser *anunnaki* nobles spanning tens of thousands of years. How are we to reconcile the lifetimes and the reigns in the texts with what we know of the biology of aging?

Just as the *anunnaki's* dazzling powers were manifestations of advanced technology, not divinity, so it was with their long lives. They were not immortal *gods*, but the beneficiaries of advanced anti-aging medicine. As we've noted, by the time Nibiru was ejected from its native orbit, the culture of the planet was already technologically advanced. In

3.4 Settling on Earth

the millions of years that followed, their scientists could well have learned to deliver lifespans that we consider impossible. It seems that what we are able to imagine only in science fiction was standard medicine for the *anunnaki* ... at least for the elite.

That their longevity was not entirely inborn but could be achieved is suggested in texts and images. Some depict a *Tree of Life*. (Figures 3.4.7 & 3.4.8) Tablets mention the *Food of Life* and the *Water of Life* brought from Nibiru for the *anunnaki*. Many imply that the *long life* was a gift that one could be granted. In one tale Enki sends an early human to the court of the king on Nibiru, saying:

Figure 3.4.7. Nannar and Ningal, his wife, with a Tree of Life symbol. From a stone carving.

Figure 3.4.8. Two men dressed as eagles with a Tree of Life.

when to Heaven [he] has ascended, and has approached the gate of An, the Bearer of Life and the Grower of Truth at the gate of An will be standing ... [the visitor] is offered the Bread of Life so that he might have the long life, but not understanding what he is being offered, and fearful of being poisoned, he declines.[10]

The Epic of Gilgameš resounds with the dilemma of mortality. Its hero intends to reach Nibiru, desperate for the *long life* of the *gods* to which he thinks his lineage entitles him, for after all, he is 2/3 *anunnaki*...his mother being one of the noble *lofty ones* of Uruk. Late in his quest, the hero of the deluge tells Gilameš what we already know: that An and Enlil had proclaimed that humans were never to have the *long life* of the *anunnaki*. (Figures 3.4.9 & 3.4.10)

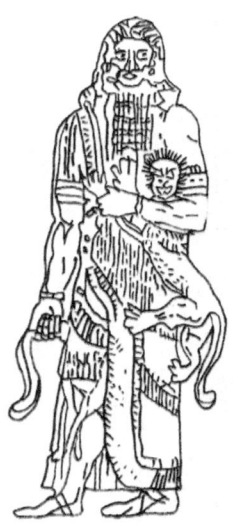

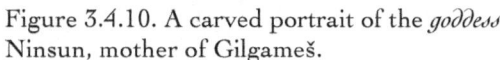
Figure 3.4.9. A carved portrait of Gilgameš holding a lion, demonstrating his stature and strength.

Figure 3.4.10. A carved portrait of the *goddess* Ninsun, mother of Gilgameš.

A greatly extended life was given to *those who came down*, but long life is not eternal life, and the *gods* were not immortal. Tablets tell of Ninmaḫ

3.4 Settling on Earth

visibly aging and of Dumuzi's being killed, as Inanna also was (though she was restored to life). The lifespans of the *gods* became an issue as their stay on Earth drew to a close, as we will discuss, yet no text survives elaborating on anunnaki mortality. There probably was at least one, though, for there's a portion of Psalm 82 that almost certainly was modeled on a Sumerian original. In the King James version:

God...judgeth among the gods... [and says that HE has said]
you are elohim, all of you children of the Most High
but ye shall die like men and fall like...princes [11]

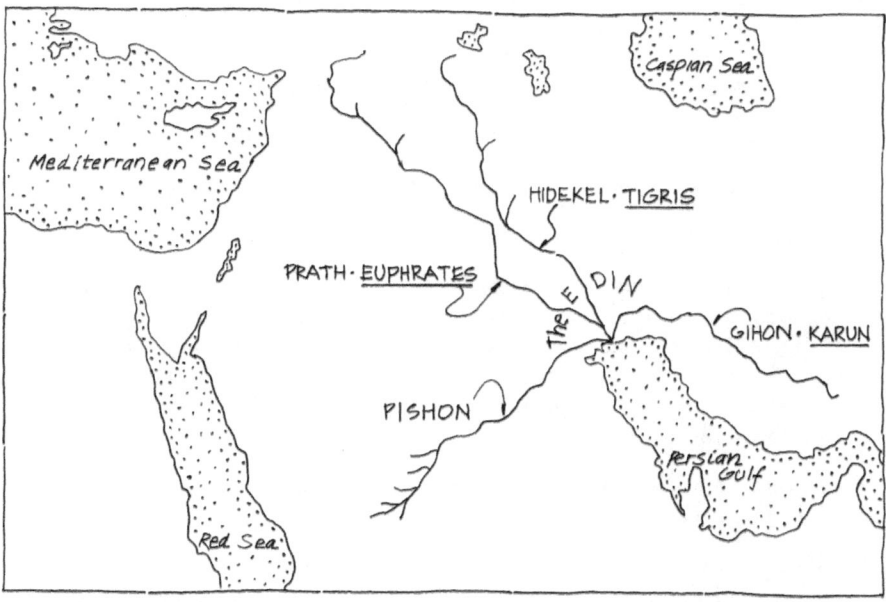

Figure 3.4.6. Four rivers converged at the head of the Persian Gulf, the historic E.DIN. Three are still flowing, one is buried in the sands. The Hebrew names of the four rivers watering the biblical Garden of Eden are shown, followed by the modern names of the surviving three, underlined.

In the next chapter we learn about a crisis that arose to some extent as a consequence of the long lives of the *anunnaki*.

[1] From *Eridu* comes the name for our planet in many languages: Erde, Aarde, Eretz, Ertz, Jord ... Earth

[2] In Mesopotamia, the assignment of land rights was often done by drawing *divine lots*. In Canaan, Joshua addressed his scouts as he prepared to assign unconquered lands to Israelite tribes:
Up, go about in the land and write it out and come back to me, and here I shall cast the lot for you before the Lord in Shiloh. (Alter translation)
Today in the West, parcels of land can still be referred to as *lots*.

[3] Four rivers watered the Garden of Eden. Four rivers flowed into the *edin* of the *anunnaki*. Two are still robust, the Euphrates and the Tigris. The third was a stronger Karun, which flows into the marsh from the east. The fourth once flowed from the Red Sea mountains and crossed Arabia. Its buried course is revealed by ground-penetrating radar. (Fig. 3.4.6 on the preceding page)

[4] The Egyptian word for divinities, NFR or NTR, also meant *watchers*.

[5] We will use the terms *anunnaki*, *lofty ones*, and *gods* interchangeably.

[6] *Ilu* evolved into *Allah* in Arabic, another Semitic language.

[7] Riding the *elevated* tracks of the New York City *el*, an ultra-orthodox man across from me was deep into a small book, as if in prayer. I imagined he was silently saying *el* from time to time. Words built on that root appear throughout sacred and scholarly Jewish texts. More than 5,000 years after *el* first was spoken, both its meanings seemed to be in use: words of devotion to the *Most High* murmured in a train *high* above the city streets.

[8] There were hundreds of *anunnaki* of lesser status, most of them children, grandchildren, nieces, and nephews of the circle of twelve.

[9] The Mesopotamian texts reporting this conflict seem to be the source of the Greeks' battle of the Titans, which includes details identical to those in the then ancient texts ... such as one chief combatant biting off the genitals of the other.

[10] The Bearer of Life and the Grower of Truth at the palace gates may have had replicas in the Edin of the *lofty ones*, since they found their way into the Book of Genesis, as the Tree of Life and the Tree of Knowing in the Garden of Eden.

[11] A translation of this remarkable passage by the poet-scholar David Rosenberg in his *A Literary Bible* reads thus:

you too are gods, heads of nations
thoughts of My Lord, but you will disappear...
your heads fall, like great nations in ruins

Crisis on Earth

Golden ingots were flown to NI.BI.RU every 3,600 years, when the shining planet approached. The mines and smelters in southern and eastern Africa were in full production.

Many texts say the mines were in the *abzu*, the roots *ab* meaning *lower* and *zu* meaning *world*. Of the several possible translations of *abzu*, the meaning of a compound word in Šumerian being determined by its context, the tablets most likely were saying two things: *place underground* and *land below the Equator*.[1] In an epic about the voyages to the mines by two *gods*, the directions and lengths of their ocean transits are consistent with journeys beginning at the head of the Persian Gulf and ending on the eastern coast of Africa.[2] Ancient mines have been discovered in southern Africa by the thousands. The remains of bones and fires found inside some caves have been dated to 60,000 BCE, and stone tools to 100,000 BCE.

The working conditions in the mines, however, were brutal. Suddenly, having borne a hard fate for a very long time, the ordinarily obedient commoners had had enough, and mutinied.

Texts describing the life of the colony before humans existed say that the *anunnaki* toiled in the mines for forty *counted periods*, a phrase that usually meant the orbital period of Nibiru, 3,600 Earth years. If there were forty orbits from the founding of the Earth colony to the miners' revolt, that would be a span of 144,000 years. Considering their extremely long lives, and knowing what it is like to work in a gold mine, one can easily imagine a rebellion by previously obedient *anunnaki* commoners. A Šumerian text about a visit by Inanna to the *abzu*, says that she saw:

Anunnaki eating food mixed with clay and drinking water mixed with dust…

The Atra-Ḫassis, a Babylonian epic based on Šumerian texts, begins:

when the gods like men
bore the work and suffered the toil
the toil of the gods was great
the work was heavy the distress was much
… suffered the toil day and night
… complaining backbiting, grumbling in the excavations …

NI.BI.RU was still in need of gold. EN.LIL left E.DIN to see for himself what was happening and was taken hostage.

The Babylonian epic quotes the leader of the rebellion:

come let us unnerve him in his dwelling
let us proclaim a mutiny
let us adopt hostilities and battle...
the lofty ones heeded his words
they set fire to their tools...
throwing them away they went
to the gate of the hero Enlil ...
some shouted let us kill him ...
let us break the yoke

Enlil, stunned to be seized and to hear demands for his death, contacted his father on Nibiru. He wanted the leader of the mutiny killed. The miners stood steadfast together.

every one of us gods has war declared
we have our ... in the excavations excessive toil has killed us
our work was heavy the distress much

AN came to Earth and convened a council. EN.LIL said he'd resign and return to NI.BI.RU unless the leader of the mutiny was executed, but to AN, the miners' case was compelling. He insisted that a solution be found.

There are hymns in which Enki, *god* of many talents and epithets, was praised as *Lord of Mining*. (Figure 3.5.1) In fact, he was in the mines and had been held captive at the start of the rebellion. Enki spoke in council.

EN.KI envisioned a way to resolve the impasse. He'd observed hominin creatures in the nearby wilds, small and primitive, yet similar to their own race in many ways. He boldly proposed a solution: he would use AN.UN.NA.KI "essence" to modify the native creatures for service in the mines. His partner in the laboratory effort would be NIN.MAH, half-sister to himself and to EN.LIL, a scientist and royal midwife.

3.5 Crisis, Again

Figure 3.5.1. Two cylinder seals with Enki receiving gold. The ingots, cast in the shape of two intersecting cones, were mounted on staffs.

Enki spoke, addressing his brethren, the lofty ones, saying there was a solution, since Ninmaḫ, a life-giving goddess, was among them ...

let her fashion a worker
let a workman bear the toil of the lofty ones
let her create a mixed worker let him bear the yoke

Asked how this could be done, Enki replied that the creature that was needed already existed, and that all they had to do was to ...

bind upon it the image of the gods
it can be done

The *anunnaki* took to the idea:

they summoned and asked the goddess
the midwife of the gods the wise Mammu
you are the birth goddess make workers
make a primitive worker
that he may bear the yoke
let him bear the yoke assigned by Enlil
let the worker carry the toil of the gods

Texts reporting on later times make it clear that Enlil was not entirely in favor of Enki's proposal. Yet no other solutions were in view and since he had just been threatened with death, Enlil must have felt that he was in no position to object. Many Šumerian tablets state specifically that the *gods* crafted man to do their work.[3] In Akkadian texts the word generally translated as *man, awilu,* actually means *workman*; and a phrase appearing many times, *lulu amelu,* really means *workman who is mixed.*

Gaining EN.LIL's grumpy consent, AN told EN.KI and NIN.MAḪ to proceed. NIN.MAḪ, meaning Great Lady, revered in Mesopotamia for her role in the origin of humankind, was also known as MAM.MU, meaning Mother Goddess, and as NIN.TI, meaning Lady Life. Her symbol was the umbilical cord cutter. (See Figure 3.5.5)

At the start of the enterprise Enki noted Ninmaḫ's pivotal role:

thou art the mother womb
the one who can fashion mankind
fashion then the workman
let him bear the yoke

The *anunnaki* were far superior to the creatures Enki had observed, the most evolved homonin on Earth, *Homo erectus,* yet apparently there was enough similarity between the two species to make gene splicing attainable. Another factor that made the goal feasible was how similar were Earth and Nibiru. The ease with which the *anunnaki* colonized Earth, breathing the air, drinking the water, and raising food, means that the two worlds are very much alike. Nonetheless, genetic compatibility between species from different worlds has weighty implications for biology.[4]

When translation of the Mesopotamian tablets began, around the turn of the 20th century, the stories telling of Enki and Ninmaḫ making the first humans could only be thought of as fantasies. Ideas about what was possible were limited by the science of the day. Our capabilities have since then expanded and continue to. Not only is in vitro fertilization common, it can now involve the transplantation of oöplasm, sperm nuclei, and even mitochondria. Animals are being cloned. Several animal species have been genetically altered. Artificial genes are assembled from DNA fragments. Genomes are now edited, DNA sequences deleted and inserted in a process with the acronym *crispr*. What else will we achieve in the near future? The accomplishments of the brother and sister *gods* are no longer difficult to imagine, especially since we've now learned there's a naturally occurring process that may be a correlate of the one employed by Enki and Ninmaḫ in their laboratory: *horizontal gene transfer* between disparate species. (Figures 3.5.2, 3.5.3, 3.5.4, and 3.5.6)

Figure 3.5.2. A cylinder seal showing Ninmaḫ with a human infant on her lap, assistants with lab equipment, and behind her, a Tree of Life.

Figure 3.5.3. Ninmaḫ and Enki at work, the winged disc of Nibiru, the planet identified with its ruler, their father AN, overhead. (From a carving.)

Figure 3.5.4. A cylinder seal showing Ninmaḫ with birth goddesses and a Tree of Life.

Figure 3.5.5. A stone carving of Ninmaḫ's symbol (appearing also in Figures 3.5.3 and 3.5.6.)

3.5 Crisis, Again

Figure 3.5.6. A damaged carving, showing Enki, enthroned, and Ninmaḫ with her symbol, the umbilical cord cutter. Between them, a flame. Behind her, laboratory gear.

After a prolonged time of trial and error, the new race was born.

The work of Enki and Ninmaḫ did not go smoothly at first. That's not surprising, given the complexity of the enterprise, and it helps to confirm the authenticity of the numerous passages about the making of *Homo sapiens* in their lab. There are reports of deficient specimens made by Ninmaḫ, including sterility in a female, incontinence in a male, and absent external genitalia in another. There is a tablet mentioning a creature crafted by Enki with hand tremors and one with hepatitis and heart failure.

There are many more texts about the successful crafting of humans, events so momentous that they were translated and copied repeatedly. The Atra-Ḥassis tells that blood was taken from a specific *god*, whose personal *essence* was to be used. In that account, Enki speaks:

let primitives be fashioned after his pattern…
out of his blood they fashioned mankind…
it was a work beyond comprehension

The Atra-Ḥassis goes into detail, with Ninmaḫ asking for certain substances:

bitumens of the abzu…clays of the abzu …

and her brother responds:

I will prepare a purifying bath
let one god be bled…

from his flesh and blood
let NINTI mix the essence of life [5]

EN.KI's wife was the first surrogate birth mother, attended by noble females.

NINKI my goddess spouse will be the one for the labor
seven goddesses of birth will be near to assist

In the saga of *adapa*, the first fully formed man, it says:

in those days, in those years
the wise one of Eridu, Ea [6]
created him as a model of men

Next, fourteen female AN.UN.NA.KI served as surrogates.

Copies of the original model had to be made. This was done in the *bitšiimti*, the *house of the breath and wind of life*. The saga continues:

The mother goddess and fourteen birth goddesses assembled ...
Ea cleaned the essence in her presence
he kept reciting the incantation...
the god who purifies the essence Ea spoke
seated before her he prompted her
after she had recited her incantation
she put her hand out to the essence

Interpreting this poetry, we gather that what was involved was genetic manipulation, in vitro fertilization, and implantation in surrogate mothers. The birth goddesses were divided into two groups:

NINTI nipped off fourteen portions of essence
seven she deposited on the right
seven she deposited on the left

3.5 Crisis, Again

between them she placed the mold ...
Into the wombs of the twice-seven birth goddesses
the mother goddess put the mixed essence ...
NINTI sat counting the months
the fateful tenth month was approaching...
the period of opening the womb had elapsed
her face radiated understanding
she covered her head, performed the midwifery
her waist was girdled, pronounced the blessing ...
the lady whose hand opens came ...
she opened the womb
her face brightened with joy...
that which was in the womb came forth

    There is a parallel account in another text:

double seven birth goddesses assembled...
the birth goddess brought forth
the wind of the breath of life...
the creatures were people
creatures of the mother goddess[7]

    And in another text:

[Ninmaḫ] summoned the anunnaki ...
she opened her mouth addressed the great gods ...
you commanded me a task
I have completed it ...
I have removed your heavy work
I have imposed your toil on the worker earthling
you raised a cry for a worker-being
I have loosed the yoke
I have established your freedom

The *divine* element in the specimen of blood that was obtained was called *teema, that which houses what binds the memory,* that is, DNA. The result of the splicing of genetic material was to be everlasting:

in the essence god and man shall be bound
to a unity brought together
so that in the end of days
the flesh and the soul
which in a god have ripened
that soul in a blood kinship be bound[8]

Finally, EN.KI was able to give the servant race fertility...but not the long lifespan of the Lofty Ones.

Like many hybrids, the new creatures couldn't reproduce. Relying on *anunnaki* surrogates wasn't feasible, so Enki continued in his labors:

with his own seed he made the perfect model of earthling, called adapa

Fertility made human beings *perfect,* i.e., *complete.* Sexual activity was termed *knowing,* as it would be in the Hebrew Bible. *Knowing* the servant race was to have, but not the *long life.* It was necessary for the slaves to be able to multiply, but Enlil was adamant that they not be endowed with the enormous lifespan of the *anunnaki.* And so:

with [knowing Enki] perfected him...
to him he had given knowing
lasting life him he did not give

This momentous decision is echoed in a conversation in the Garden of Eden between the Hebrew God and a group of other *gods.* Since God has peers, the passage must be of Mesopotamian, not Jewish, origin. The *long life* is not to be given to humanity, as far as both the chief of the Mesopotamian *gods* and the Hebrew deity are concerned.[9] After it is revealed that the humans have partaken of the Tree of Knowing, God proclaims:

3.5 Crisis, Again

... Behold, the man is become as one of us, to know ...
now, lest he put forth his hand, and take also of the tree of life,
and eat, and live for ever ... [he is cast out of Eden]

Next, we discuss developments in the *anunnaki* settlement following the appearance of human beings.

Figure 3.5.7. A Šumerian carving with elements that will appear in the Book of Genesis: a fruit-bearing tree; a snake (like the crescent Moon, a symbol of Enki); and a deity overseeing the scene. In Šumer that is An, represented here by the Planet of the Crossing, with which he is identified.

Figure 3.5.8. Two cylinder seals showing Enki as a serpent. The seven-pointed star, representing Earth, is another of his symbols. In scene *a*, he faces Enlil.

---

[1] Double meanings were common in Šumerian texts. There even were occasional triple meanings. The *abzu* may have contributed to the concept of an *underworld* among the Greeks, whose culture absorbed and modified a great deal from Mesopotamia. The Greek idea of the spirits of the deceased existing in a world under the surface led scholars to think that Mesopotamian accounts of the adventures of living *gods* in the geographic *abzu* were mystical tales about imagined deities in a world of the dead.

[2] The biblical accounts of King Solomon's voyages for gold read as if they went from the head of the Gulf of Aqaba to southern Africa.

[3] The Šumerians used terms signifying *making* and avoided the word for *creating* when referring to the *anunnaki's* bringing humans into existence. They were apparently respecting a distinction that the *anunnaki* made.

[4] Discussions of the genetics involved in the *anunnaki* crafting of *Homo sapiens* will involve ongoing developments in science, such as that of the astrobiologist Charles Cockell's work on the physics underlying the morphology of life. It will inevitably touch on theories and discoveries outside the mainstream, such as Rupert Sheldrake's *morphogenetic field*, and Wilhelm Reich's *biogenesis*.

[5] The word in Akkadian, the language of the Atra-Ḫasis, here rendered as *essence of life*, is ordinarily translated as *clay*, its literal meaning. If the scribes were saying *clay* they were using the word as metaphor; clay could have no role in genetic engineering. But the same word in Šumerian means *that which is life* or *essence of life*, a good prescientific way to say *genes*. It was common for scientific terms in Akkadian, Assyrian, and Babylonian texts to be insertions of Šumerian words. As one tongue succeeded another in Mesopotamia, Šumerian remained the language of science and scholarship. Passages like this one gave rise to the mistaken idea that the peoples of Mesopotamia said that their *gods* created humanity using clay, and to an enduring poetic device: *man is made of clay*.

[6] One of Enki's many epithets. It means *He whose house is water*.

[7] The Mesopotamian *mother goddess* is alluded to in the tale of the creation of humankind in the Book of Genesis. The Hebrew names of Adam and Eve, *Adam* and *Ḥava*, mean *Earthman* and *Life*. Since the first human female is the mother of humanity, it makes sense that the Bible calls her *Life*. In doing so it echoes the Šumerian epics, since one of the *mother goddess's* epithets was Ninti, *Lady Life*. And that name sheds light on the story of Eve being made from the rib of Adam.

The literature of Šumer was replete with plays on words. The root *ti* meant *life* but it could also mean *rib*. The epithet *Lady Life* could therefore be read as *Lady Rib*. Only learned Jews would have known that the biblical episode demonstrating God's mysterious, supernatural powers contained a reference to the then ancient texts reporting the artificial origin of humanity. The authors of Genesis saluted the culture from which theirs had emerged with a pun! (The first discussion of this connection between the narratives was published around 1915.)

The spirit of Enki is present in the drama in the Garden of Eden. The Hebrew root for serpent, NHS, also can mean *one who solves secrets*, one of Enki's Šumerian epithets. Furthermore, the serpent was one of Enki's symbols in Mesopotamia. He could even be depicted as a snake. (See Figs. 3.5.7 and 3.5.8)

[8] Paleogeneticists have found no evidence suggesting that elements of one genome got inserted into another. Since, as the texts say, the *essences* were intentionally *bound to a unity*, and since no humans existed before the graft was achieved, it is conceivable that scientists never will find any such evidence.

[9] In Mesopotamian literature, the opposition between Enki and Enlil often plays out in their differences over mankind. Enki, the inventor, the scientist, is our champion; Enlil, the ruler, the moralist, is dubious about us, at best. God's ambivalence toward mankind (and toward His chosen people) in the Hebrew Bible reflects the opposed feelings toward humanity in the two chief *gods* of Mesopotamia. The conflict between their clans affected the course of human life so profoundly that it begged to be reflected in the new theology.

Giants in the Earth

The new Earthmen were distinct from the two species that had been blended to bring them into existence, the four-to-five-foot-tall, dark, furry, forward-leaning African hominin, and the fair, seven-foot-tall, smooth-skinned, erect being from NI.BI.RU. Intermediate in height between the two, the human beings had features of each ... a head of dark terrestrial hair and a smooth alien skin, for example.

The AN.UN.NA.KI commoners in Mesopotamia asked that humans be brought out of Africa so that they, too, would be relieved of labor. EN.KI objected, so EN.LIL assaulted his compound.¹ His attack succeeded. EN.LIL then took "black headed ones" to E.DIN, where they became laborers, farmers, builders, and cooks.

Enki had erected a magnificent residence near the African mines.

the lord of the abzu king Enki built his house of silver and lapis lazuli
... the creatures of bright countenance
stood all about He Who Makes Things

As he prepared his attack, Enlil cut communications with Nibiru.

the lord Enlil whose decisions are unalterable
verily did speed to separate heaven from earth
in the bond-heaven-earth he made a gash
so that the crafted ones could come up [from Africa to Mesopotamia]
from the place-where-flesh-sprouted-forth

Enlil deployed a powerful weapon in the attack.

the house which is not submissive to the lord
the ax-that-produces-power makes it submissive to the lord ...
he set the earth-splitter ...
and drove it into the place-where-flesh-sprouted-forth ...
from the ground people were breaking through toward Enlil
he eyed his black headed ones in steadfast fashion

The ordinary *lofty ones* in Mesopotamia rejoiced.

the anunnaki stepped up to Enlil
raised their hands in greetings
soothed Enlil's heart with prayers
black headed ones they requested of him
to the black headed people to give the pickax to hold ...
with picks and spades they built the shrines [and] the canal banks
they grew food for the people and for...the lofty ones

Enlil's bringing Earthman (*Adam* in Hebrew) to work in the Edin is echoed in Genesis.

And the LORD ... took the Adam and HE placed him in the garden of eden, to till it and to tend it

There are many carvings from Šumer (as well as later images from Egypt) showing humans in the presence of much bigger *gods*. The size difference between *gods* and men has been interpreted as a visual metaphor reflecting their relative levels of importance. Yet if the images are regarded as being to some extent realistic, they confirm textual references to the height of the *anunnaki*. (Figure 3.6.1) There is also hearsay testimony that tends to confirm the extraordinary size of the *lofty ones*. It comes from Herodotus who, in his report on 5th century BCE Babylon, said:

atop the ziggurat in the city's sacred precinct there is a spacious temple which contains a couch that is unusually large and richly adorned, with a golden table beside it. The people say that when the god descends from the sky and stays in his temple, he sleeps on the couch.

While the noble AN.UN.NA.KI males had female partners, hardly any of the commoners did. The ordinary AN.UN.NA.KI began to take human women as wives ... resulting in an unplanned second round of hybridization between the terrestrial and celestial species. Many of the fruits of those unions had greater size, intelligence, and longevity than humans had ever known.

3.6 Giants in the Earth

Figure 3.6.1. A carving in stone from Nippur c. 3,000 BCE. A priest offering a vial to a *god* — who would tower over the naked human were he to stand.

The first humans were quite distinct in appearance from both of humankind's parent species: bigger and smoother-skinned than *Homo erectus*, smaller and darker than the *anunnaki*. But the distinctions between Earthmen and *gods* became less clear when the unplanned interbreeding produced *demigods*. This was a development of such consequence that the Book of Genesis transmitted the Mesopotamian accounts virtually unaltered, saying that in the age before the Flood …

…the sons of the gods saw the daughters of men that they were fair, and they took them wives…those who came down were in the earth in those days, and also after that, when the sons of the gods came in unto the daughters of men, and they bare children to them, the same became mighty men which were of old, men of renown [2]

The mixed offspring of these marriages naturally had more prominent *anunnaki* characteristics than did the original Earthmen. The *might* of the biblical *men of renown* was a reflection of the abilities and stature of these *demigods*, who were clearly superior to ordinary humans. (Figures 3.6.2 and 3.6.3) This means that the extraordinary lifespans of the descendants of Adam, such as Methusaleh, grandfather of Noaḥ, are based in fact. The longevity of the new breed of elite humans resulted from their having an enhanced endowment of *anunnaki* genes. They benefitted from the portion of the *long life* of the *gods* that was genetically encoded.

There is a parallel account of the mating of *gods* and humans in the Book of Jubilees, a text excluded from the Hebrew canon and known only through translations into other tongues. In one passage:

Two hundred watchers descended to Earth and…

each one of them chose for himself one, and they began to go in unto them and defile themselves with them…and the women bore giants

Figure 3.6.2. An early Šumerian carving depicting two kings being attended by their subjects. Note the three distinct sizes of human beings

3.6 Giants in the Earth

Figure 3.6.3. A small portion of the inlaid scenes on the exquisite *Standard of Ur*, a box-like tomb artifact. A feast scene is shown with persons of three heights: the huge one dressed elaborately; two of the elite, not quite as tall; and the small attendants.

Until recently an account of humans interbreeding with another species could only have been read as fantasy. Yet geneticists have been finding numerous examples of interbreeding in nature, and the understanding of what separates species, once clear, has gotten murky. And as we have recently learned, *Homo sapiens sapiens* clearly once did interbreed … with *Homo sapiens neandertaliensis*.

The height of the *demigods* would be a trait they'd pass on. There's an episode in Exodus that confirms that they did, an event that takes place many generations after the birth of the first *men of renown*. As the Hebrews approached Canaan, Moses sent scouts ahead. They saw huge men:

we came unto the land whither thou didst send us
and truly doth it flow with milk and honey…
we did see there the giants
the sons of anak, the nefilim…
and we were like grasshoppers in our eyes
and so were we in their eyes

The phrase *sons of anak* appears in other Bible passages, too, as does the word *annakim*…Hebrew renderings of *anunnaki*. And there are several other episodes in which the Israelites encounter gigantic men as they ventured into the western Mesopotamian diaspora north of the Sinai.

Cities were founded on the plain and uplands of the rivers Tigris and Euphrates, as settlement moved inland from ER.I.DU, which was

near the head of the Persian Gulf. The overall authority for each city rested with one of the twelve highest Anunnaki lords. He and EN.LIL together appointed a noble of lesser rank to administer the city as its king. Kingship had been granted to the colony by AN. On NI.BI.RU AN's insignia were the tiara, for his royal stature; the scepter, for his power; and the shepherd's staff, for the guidance he provided. Replicas of the symbols of his authority were given to the kings on Earth.[3]

The initiation of kingship on Earth was a momentous event. The ceremony was held on sacred ground in the original place of settlement, the residence of Enki, *Lord of the Earth*, founder of the colony:

when kingship was lowered from heaven
kingship was in Eridu
in Eridu Alulim became king and ruled eight šars

The levels of Earth's social order were as follows:

- First: Enlil, closely followed by Enki.
- Second: ten highly ranked *anunnaki* lords, the *gods* of the great cities.
- Third: dozens of less highly ranked nobles, *gods* of other locales.
- Fourth: the lesser nobility, the kings and functionaries.
- Fifth: ordinary *lofty ones*, the *anunnaki* commoners.
- Sixth: those of mixed *anunnaki* and human parentage. Highest among them were the *demigods* who had noble *anunnaki* forbears.
- Seventh: the original servant race.
- Eighth: enslaved humans from another city, captured in war.

Carvings of bound captives make it clear that the status of the last group was harshly enforced. However, there is nothing to suggest that the subservience of the main human population involved coercion or cruelty. Quite the opposite. The people had a positive attitude toward serving their lords. Life on Earth had never been any different; it was the natural order.

__Enthralled with the tall, brilliant, skilled, beautifully clothed, fair Lofty Ones, the humans living in the cities, materially dependent, inferior physically as well as intellectually, short-lived, dark, and naked, did not need to be coerced into serving their superiors. In addition to being the laborers of the cities, humans were the foot soldiers in the armies of the Lofty Ones. For this role, too, no coercion was needed. To fight and die for one's beloved god and to kill the followers of his enemy were glorious deeds.__

As we will discuss, the roles of de facto slave and dispensable soldier were imprinted early on the identity of humankind...with fateful effect.

The Anunnaki, flying from place to place and into the heavens in their "sky chambers" and bearing their "thunderbolt" weapons, claimed divinity for themselves. In fact, several of the most highly ranked of the Lofty Ones claimed to be the personifications on Earth of the celestial deities, the planets of the Solar System and the signs of the Zodiac.

From the descriptions of the *gods'* weapons, aircraft, and rockets, it's clear to us that their physical powers derived from technology. The people, though, were led to see their abilities as aspects of divinity. A few of the highest ranking *anunnaki* nobles bolstered their standings by saying they were personifications of the planets. The *anunnaki* apparently believed that the planets of the solar system were not merely material bodies, but were entities with personality and consciousness, celestial divinities. By claiming identity with planetary deities, some of the noble *lofty ones* made themselves even more awesome to their worshippers. A prime example is Irnini, also called Inanna, meaning *Beloved of An* (her great-grandfather), who claimed to be the personification of the brightest planet in the sky, Laḫamu in Šumerian, the planet we call Venus. (In the later languages of Mesopotamia Inanna was called Ištar, Aštarte, and Aštoreth.) [4]

We know through discoveries made by archaeologists and paleoanthropologists that humans lived in many places outside of the cities of the *anunnaki*, at levels of cultural development varying greatly from place to place. They were the descendants of those who left the domains of the *anunnaki*, gradually spreading over the entire planet. They were of no concern to the *lofty ones*; they are not mentioned in the tablets.[5]

The way we see the relationship between civilized and uncivilized humanity is backward. The nomadic and indigenous peoples of the world are not cultures in the process of a long journey upward from primitive to civilized...the kind we assume our ancestors took. They are, rather, the offspring of those who, for their own reasons, moved away from the areas dominated by the *anunnaki* and settled into ways of life that pleased and suited them. They are not in early stages of development that would in time lead them toward civilization. Their ancestors were civilization's escapees.[6]

Humans probably left the settlements in Mesopotamia and Africa in small groups over the course of tens of thousands of years. They would have set out with various levels of skill and personal endowment. The cultures of humans living far from the cities as hunter-gatherers, nomads, and farmers, therefore, developed from many different starting points of cultural advancement, and at widely separated times. Some early bands could have wandered away from the mines in Africa without ever having learned much from Šumerian culture. Others could have gotten away from the major Mesopotamian cities quite accomplished in crafts and farming.[7]

Paleoanthropologists assume that all cultures evolved from the same zero point in time and space, their lines of advancement beginning with the instinctual abilities of an advanced African homonin. But if different groups of humans had different levels of cultural advancement when they left the domains of the *anunnaki* in Africa and in the Middle East, and if they set off at different times, it's no wonder that scientists are unable to come to a consensus regarding the sequence of development of the prehistoric tools, ceramics, and artwork that have been found all around the world.

In the next chapter we consider how the *anunnaki* responded to the most momentous event they experienced on Earth.

---

[1] Violence initiated by one of the royal brothers against the other is rare in the annals of Mesopotamia; mostly it erupts between members of their clans.

[2] Two Hebrew phrases are rendered here with grammatical accuracy, *the sons of the gods* and *those who came down*. The traditional translations of the phrases are, respectively, *the sons of God* (which makes no sense) and *giants* (as mentioned in the Acknowledgment). In the chapter Words of the Bible we'll explore these two purposeful misrepresentations of biblical terms.

³ In the West, the crown and scepter remained with the kings while the staff went to the bishops, reflecting the division of authorities between Enlil and Enki.

⁴ When people saw Venus, the *evening star*, the brightest point of light in the night sky, they were led to think of Inanna, the most powerful female *god*.

⁵ If the *anunnaki* had any interest in the fate of humans beyond their dominion, they would have appeared in some way in the literature of Mesopotamia. For example, the cave called Šanidar in the highlands north of the upper Tigris, quite near to Mesopotamia, was continuously occupied from 100,000 to 13,000 BCE. Its community had to have been known to the *lofty ones*, yet there is no mention in the tablets of this or any other human settlement not ruled by them. This was true even for highly developed cultures in the vicinity of Mesopotamia, such as those to the northeast in the Zagros Mountains. Except when they were met in war, humans outside *anunnaki* control were never acknowledged.

⁶ In the Mesopotamian texts unearthed to date, there is only one telling of a departure. The episode was obviously significant, since it was retold in the Book of Genesis. The tablet says a group was exiled from Edin led by a man named Kain, who had killed his brother, Abael. Kain had been taught farming by one of the sons of Enlil, and Abael had been taught shepherding by a son of Enki, so the tale bears the imprint of the tension between the brother *gods*. The exiles settled in a land called Dunnu. In the biblical tale the names of the brothers are the same, their occupations are the same, and the name of the place of exile is also actually the same. Genesis tells that after Cain was expelled from Eden he settled in the *Land of Nod*. In Šumerian, the order of a compound word's roots could be reversed without changing its meaning. So Dunnu and Nudun would have the same meaning … and it's a short step from Nudun in Šumerian to Nod in Hebrew.

⁷ The prehistoric mound builders in the southern United States lived in cities of tens of thousands of inhabitants, with ceremonial plazas and earthen mounds one hundred feet high. They built from memories they carried of the sacred precincts and ziggurats of Mesopotamia. A cross within a circle was a sacred symbol for the tribes of the Bakongo culture of west central Africa. Their forebears had handed down the Šumerian representation of the *Planet of the Crossing*. The Dogon tribe of Mali must have descended from a group who left the Egyptian domain of the *anunnaki* carrying some of the culture's astronomical sophistication, e.g., a detailed understanding of the Sirius star system.

Deluge

The AN.UN.NA.KI were thriving, supported in luxury by their enthralled human servants. But disaster loomed. The Lofty Ones learned that on its next passage NI.BI.RU would come close to Earth, wreak havoc, and cause a watery catastrophe.

After they learned what was about to happen, the *anunnaki* had to be on high alert. After all, they were on the planet that in the remote past had suffered a cataclysmic collision when Nibiru drew too near. Not only that, their home planet soon was going to run the gauntlet of the Asteroid Belt.

Before the deluge would strike, the Lofty Ones could take to their spacecraft ... yet what of the humans? EN.LIL had long before then come to regard humankind as an abomination, out of disgust for the interbreeding between humans and AN.UN.NA.KI. He'd even tried to decimate civilized humanity, but EN.KI had blocked his cruel campaigns. Now a natural event was going to do the job for him ... as long as the people were kept in the dark. EN.LIL directed the ruling circle to swear an oath not to disclose the disaster to come, thus sealing the fate of the peoples of Mesopotamia.

Major texts tell of Enlil's disgust with the servant race and quote the harsh orders he gave to bring about humanity's demise. He had reluctantly agreed to the creation of humans, but now he'd had enough.

in the land like wild bulls they lay
the god was disturbed by their conjugations
the god Enlil heard their pronouncements and said to the great gods
oppressive have become the pronouncements of mankind
their conjugations deprive me of sleep[1]

For the humans and their livestock Enlil ordered:

aches, dizziness, chills, fever...disease, sickness, plague, pestilence

There was a *man of renown* devoted to Enki, a man who'd have a pivotal role in what would later unfold. He called to his *god*.

living in Enki's temple ... his mind alert to his Lord ... appealing to him
Ea, O Lord, mankind groans
the anger of the gods consumes the land
yet it is thou who hast created us
let there cease the aches, the dizziness, the chills, the fever

In response to his follower's entreaty, Enki intervened. In a way not yet known to us he rendered ineffective the afflictions that Enlil had imposed. No text giving the specifics of Enki's actions has been discovered, but clearly once again he frustrated his brother, who fumed:

the people are not diminished
they are more numerous than before

Enlil then set about the devastation of humankind through starvation, to be achieved by drought. His pronouncements were ominous:

let the rains be withheld above by the rain god
below let the waters not rise from their sources
let the wind blow and parch the ground
let the clouds thicken but hold back the downpour

How much were the harsh conditions mankind suffered a result of the weather-modification Enlil ordered, and how much were they natural? Earth was in a phase of glaciation, and much of the planet's water was being drawn into the masses of ice that were forming. There's evidence, such as widespread population decline, of prolonged, intense drought.

Enlil demanded that seafood be made unavailable. The *Lord of the Deep*, Enki, heard from his brother, the *Lord of the Command*:

draw the bolt, bar the sea...guard [the ocean's] food from the people

Enki's loyal follower cried out again for help.

3.7 Deluge

In the house of his god...he set foot...
every day he wept bringing oblations in the morning...
he called the name of his god...

For a very long time Enki appears to have given no response. Perhaps the *Lord of Earth* was bound by an agreement that has not been found. For seven passes of Nibiru, that is, for more than 25,000 years, humanity was in distress. Finally it was Enki's turn to have had enough. He called for a campaign of civil disobedience:

make a loud noise in the land...
do not revere your gods
do not pray to your goddesses

Enki called elders to assemble in his temple
 told of his opposition to the actions of the other gods,
exonerated himself, and outlined a plan of action.

Of the tablets telling of Enki's action, only fragments survive:

in the night...by the riverbank...*from the lower world [Africa] Enki* ...brought the water warriors...*commands were shouted*...go...the order...

No intact texts have been found giving details of the insurrection, yet from Enlil's response we know it was effective. He summoned Enki and confronted him in an assembly of *anunnaki* nobles:

...filled with anger...
all of us great anunnaki
reached together a decision...
I commanded that in the bird of heaven
Adad should guard the [skies]
that [Nannar] and Nergal should guard the [ground]
that the bolt, the bar of the sea

you should guard with your rockets
but you let loose provision for the people...
He demanded: stop feeding your people...
He ordered that Enki no longer
supply grain on which the people thrive...

Enki's reaction to being publicly chastised took the *gods* by surprise:

The god was fed up with the sitting
in the assembly of the gods laughter overcame him

After the shouting following Enki's derisive outburst died down...

Enlil reminded all of the unanimous decision. He reviewed the origins of the primitive workers. He recalled the many times that Enki had ignored rules. He spoke of how mankind would be eliminated by the deluge that was coming, and of how the catastrophe needed to be kept secret from the people. He called on the assembly of nobles to bind themselves to secrecy.

Enlil opened his mouth to speak
and addressed the assembly of all the gods
come all of us and take an oath
regarding the killing flood
An swore first Enlil swore
his sons swore with him

An's presence reflects the importance of the convocation and confirms that Nibiru was approaching; a voyage to Earth was feasible only when the *Planet of the Crossing* was within the known Solar System. Enki resisted:

Why will you bind me with an oath?
Am I to raise my hand against my own humans?

3.7 Deluge

EN.KI initially refused the oath, but eventually gave in.

An, Enlil, Enki and [Ninmaḫ]
the gods of Heaven and Earth
had taken the oath

However, EN.KI couldn't really accept the total annihilation of his Mesopotamian children. He designed a vessel that could save a few souls from the city of Šuruppak so that the population of civilized humanity could in time be restored. The craft would also carry "seeds of life", genetic material from the culture's animals and plants. He gave instruction to an esteemed devotee, using a trick to avoid overtly breaking the oath. Keeping the craft's true purpose secret, the man enlisted help to build it.

The Book of Genesis says the Earth was covered by water that came in the form of unrelenting rains. Of course, no ordinary natural event could cause the volume of water on Earth to suddenly increase and totally cover the continents, only to quickly drain away. Except for the religiously orthodox, everyone understands that the biblical Flood has prominent fictional aspects. Yet a deluge surely occurred.[2]

The first archaeological evidence for a Mesopotamian inundation came in 1929 in a shaft dug into the ruins of Ur. It revealed that under a three-foot-thick layer of the usual debris of civilization, there was an undisturbed layer of hard-packed clay over eight feet deep. The material was so uniform it could only have been brought by water ... and was so laced with the remains of countless tiny marine organisms, that the water could only have come from the sea. The archaeologist directing the dig was then dumbfounded to find, under the clay, another layer of urban debris, the remains of Ur's first settlement. His wife brought him out of his confusion, exclaiming that they'd found the Flood of the Bible. Other digs revealed an area of inundation extending inland four hundred miles from the head of the Persian Gulf and a hundred miles wide. The deposits of clay were progressively thinner the farther they were from the sea.

Documentary evidence for a great flood is substantial. On Mesopotamian tablets, such as the lists of the kings and their reigns, there are many explicit references to events that took place and people who lived before the flood. The flood divided Šumerian history in two. One king boasted that he could:

read the enigmatic inscriptions from before the deluge.

Another king said he was exalted because he was:

of the seed preserved from before the deluge.

The ancestry of one of the kings contained this momentous language:

on that day, on that remote day
on that night, on that remote night
in that year, in that remote year
when the deluge had taken place ...

Scientific texts said that the information they held came from:

the olden sages before the deluge.

This is the sequence of events in the flood epics of Mesopotamia: • The golden planet approaches • The Anunnaki learn of the impending flood • A powerful gale blows from the south • A loud roar fills the air • Clouds darken the sky • The Lofty Ones ascend • After massive rains ... a wall of water.

We can deduce what happened. Electrical and magnetic forces resulting from the close approach of Nibiru disrupted the atmosphere, producing torrential rains, and perhaps a rapid increase in warming. Gravitational forces caused earthquakes and abnormal tides. There is only one phenomenon that could have then caused water to sweep over Mesopotamia in the manner reported by the texts: a mega-tsunami.[3]

The most probable cause of so mountainous a wave is a breakup of the Antarctic ice cap, major portions of it sliding into the ocean. The wave from such masses of ice plunging into the sea would dwarf the tsunamis we have seen in our times. The northbound surges in the Atlantic, Pacific, and Indian Oceans would be so tall that the only people to escape death would be those living far to the north, well inland, or at relatively high elevations.[4]

No complete Šumerian account of the deluge and the events leading up to it has been found, but with Akkadian, Babylonian, Assyrian, and Canaanite texts to supplement the partial Šumerian ones, a full, consistent story can be compiled. In all the versions of the flood tale there's a human hero. He was Ziusudra to the Šumerians, Utnapištim to the Akkadians, and Atra-Ḫasis to the Babylonians.⁵ We'll refer to this *man of renown* as Ziusudra, the name by which he was known in his own time. He was a person of high standing in Šurrupak, perhaps even its king.

The most complete of the Mesopotamian deluge sagas is given in Ziusudra's voice in the Epic of Gilgameš. It begins with a portentous dream Ziusudra had while residing in Enki's temple in Šurrupak.

the gods commanded total destruction
Enlil imposed an evil deed on the humans

Ziusudra called to Enki, pleading to his lord, desperate to know what evil was approaching. Enki found a stratagem by which he could comply in form with the oath he'd taken, while ignoring it in substance. He placed Ziusudra on the other side of a reed partition and pretended that he was speaking to the wall. He thus informed Ziusudra of what was to come, and of all that his *god* expected of him:

wall, listen to me, reed wall, observe my words
on all the habitations, over the cities
a storm will sweep
the destruction of mankind's seed it will be
this is the final ruling
the word of the assembly of the gods
the word spoken by An, Enlil and [Ninmaḫ] …
reed hut, hearken, wall, reflect
man of šuruppak, son of ubar-tutu
abandon your house, build a ship
give up possessions, seek thou life
forswear goods, the soul alive
aboard the ship take thou
the seed of all living things

Genes, *the seed of all living things*, were taken aboard … not pairs of living creatures as in the Book of Genesis. This assignment makes sense, for Ziusdura was serving the *god* who was the chief scientist on Earth. The vessel was to be a *magurgur*, meaning *boat that can turn and tumble*. It was to have no openings and be sealed all over with pitch. Clearly, to ride out a mega-tsunami it had to be submersible. (In the Babylonian epic the craft is a *tzulili*, a word close to the modern Hebrew for submarine, *tzolelet*.) Enki told Ziusudra what the signal to board would be:

when Šamaš who orders trembling at dusk
will shower down a rain of eruptions
board thou the ship batten up the entrance

Šamaš, *god* of rockets, would direct the *gods'* ascent from Sippar, the city he ruled. Lift-off would be in darkness; Ziusudra would be able to see the exhaust flames in Šurrupak, about one hundred miles to the south. The Assyrian deluge epic tells that as the *sky chambers* came into use:

the noise of the deluge…set the gods trembling…
the anunnaki lifted up…setting the land ablaze with their glare

The Babylonian flood epic says of Ziusudra's ordeal during the storm:

[he] was in and out, he could not sit, could not crouch…
his heart was broken, he was vomiting gall…
the appearance of the weather changed
the rains roared in the clouds the winds became savage…
the deluge set out its might came upon the people as a battle
one person did not see another
they were not recognizable in the destruction
the deluge bellowed like a bull

In the Epic of Gilgameš, Ziusudra describes the flood:

with the glow of dawn
a black cloud arose from the horizon…
everything…turned to blackness…
for a day the south storm blew
gathering speed as it blew
submerging the mountains…

3.7 Deluge

six days and six nights blows the wind
as the south storm sweeps the land
when the seventh day arrived
the deluge of the south storm subsided

A tiny tablet in Akkadian, found in Ašur, links Nibiru's passage through the inner Solar System with the deluge. It contains so many Šumerian terms it must have its source in an original from Šumer.

his weapon is the deluge
god whose weapon brings death…
supreme, supreme, anointed…
who like the sun the land crosses…
who the circular band hammered together…
lord who at new year time
within Tiamat's battle place reposes…
this is the name of the lord
who from the second month [through the twelfth]
the waters had summoned forth

The tablet speaks of the Asteroid Belt, calling it the *circular band*, that the celestial deity, said to be shining *like the Sun* (Nibiru, sheathed in reflective gold), had previously *hammered together*. It says that the planetary *god* passed through the asteroids, *Tiamat's battle place*, at the start of the new year, and that its effect on Earth, *the waters summoned forth*, extended from the second month to the end of the twelfth. This implies that there were places where the geography kept water from quickly returning to the ocean, so that it took nearly ten months for it all to drain off.[6]

As NI.BI.RU passed over, the AN.UN.NA.KI watched in horror and grief as all they'd built and nurtured in Mesopotamia was obliterated.

Seen from the chariots of the lofty ones…the flood sweeps over all

The conditions in the orbiting *anunnaki* spacecraft were dismal:

the gods cowered like dogs
crouched against the outer wall
Inanna cried out like a woman in labor:
the olden days are alas turned to clay...
the anunnaki gods weep with her
the gods all humbled sit and weep
their lips drawn tight...one and all

   In another craft:

the anunnaki, great gods
were sitting in thirst, in hunger
Ninti wept and spent her emotion
she wept and spent her feelings
the gods wept with her for the land
she was overcome with grief...
where she sat, the gods sat weeping
crouching like sheep at a trough
their lips were feverish of thirst
they were suffering cramp from hunger...
Ninti saw and she wept...
my creatures have become like flies
they fill the rivers like dragonflies
their fatherhood taken by the rolling sea

   The king of Nibiru directed the *lofty ones* to return while the home planet was still close. But Ninmaḫ was reluctant to leave. In her vessel the gods debated the merits of An's command:

shall I ascend to Heaven
to reside in the House of Offerings
where An the Lord has ordered to go?

3.7 Deluge

As the water drained off, they spotted the vessel of salvation. EN.LIL was furious over the violation of the oath. He was urged to relent and he did ... and pledged to never again harm humankind.

The vessel was sighted. The *lofty ones* landed close by it. Enki had a good idea where the craft would rest. Water surging up the Persian Gulf would carry a ship toward the eastern Turkish highlands and a text tells that a navigator was on board, with instructions to direct the craft to:

the mount of salvation.

No tablet has been found that locates the landing place.[7] Discovering the band of humans was a relief to the shaken and exhausted *anunnaki*. As ever, the role of humanity was to serve the *lofty ones*. Ziusudra's party slaughtered and roasted animals for them.

[the gods] smelled the sweet savor
gathered like flies over the offering

But discord was never absent for long. Ninmaḫ swore:

by the great jewels An had fashioned for her,
that she would not forget their ordeal and what had happened, saying
let not Enlil come to the offering for he unreasoning
by the deluge my humans consigned to destruction

Indeed, as Nibiru approached Enlil had pronounced:

let them perish
let the seed of earthling be wiped off the face of earth

For his part, Earth's supreme leader wasn't inclined to rejoice:

When Enlil's craft descended and he saw the vessel
he was filled with wroth against the igigi
has some living soul escaped?
no human was to survive destruction [8]

The *igigi*, the *gods* assigned to live off planet, had not taken part in the oath-taking and were the logical objects of Enlil's suspicions. But Ninurta guessed who had saved the band of humans and said to Enlil, his father:

who other than Ea can devise plans
It is Ea who knows every matter

Enki then cajoled Enlil, making the case for acceptance:

thou wisest of the gods, thou hero
how could thou unreasoning
bring about such a catastrophe?

Enlil relented, brought around by the arguments of Enki, Ninmaḫ, and Inanna, as well as by the realities of the situation. His turnaround was complete; he had Enki's follower Ziusudra taken to one of the domains of the *gods* (whose vital location we will discuss), where he was endowed with *the long life*. As Zisudra tells Gilgameš much later:

Enlil went aboard the ship
holding me by the hand he took me aboard
he took my wife aboard and made her kneel by my side
standing between us he touched our foreheads to bless us
hitherto Ziusudara and his wife like gods shall be unto us
far away shall the man Ziusudra reside...
The land Tilmun the place where [Šamaš] rises
they caused him to dwell...
life like that of a god they gave him
breath eternal like a god they granted him

This account of the hero of the flood being awarded the lifespan of the *gods* is consonant with his name in the earlier epics. The Addakian epithet Utnapištim and the Šumerian epithet Ziusudra both mean *he of life days extended*. Furthermore the young king appears to be not at all surprised to be talking with the hero of old, thousands of years after the deluge.[9]

3.7 Deluge

Enlil's kindness toward Ziusudra was later echoed in Genesis:

and the LORD blessed Noaḥ and his sons and said unto them:
be fruitful and multiply and replenish the Earth

The flood epics of Mesopotamia had different points of emphasis and different tones, yet they were in agreement in core content. (1) Enlil found the sexual unions of *anunnaki* and humans intolerable and tried to lay waste civilized humankind. (2) Enki foiled his brother's initiatives. (3) Enlil was pleased to learn that the humans in his domain would be destroyed by a natural calamity if kept uninformed. (4) Enki slyly defied him and helped a renowned human to survive the deluge with kith and kin, along with the means to restore civilization's plants and animals. (5) As the waters receded, and the *lofty ones* returned from orbit, Enlil accepted what his brother had done and pledged not to assault humankind ever again.

The flood was a focal event in the history of Mesopotamia and had to be made prominent in the scriptures of the Hebrews, whose culture had its origin there. The scribes of Genesis had to adapt historical texts involving the olden *gods* in a way that would bolster the new theology of one God. The deluge was too important to forget, yet it was too terrifying to recall clearly, and in addition the involvement of the *anunnaki* was problematic.[10]

The Jews received a radically revised version of history. The biblical tale condenses events taking place over a long period into a single episode. It turns a conflict of wills between two ruling *gods*, in which the first one, powerful but not all-powerful, relents ... into a tale in which a unitary God inexplicably changes His mind. It takes the theme of a moralistic *god's* disgust with the race of servants (for behavior they really couldn't help getting caught up in) and replaces it with God's fury over how sinful humans had become. The biblical tale takes a disaster caused by a real planet, an event that could recur, and reports it as the will of an omnipotent deity who promises never to do such a thing again. It replaces a realistic means of insuring that life will flourish after the disaster (taking aboard *the seed of living things*) with an unrealistic account involving breeding pairs of animals. And it takes the natural drowning of the cities of Mesopotamia and turns it into the supernatural flooding of the entire planet. Yet in closing, the biblical account and those of the Mesopotamian scribes converge: the deity in Genesis and the chief *god* of Mesopotamia both pledge to never again inflict violence on humanity. The Bible's literary accomplishment is masterful.

We can calculate the dates of the Flood and other nodal events by compiling information from a number of texts, notably the king lists, and from accounts of the eclipse that will figure in our discussion later. From the time of the first ruler, kingship beginning when Enlil arrived, to the deluge, there were ten supreme kings, ruling for a total of 432,000 years.[11] A text tells that from the founding of the Earth colony to Enlil's arrival, there were 8 orbits of Nibiru, or 28,800 years. Thus ...

- The arrival of Enki and the first settlers: 452,156 BCE
- The arrival of Enlil and the start of kingship: 443,356 BCE
- The Deluge: 11,356 BCE[12]
- Most recent passage of Nibiru: 556 BCE

This date for the flood falls within a period when an ice age was fading. The natural rise in temperature and atmospheric and surface moisture during de-glaciation facilitated the collapse of the Antarctic ice pack, which was triggered by the effects of Nibiru's close approach.

There are recycled accounts of the watery violence caused by Nibiru elsewhere in the Hebrew Bible: passages in Psalms 29, 77, and 104 and grim prophecies, such as that of Amos, about the coming Day of the Lord. Out of theological necessity, Amos didn't mention a planet, yet he was clearly referring to the next approach of Nibiru, which educated persons knew was to take place not that far in the future. His words about the chaos the Lord of the Universe would bring about echoed the Mesopotamian accounts of the destruction twice wreaked on our world by the original Lord of Heaven: the collision that moved the planet and produced the Asteroid Belt, and the global flood. If his predictions proved accurate, people would think of the approaching golden planet as the physical agent of their all-powerful God. In the King James translation:

Woe unto you that desire the day of the LORD! To what end is it ... the day of the LORD is darkness, and not light ...
shall not the land tremble for this, and every one mourn that dwelleth therein? And it shall rise up wholly as a flood; and...the LORD GOD of hosts is he that toucheth the land, and it shall melt...it is he that calleth for the waters of the sea, and poureth them out upon the face of the earth: the LORD is his name.

As we'll discuss in the last chapter of The Mesopotamian Tale, on its next visit Nibiru did not come close to Earth. That transit was a nonevent compared with the one that caused the deluge. Yet the prophecies of Amos and his ilk were retained in the final version of the Hebrew Bible, which was being fashioned at that very time. The learned editors knew that Nibiru would keep returning and that another catastrophic *day of the Lord*

3.7 Deluge

was possible, as indeed it is. They must have concluded that there was value for the Jewish faith in keeping alive some awareness of the threat.

Evidence is coalescing for a sudden rise in global sea levels apparently caused by a torrent from the north that took place at around the time of the mega-tsunami from the south. Known as the Younger-Dryas event, it involved an enormous volume of melt-water produced by a cloud of meteorites striking the massive North American icecap. How much of the continental margins were submerged, and how long it took for glaciation to bring sea levels back down, is not firmly established. This event could be the historic source of the theme of the drowning of the entire planet in Genesis.

[1] Enlil's dark intentions are echoed in God's words in Genesis:

And GOD saw that the wickedness of man was great in the earth ... and the LORD said, I will destroy man whom I have created from the face of the earth

Enlil's attitudes and campaigns are also reflected early in Exodus, when Pharaoh's fear and disgust over the Israelite's fecundity leads to his horrific proclamations.

[2] The Younger-Dryas event, a recently discovered planetary catastrophe caused by meteor impacts, almost certainly raised sea levels worldwide. The time of its occurrence might have been close to the time of the Mesopotamian deluge.

[3] The archaeological findings at Ur are consistent with the local geography. For ages, the Persian Gulf had received sediment brought by the rivers converging at its head. Water surging from the Indian Ocean would have been funneled by the land bordering the gulf, increasing its force and causing it to plow up the sediment at the head of the gulf...so that Mesopotamia was not only drowned, it was buried in mud. (In 2018, augmentation of a tsunami by the funneling effect was seen in the Bay of Palu, in Indonesia.) The archaeologist was so excited about the potential impact of discovering the historical basis for the Flood of Genesis that he wrote his telegrams to colleagues at the University of Pennsylvania in Latin. The evidence he'd found drew popular attention when he and his wife returned to Philadelphia, but in time his peers dismissed their discovery. It was all merely the result of river flooding, they decided. That explanation made no sense, but the discovery was too inconvenient to be appreciated for what it was.

[4] We are now witnessing phenomena consistent with the massive slippage of ice that we posit. (1) Starting in 2014, scientific publications have made it clear that the western Antarctic ice cap is in an irreversible process of deterioration. This is a result of climate change, though the situation is complex and the precise causal chain is unclear. Some scientists have concluded that catastrophic disintegrations of the Antarctic ice cap probably occurred in the past. (2) With increasing Arctic temperatures, melt water is flowing beneath the Greenland ice cap, speeding the movement of its glaciers toward the sea. The relationships between ice and rock in Greenland and Antarctica are different, so there won't be a precipitous collapse of the Greenland ice, but vulnerability in the southern ice can be inferred from what we observe in the north. (3) In the early 21st century it has become obvious that a warming atmosphere holds increased amounts of water and produces extreme precipitation, Earth had been in a warming phase, as we'll soon discuss.

[5] There are Akkadian accounts of the deluge in which Enki refers to his faithful follower as being *atra-ḫasis*, meaning *exceedingly wise*. That phrase became the epithet by which he was known in Babylonia; it's the title scholars have given to the Babylonian flood epic.

⁶ This account corresponds well with the timing given in the Book of Genesis, where it says that the events of the Deluge began on the seventeenth day of the second month and lasted until the first day of the new year.

⁷ The double peaks of Ararat, the highest points in the entire Middle East, have since medieval times been thought to be the resting place of Noah's Ark.

⁸ In the flood epics, as in every Mesopotamian text ever found, no mention is made of humans living on their own far from civilization. It is certain that many of them survived the tsunami. Apparently, they were of no interest to the *anunnaki*.

⁹ The flood epics suggest that Ziusudra was a *demigod* with enormous longevity, so his being granted the *long life* may not have been an extraordinary gesture. The case for Ziusudra's *anunnaki* lineage gains support from a fragment of the apocryphal *Book of Noah*. It says that Noah's father was startled by his son's appearance at birth, fearing that his wife had conceived him with a *god* ... an unusual thought in a Hebrew text and almost certainly not of Jewish origin.

¹⁰ In their account of the Deluge the authors of Genesis did something on a mass scale that occurs naturally in individual lives: create what Freud called a screen memory. In this development, traumatizing experiences are not blocked from consciousness by amnesia, but instead are turned into an acceptable, partly accurate memory, through a process of insertion and deletion.

¹¹ Each reign of a supreme king was a multiple of 3,600, e.g., 28,800, 36,000, and 43,200 years. The installation of the kings must have coincided with Nibiru's approaches, when travel between the two planets was feasible. That suggests that An, who had granted kingship to the colony, presided at the coronations.

¹² A curious, enigmatic biblical passage appears to confirm this date. In Genesis 6, God says that He intends to do away with mankind:

And the LORD said, My Spirit shall not always strive with man, for that he also is flesh: yet his days shall be a hundred twenty years

What does *his days shall be 120 years* mean? No lives of 120 years are mentioned in the Bible, other than that of Moses, and it's not evident whose days are being cited. The meaning of the passage can be clarified by The Mesopotamian Tale. At the time of the deluge, Enlil's *spirit* surely was not *striving with man*. At that moment he had been on Earth for 432,000 years, a span determined by the king lists. That number of Earth years is 120 of Nibiru's *years*, if *year* means the time it takes for a planet to fully circle the Sun: $120 \times 3,600 = 432,000$. The enigmatic passage, therefore, echoes the historical fact that at the time of the flood, Enlil, no longer tolerant of humankind, had been on Earth 120 of Nibiru's years.

Rebuilding

If the AN.UN.NA.KI were to once again have the way of life they'd been enjoying, the tasks ahead were staggering. As EN.KI and EN.LIL contemplated rebuilding the cities, restoring agriculture, and resuming gold shipments, they came to a momentous decision. No longer would humans be restricted to relatively low-level tasks. As the population was rebuilt, promising humans would be endowed with the knowledge and skills needed to restore and maintain civilization.

Those growing up with the biblical story of the Flood that destroyed the world are naturally curious about the actual deluge. The water's impact was massive and widespread, but it had its limits. For instance, *anunnaki* structures outside Mesopotamia and well above sea level were untouched. These included massive walls high in the Andes, which we will discuss in the chapter Great Stones, and magnificent masonry temples in the highlands of Anatolia. And descendants of the humans who'd left civilization long before the deluge were unharmed because they were dwelling in locations far enough from the sea or high enough above it.

Much of what the *anunnaki* had built in Egypt was salvageable. The cities along the Nile were swept by waters surging from the Red Sea, but geography saved them from being buried deep in mud[1]. Egypt's major buildings were made of stone and could be restored. Texts tell of rebuilding after a great inundation. The *god* in charge of the restoration had come from the *celestial disk* long before the flood and had built dams, canals, and works of architecture.[2] The texts say that this builder and teacher *god* created mankind, paralleling the Mesopotamian creation epics. Of course this was Enki. In Egypt he was Ptaḥ, meaning *developer*, a name echoing one of his Šumerian epithets, *he who makes things*, Nudimud.[3]

The destruction in Mesopotamia, in contrast, was total. The texts make it clear: the *anunnaki* heartland was utterly destroyed. The cities were crushed by the mountainous waves, the soft bricks dissolving, the ground becoming smothered in sediment. After the seawater receded, the principal rivers and their tributaries were left choking in disarray.

...nothing was produced
the small rivers were not cleaned
the mud was not carried off...
in all the land there were no crops

only weeds grew…
the Euphrates was not bound together
The Tigris was confounded jolted and injured

Time was needed for the people to grow in numbers sufficient to maintain a restored civilization. The fullness of culture that the *gods* envisioned after the deluge, with their human followers more capable than they'd ever been, needed several thousand years to come to fruition.

The mud on the flatlands had to dry sufficiently before planting would be feasible, so farming was first established in the hill country to the north and in the mountainous regions to the west. Texts tell of Enlil distributing grains in those two areas. Later, when the soil on the plain was dry, he began to operate there, assisted by other *gods*:

Šumer, land that knew not grain, came to know grain…
the land with wheat and barley did become acquainted (Figure 3.8.1)

Figure 3.8.1. An Akkadian cylinder seal showing Enlil with crops; grain decorates his throne. One *god* approaches with crops, one with implements, one with seeds.

During this critical time, Enki and Enlil worked together:

Seeds were a gift of An, from his Celestial Abode. The skills of agriculture were gifts of Enlil and his son Ninurta. Those of animal husbandry were gifts of Enki…
the wooly creature they placed in a sheepfold

3.8 Rebuilding

the seeds that sprout they gave to the mother
for the grains they established a place
to the workmen they gave the plow and the yoke...
the young woman sprouting abundance brings
she lifts her head in the field
abundance has come from heaven
the wooly creature and grains...come forth in splendor
abundance was given to the congregated people

The human population slowly increased. Immigration may have played a role, though none is mentioned in the tablets. The authors of Genesis, however, did note influx. Some generations after the Flood:

[people] journeyed from the east, that they found a plain in the land of [Šinar] and they dwelt there

There would be human scribes, scientists, technicians, teachers, artists, musicians ... and even kings, for AN decreed that kingship would again be granted to Earth. Each city would have its ruling Lofty One and he, as before, along with EN.LIL, would summon a king to the throne. Only now the sovereign would be a "man of renown", descended from the marriages of high-ranking AN.UN.NA.KI with humans distinguished by lineage.

As the numbers of people grew and the cities were rebuilt, decisions had to be made about governance. An came to Earth to oversee the process. In a text known as the Epic of Etana:

the great anunnaki who decree the fate
sat exchanging their counsels regarding the land
they who created the four regions
who set up the settlements
who oversaw the land
were too lofty for mankind

Humans with skills and responsibilities would have dealings with the *gods*, yet it would be unseemly for them to have direct contact with the greatest of the *lofty ones*. Intermediaries were needed between the *anunnaki* lords and the people responsible for maintaining the cities. *Demigod* kings were to provide the connection. The symbols of kingship were again brought from Nibiru, as they had been at the time of Enlil's arrival.

The tiara, the scepter and the shepherd's crook
lay before An in heaven...[and]
kingship descended from heaven

Following the flood, the lands ruled by the AN.UN.NA.KI were divided into domains. Three were assigned to members of the clans of the two royal brothers. The one around TIL.MUN was not; it was awarded to NIN.MAH, who, as sister to both royal brothers, would keep it neutral.

Statutory authority was assigned over the separate regions that were established. Four domains were defined. (Figure 3.8.2)

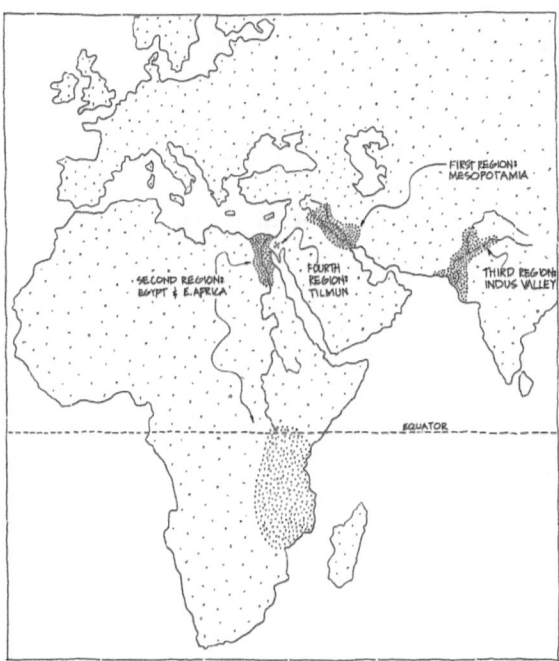

Figure 3.8.2. The four domains established following the deluge.

3.8 Rebuilding

- Mesopotamia and its neighboring lands, the first region to begin rebuilding, was granted to the sons of Enlil: the plain of the two rivers and the country to its west, to Nannar; the highlands to the north, to Ninurta; Anatolia and the Aegean islands, to Iškur. Sippar remained the domain of Šamaš, as it had been from the start, (The deep mud, though dried, was too soft for the city to resume service as a launching site. It became the seat of Šumer's high court.)
- Africa, the second region to start rebuilding, a thousand years later, was given to the sons of Enki: the prize, Egypt, to the firstborn, Marduk; the eastern mining region, to Gibil, whose name, meaning *burns soil*, refers to smelting; southern Africa, to Nergal; the great lakes and headwaters of the Nile, to Ninagal; the plain of Sudan, to Dumuzi. Ningišzidda's domain is not known. (Figure 3.8.3)
- Several hundred years after the start of reconstruction in Africa, development was begun in a newly established third domain in India. It was granted to Nannar's daughter, Inanna.
- Limited rights were granted to *gods* in a fourth region. As we'll soon discuss, neither clan was given exclusive authority there.

Figure 3.8.3. A Šumerian cylinder seal showing Enki facing his six sons.

Once the flatlands dried, permanent buildings could be erected. Deeply invested in tradition as they were, the *anunnaki* set out to recreate their buried cities, keeping the original street layouts and the sanctified designs of the major structures.[4] One text states:

let the bricks of all the cities be laid on the dedicated places
let all the [bricks] rest on holy places (Figures 3.8.4 a and b)

Figure 3.8.4a. A spike, held by a great *god*. With elaborate ritual, kings placed copper figurines of this kind in the foundations of major buildings. The figurines depicted the placing of giant spikes, something that was actually done by *gods* in the most important structures.

Figure 3.8.4b. A small stone carving with a woman revering the *god* Ningišzidda placing the spike for the zigurrat of Lagaš.

a

b

A tablet describing a major project said:

The everlasting ground plan, that which for the future the construction determined *I have followed*. It is the one which bears the drawings from the olden times and the writing of the upper heaven

Eridu, the first site place of anunnaki settlement, was the first to be restored. Enki's precinct had always been holy; within the rebuilt compound a temple to the *Lord of Earth* was erected, the *Eengurra, House of the Lord whose Return is Triumphant* It was the first significant building of the age following the flood. (Much revered, Enki's temple was rebuilt several times over the following centuries.) It was the site of a convocation of *gods* concerning the rebuilding of old cities and the founding of new ones. An, having journeyed from Nibiru for the occasion, addressed the assembly:

great gods who have hither come..
my son for himself a house built the lord Enki
Eridu like the mountain on Earth he raised
his house in a beautiful place he built
to the place Eridu no one uninvited can enter...
in its sanctuary from the Abzu
the divine formulas Enki has deposited

3.8 Rebuilding

Competition was present, as always. Enlil said that Enki was keeping the formulas needed to reestablish civilization to himself. Their father decreed that the formulas be shared, and Enki obeyed his command.

Kiš, within the domain of Enlil's heir, Ninurta, was the first rebuilt city of the new age. It was made the seat of the first king to dominate the region and became the administrative center:

may the city be the nest
the place where mankind shall repose
may the king be a shepherd...
after the flood had swept over Earth
when kingship was lowered again from heaven
kingship was in Kiš

The rebuilding of Ur, *the city,* began under the rule of Nannar. In time Ur would grow to become the economic hub of Šumer and a prime center of worship. With much ceremony, the construction of its ziggurat began. (Figures 3.8.5 through 3.8.7)

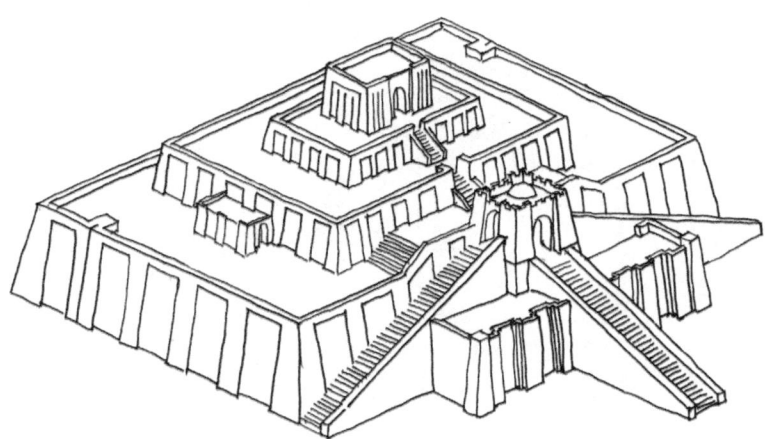

Figure 3.8.5. An archaeologist's conception of the ziggurat of Ur, based on documents and on the surviving ruin. The structure was restored by King Urnammu c. 2125 BCE at the direction of Nannar. The mass was of mud brick, the sheathing of baked brick and bituminous mortar.

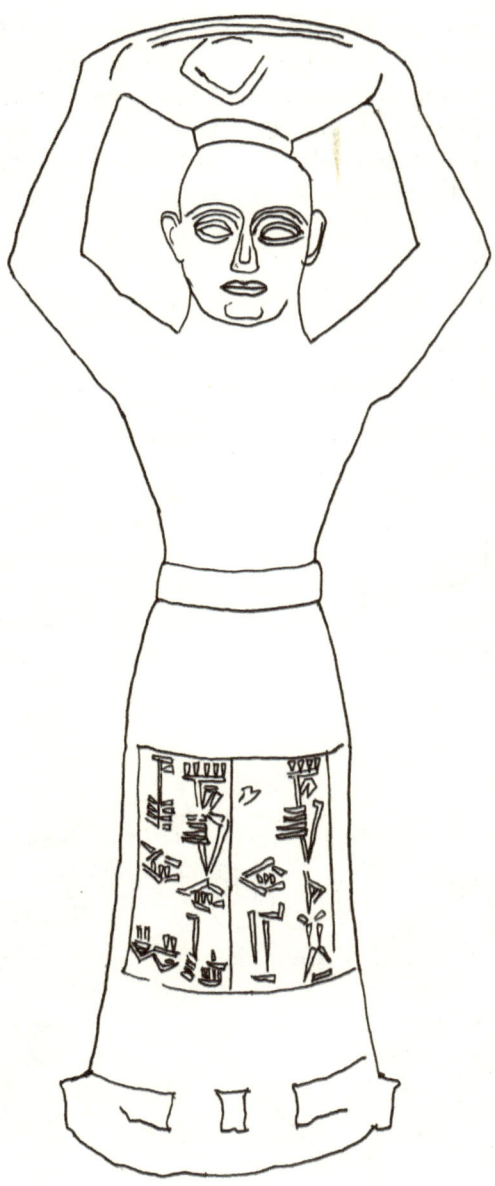

Figure 3.8.6. Now on display in J. P. Morgan's library, a statue of Urnammu, who ruled at the start of Ur's restoration and who rebuilt its ziggurat ... the first brick of which he cast, with great ceremony. He is in the lowly role of a carrier of a basket of mud for construction, symbolizing his subservience to his *god*. The inscription reads, *Urnammu, King of Šumer and Akkad, the one who built the temple of Enlil.*

3.8 Rebuilding

Figure 3.8.7. A partial reconstruction of the ziggurat of Ur, directed by an archaeologist. Atop the first stage the ruins of the second stage are visible. The oral tradition of the local Arabs held that the third stage ruins could once be seen. An automobile nearby suggests the scale of the structure.

The *gods* dictated all matters of war and peace, as before the deluge. The kings boasted of lands conquered and peoples subjugated on the orders of their *gods*. As before, no city remained dominant for long. One would gain power through violence and intrigue; then another did the same. Many texts tell of the dynastic conflicts, sexual liaisons, and battles that were involved, as well as the immense loss of human life.

Life in the cities centered as before on worshipping and supporting the *gods*. In the sacred precinct of each city, priests presided over prayers, sacrifices, and festivals and tended to the *gods* when they were in residence. One well-documented aspect of the attention lavished on the *lofty ones* was the fine cuisine. In one text:

Loaves of barley bread ... loaves of emmer bread.
A paste of honey and cream.
Dates, pastry ... beer, wine, milk ... cedar sap, cream.
Roasted meats with libations ...

A text about the culinary service to the *gods* in Uruk specifies the five beverages that were to be served with meals, and gives the recipe for a cut of bull to be prepared for the *lofty ones*:

Fine flour ... made into dough in water, prime beer and wine ... *mixed with fats*
Aromatic ingredients from the hearts of plants ... *nuts, malt and spices*

Some of the populace ate well, too. In a poem praising *coq au vin*:

In the wine of drinking
In the scented water

In the oil of unction
This bird have I cooked
And have eaten

Anunnaki nobles of lesser rank had authority in minor settlements and over specific functions. Many were female: Ninkaši, *Lady of the Straw*, mistress of brewing; Nidaba, overseer of the scribes; Nnmulmula, astronomer to the temples; Nina, supervisor of waterworks; and Nanše, mistress of the calendar (Figure 3.8.8).

Figure 3.8.8. A cylinder seal from Ur. The son of a prominent trader is brought before Nannar, *god* of the Moon, by a *goddess*. Overhead, Nannar's symbol, the crescent moon. The radiating cross represented Nibiru, and therefore An, its ruler.

Administering city life in those days seems not to have been any easier than it is today. Tablets from several different periods call for the return to former levels of respect, justice, truthfulness, and modesty.

The scribes of Šumer recorded what the *gods* told them about the times before the flood: the events involving Nibiru and Tiamat, the colonization by the *anunnaki*, the crafting of mankind, the founding of cities, the royal dynasties, and the warfare. Those histories were translated and copied by the scribes of successive Mesopotamian cultures who were directed, in addition, to record what was taking place in their own time.

A division evolved between the authority of power and the authority of learning. Kingship was the provenance of Enlil. The kings ruled in his name. He initiated the laws.[5] Wisdom was the provenance of Enki, who

3.8 Rebuilding

oversaw all scientific and technical pursuits. The priests of the ruling *gods* were granted advanced learning in various fields. Enki directed their education.[6] Texts tell how the first human priest was groomed:

showed him [divination using] oil and water
secrets of An Enlil and Enki
they gave him the divine tablets
the engraved secrets of heaven and earth
they taught him to calculate with numbers

It would take time for the mud left by the flood to dry so that the cities could be rebuilt, food production could rise, and the population could be restored ... about four thousand years. A new spaceport, though, was needed quickly, because the two in Mesopotamia had been deeply buried in mud. A new facility was built in the mountains immediately to the west of Mesopotamia. While a base serving the Anunnaki ruling Egypt had survived in the central Sinai, it was too distant from the settlements being restored.

Tilmun, *land of missiles*, was within the fourth region. It was meant to be dynastically neutral, ruled by neither of the clans of the brother *gods*. Ninmaḫ, who had never before ruled an area of settlement, was granted authority there. As the half-sister of both Enlil and Enki, she was one who could keep the peace and maintain the neutrality of Tilmun. Šamaš would supervise Tilmun in technical matters, but would have no statutory authority. His assignment was a natural one; he was the *god* of rocketry and had ruled Nippur and Sippar, the spaceflight centers lost to the flood. Tilmun was a restricted area, entered only by permission. *Sand dwellers*, as the remote predecessors of the Bedouin were known, could inhabit the surrounding areas, but no humans were to enter Tilmun itself. Fierce beings with awesome weapons enforced that restriction.

An environmental disaster that we'll soon discuss, centered in and near Tilmun, sealed the fate of Mesopotamian civilization. To better understand what unfolded, we need to establish that the base was in the Sinai. For reasons that will be obvious, Tilmun's remains have not been found, so we must rely on textual sources to determine its location. Taken together, they tell that the facility was located in the central portion of the Sinai peninsula.[7]

- Tilmun was said to be mountainous; there are mountains on the peninsula's central plateau, the probable site of the base, as well as on its northern and southern edges.

- Tablets say that Tilmun was located at the mouths of two bodies of water. The tip of the Sinai peninsula overlooks the mouths of the Gulf of Suez and the Gulf of Aqaba. (see Figures 3.8.2 and 3.4.6.).

- Šurbanipal, king of Assyria, said that he: laid [his] yoke from Tyre ... on the [Mediterranean] sea as far as Tilmun on the [Red] Sea.

- Šarrukin I of Akkad passing along the Mediterranean coast of the Sinai in a campaign against Egypt, said: I washed my weapons in the sea...and Tilmun my hand captured.

- The Dead Sea is close to the northern edge of the Sinai. Šarrukin II spoke of conquering lands stretching from: the shore of the [Dead] Sea as far as the border of Tilmun.

- Sumerian texts speak of Tilmun as a source of copper and gemstones; Early Egyptian texts speak of lapis lazuli and turquoise in the Sinai.

- In the Epic of Gilgameš, the questing king, seeking access to the heavens, sets out for a launch facility other than the one at Baalbek, which he had failed to enter. He comes upon the Dead Sea, the...

low lying ... Sea of the Waters of Death.

Overlooking the water Gilgameš sees a city dedicated to the *god* of the Moon. Crossing difficult terrain, he reaches Tilmun. This narrative accurately reflects the geography. The Dead Sea is just north of the Sinai; Jericho, *Moon City* in Akkadian and Hebrew, overlooks it; and the portion of the Sinai closest to the Dead Sea is mountainous.

- Nannar had authority over the Sinai peninsula and over the lands to its north. Texts call the southern portion of Nannar's domain *Gateway to Heaven*, a fitting phrase for a region with a launch facility. (Nannar's Akkadian name was *Sin*. The peninsula was named in his honor.)

- Ninmaḫ was proud to have as her domain a place of such importance.

3.8 Rebuilding

the gods have given unto my hand
the pilot guiding instruments of heaven earth
mother of the sky chambers am I ...
a mistress I am now
alone will I stay there reigning forever

Ninmaḫ received a new epithet, Ninḫursag, *Lady of the Peak Mountain*. The mountain with which she was identified, now known as Mount St. Catherine, the Sinai's tallest, is holy in both Christianity and Islam.[8]

• Ninurta, Ninmaḫ's son, had done extensive land restoration in Mesopotamia and was pleased to give his mother a comfortable lifestyle in her new domain. In a long poem he lauds what he developed:

the peak mountain ...
shall provide you with the shiny ores
its mines will as tribute copper and tin give you

• Since the Sinai was rich in minerals, Enki, *god* of mining, was familiar with it. His daughter Ninsikilla lived there with her husband, Enšag, who had certain responsibilities at Tilmun. Ninsikilla complains to her father:

tilmun the city thou has given...
has not waters of the river...
unbathed is the maiden

Enki, ever the problem solver, gives an order to the *god* of rocketry:

let divine [Šamaš] position himself in the skies
a missile let him tightly affix...
and from high direct it toward the earth...
from the source whence issues earth's waters
let him bring thee sweet water from the earth...

The scribe gives an account of what happened next and, perhaps in anticipation of disbelief, ends with a confirmation:

[Šamaš] positioning himself in the skies a missile tightly tied...
from high directed it towards the earth...
he let go of his missile from high in the sky
through the crystal stones he brought up water
from the source whence issues Earth's waters
he brought her sweet water from the earth ...
verily it was so...[Tilmun became a] land of crop raising fields and farms which bear grain.

The key to unlocking the meaning of this text is this: hydrologists have detected fossil water beneath the Sinai, the remains of lakes from earlier geologic ages. (Egyptian oilmen unintentionally tapped into some of it.) The water under the Sinai is at high pressure in reservoirs three thousand feet down, held in place by the rock overburden. Enki must have found a spot where an explosion would open a path for water to rise to the surface and directed Šamas to strike it with a missile.

Knowing Tilmun's location is vital since, as we are about to see, it helps explain the sudden collapse of Šumerian culture. In the next section it will be clear why no physical evidence of the base has yet been found.

¹ The Strait of Gibraltar limited the flow of water from the Atlantic, so the rise in sea level at the distant end of the Mediterranean Sea was not forceful, but gradual.

² The *god's* earlier projects in marshy areas along the northern Nile are the basis for lower Egypt's ancient designation as *the raised land*. Enki directed work there just as he had done in Šumer when the Earth colony was first founded.

³ When texts from Egypt and Mesopotamia are correlated, Ptaḫ's reign in Egypt is found to begin c. 20,000 BCE, long before the deluge. In Mesopotamia, texts on hard clay tablets survived the flood. Not so in Egypt. The use of papyrus after the flood suggests that it had long been the *lofty ones'* medium there before the flood.

⁴ After World War II, flattened parts of old cities, great ones such as London, and small ones such as Amiens, could have been given layouts better suited to modern life. Instead, reconstruction often respected old roads and streets, with many new buildings made to conform to the shapes of obliterated ones. Apparently it was important after such a catastrophe that the crushed areas not be totally replaced, but restored to the extent feasible. So it may have been for the *anunnaki*.

⁵ Enlil, the most powerful of the *gods*, was the primary lawgiver in all the Mesopotamian cultures. His role resonates in the lengthy Covenant in the Book of Exodus, where God declares prohibitions and consequences, using language that reads as if lifted from one of the legal codes of Mesopotamia.

⁶ Science and scholarship became bonded with religious authority; the bond persisted after the departure of the *gods*. It was the source of the power of the Roman Catholic Church in matters of science, and for its role in the birth of the universities. It would be many centuries before a seat of higher learning in the Western world was founded that was not under the auspices of a church.

⁷ Most texts use the name Tilmun to designate the spaceport and its immediate vicinity, but some texts use it to refer to the entire peninsula. As a result, standard scholarship is sometimes mistaken about its location.

⁸ The name Catherine derives from ancient Armenian: *gadarine*, *she is of the peak*, *gadar* meaning *peak*, and *ine* almost certainly meaning *she is*, as it did in ancient Greek. Thus, the mountain's name is of Middle Eastern origin and echoes the new epithet bestowed on Ninmaḫ, *Ninḫursag*, meaning *lady of the peak mountain*. Identified with the most beloved of the female *lofty ones*, the mountain was holy long before the monotheisms arose. (Scholars who suggest that the mountain was named for St. Catherine of Alexandria are making an understandable error.)

Conflict and Catastrophe

The AN.UN.NA.KI mining colony had not been long in existence when a great battle between nobles took place. From that moment on, warfare among the Lofty Ones was never long absent. If there was no war in progress among the noble AN.UN.NA.KI, one was surely brewing. The city of a ranking Lofty One would win dominance over the other centers; sooner or later its forces would suffer defeat and another city and its lord would come to rule supreme. Alliances were made and broken. Rivalries waxed and waned. The flood interrupted this brutal drama, yet as the populations of the cities recovered, the armies were rebuilt and the Lofty Ones returned to their bloody ways.

In many respects, *anunnaki* nobles truly were noble, having high principles and strong values regarding honor, respect, and responsibility. Yet their shortcomings could be glaring. At times, they were heartless, arrogant, jealous, and lustful. The leading *gods* never ceased their intrigues and wars, always eager to amass prestige and dominion. The tales of the *gods'* sexual excesses were many, the frankness of the accounts suggesting that such behavior was the norm. The *anunnaki* were *lofty* in learning, skill, and physiology; in morality many of them often were not.

For us, the most telling aspect of the *gods'* moral inadequacy is their manipulation of the love felt for them by their human worshippers, who out of devotion willingly went forth to die in battle. The tablets telling of the wars speak of the *gods'* alliances, the geography, the sacking of cities, and the horrific human toll. An entire army might be wiped out when the opposing *god* intervened and used his personal weapon against it.[1]

The founder of the Akkadian empire told of being led in bloody conquest by Inanna. His grandson served the ambitions of Nannar (the father of Inanna) with notable success, yet when he went to war without his *god's* permission, he was destroyed. The Hittites, having adopted Mesopotamian ways, articulated their principles of warfare, making it clear that they went into battle on the orders of Iškur. The Egyptians took pride in the cruelty that Ra (Enlil's son Marduk) ordered. (Figure 3.9.1)

As discussed earlier, *anunnaki* nobles presented themselves to humanity as divine beings. A few in the ruling circle of twelve went further and said they were the embodiments of the celestial *gods*, the planets. Some of them in addition were identified with signs of the zodiac. We can discern no purpose for the *gods* on Earth to link themselves with the planetary *gods* and with the star-beings of the zodiac, other than to put humankind in even deeper awe of them. Thus the people were made more malleable. After the deluge, the ruling *lofty ones* and the kings who served them rebuilt the armies, and the wars of the *gods* resumed. This book's third appendix delineates the conflicts in the period that extends from the rebuilding of Šumer to the moment in time we next consider.

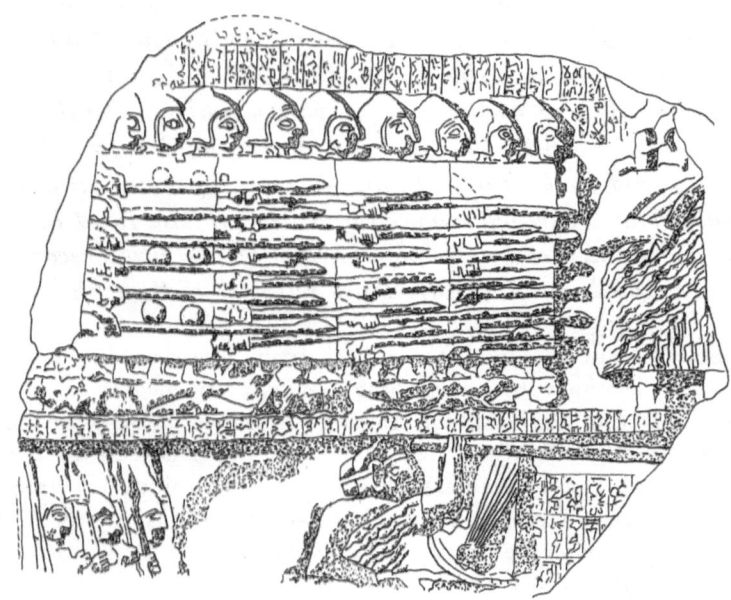

Figure 3.9.1. Šumerian battle scenes. A fragment of a stone relief.

MAR.DUK, eldest son of EN.KI, made a startling announcement. His astrologic sign was Aries, the Ram, and since Earth was entering the Age of Aries, he proclaimed that it was time for him to ascend and be acknowledged as the chief of all the Lofty Ones.

Meaning to undo what he saw as the original theft of his father's rights by his uncle, MAR.DUK began drives of conquest, rousing fresh hostility between the two clans. EN.LIL was shocked when he realized that MAR.DUK intended to attack the Sinai spaceport...and that his army appeared unstoppable.

The prospect of his belligerent nephew having control of one of the two launch facilities so alarmed EN.LIL that he resolved to deny MAR.DUK the base with the only means available to him: destroying it. Dismissing dire warnings from his brother EN.KI, he empowered two of MAR.DUK's rivals to use the colony's long-hidden weapons of terror, seven powerful bombs. He also authorized the simultaneous destruction of five small cities just north of the Sinai, with the aim of killing MAR.DUK's son.

3.9 Conflict and Catastrophe

At this turning point in the wars of the *gods*, Enlil prepared to act against Marduk and against his son, Nabu. Under father and son the *cities of the plain* were allied. These were towns located near the southern end of the Dead Sea. It's fascinating how, at this critical moment, the Mesopotamian and Hebrew narratives overlap, complementing each other in a two-voiced account of events. For example, five allied towns are named in the Book of Genesis. Two are famous: Sodom and Gomorrah.

Texts from Mesopotamia tell of a war of kings serving Enlil and Nannar against the *rebel lands of the west* (i.e., west of Mesopotamia proper) where the *cities of the plain* were located.² Genesis calls this conflict the *war between the kings of the east and the kings of the west*, and tells that the patriarch Abraham and his horsemen took part in it at the direction of God.³ The historic Abraham, with cavalry under his command, had to be serving Enlil. That would fit with what we know of him: a wealthy man of Šumer, son of Teraḫ, priest in Ur, the principal city of Enlil's domain.⁴

The God of the Universe was brought into the tale of the biblical Abraham's journey to Canaan for theological reasons, though the historic Abraham was ordered to go there (c. 2,050 BCE) by the chief *god* of Mesopotamia, because of his precarious political and military situation.

The *cities of the plain* would be stepping stones to the Tilmun spaceport, so Marduk's forces in southern Canaan had to be defeated. Genesis says that sin led to God's destruction of Sodom and Gomorrah; the sin that led to Enlil's orders was the cities' allegiance to Marduk. Genesis says that Abraham was sent north from the cities just before God destroyed them. That implies that the attack on Tilmun and on the towns, carried out under Enlil's authority, was coordinated with a thrust by the historic Abraham against forces to the north loyal to Marduk.⁵

Enki made a pact with Ninmaḫ that shifted the rule of Tilmun from herself to Marduk's son. That empowerment of his brother's clan could only have further provoked Enlil. The circle of twelve *gods* met in a council of war and contacted An on Nibiru. Nergal journeyed to Babylon in hopes of persuading Marduk to give up his campaign for supremacy and to once again leave Mesopotamia for his other seat of power, Egypt. Predictably, Nergal's appeal failed and he urged war on Marduk.

Growing angry, Enki announced in council that he stood by his eldest son. Nabu and Nergal shouted at each other. Nergal threw accusations at Enlil, and even argued with Enki, his father, who ordered him out of the chamber. He bolted, intent on obtaining the *weapons of terror*. Gibil, whose African domain adjoined Nergal's, alerted Marduk that Nergal was searching for the bombs. Marduk, alarmed, asked Enki to take possession of them. Enki implored the other great *gods* to stop Nergal, but they were in disarray and took no action.

By the time Ninurta met up with Nergal, his cousin and ally was arming the weapons. The pair consulted An, who set three conditions for their use. One, the weapons could be deployed only against targets he approved. Two, the *anunnaki* stationed at Tilmun had to be warned. Three, no human settlements were to be attacked. Nergal replied with fury. In his drive to defeat Marduk and Nabu, he would not spare their followers. He objected to warning Tilmun ... then relented on that issue. On and on went the argument. Nergal agreed not to attack the cities in Šumer loyal to Marduk, but held to his intention to flatten the *cities of the plain*. With the destruction of Tilmun they'd no longer have tactical worth, but Nabu, an object of Nergal's wrath, was thought to be in one of them. An and Enlil gave in regarding the cities; Ninurta was speechless.

The two allies began their mission. Ninurta did his part, blasting Tilmun, while Nergal, against the pleading of his cousin, destroyed the five cities. In the epic about these events, Ninurta is *annihilator*:

Annihilator to the mount ... [the launch facility] set his course
the awesome seven [weapons] without parallel trailed behind
at the mount most supreme the hero arrived
he raised his hand the mount was smashed
the plain by the mount most supreme he obliterated
in its woods not a sapling was left standing

Nergal, whom the epic calls *scorcher*, used the royal road along the eastern coast of the Sinai to guide his flight north toward the five cities.

then emulating Annihilator
Scorcher the king's highway followed
the cities he finished
to desolation he overturned them
in the hills he caused starvation
their animals he made perish

A tablet in Šumerian and Akkadian states:

Lord bearer of the scorcher that burnt up the adversary
who obliterated the disobedient land

3.9 Conflict and Catastrophe

who withered the life of the followers [of the] evil words
who rained stones and fire upon the adversaries

About the attack on Tilmun, a Babylonian king later says:

the lord of the gods became *enraged*
he conceived wrath, he gave the command
the gods of that place abandoned it…
the two, incited to…evil made its guardians stand aside

On another tablet:

Enlil who sat enthroned in loftiness
was consumed with anger
the devastators again suggested evil
he who scorches with fire
and he of the evil wind
the two made the gods flee
made them flee the scorching…
that which was raised towards An to launch
they caused to wither
its face they made to fade away
its place they made desolate

Mesopotamian texts suggest that some of the five cities lay in a plain south of the Dead Sea, separated from its waters by a natural dike that collapsed as the weapons exploded … so they were drowned as well as obliterated. That is consistent with our knowledge of this body of water.

Within memory, there was a bay at the southern end of the Dead Sea shallower than the main body of water. At present, so much of the water that used to flow into this salt lake from the River Jordan is being diverted for human use, that the water level has dropped, exposing the floor of what once was that southern basin.[6] (Figures 3.9.2 and 3.9.3)

Figure 3.9.2. From an 1823 traveler's drawing: the southern portions of the Dead Sea, showing the narrow strait that connected the main body of the lake with the shallow bay called the Backwater.

Figure 3.9.3. From a 1989 Space Shuttle photo: the Dead Sea. Reduced flow from the Jordan having lowered the water level, the lake's most southerly portion was left dry, and a new southern end to the body of water was established ... much like the one that apparently existed before the *cities of the plain* were destroyed. (A pipeline supplies water to the southern basin where two ponds now produce mineral salts.)

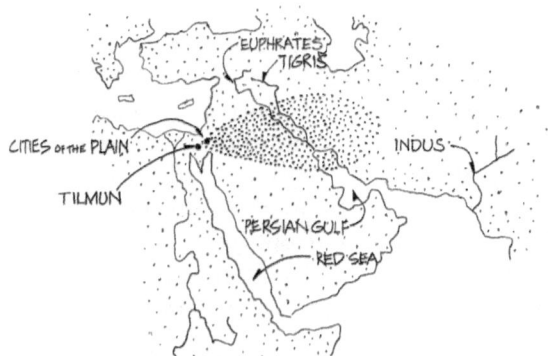

Figure 3.9.4. The Cloud of Death.

3.9 Conflict and Catastrophe 125

Enlil's initial refusal to allow the cities to be destroyed was in keeping with his pledge after the flood, to never again act against humanity, but the prospect of killing Nabu led him to yield to Nergal's rage. Not only was Nabu an effective proselytizer for Marduk, his father, his very existence broadcast violations of an unwritten taboo. Nabu's mother was the first human taken as a wife of a ruling *god*. Enlil had had to come to terms with *anunnaki* commoners' marrying humans, but his nephew's taking a human wife must have been beyond bearing, and to make matters worse, Nabu had done the same. The sexual transgression leading God to punish Sodom and Gomorrah in Genesis had an historical source: Enlil's revulsion over the sexual liaisons of the *gods* whom the cities were serving.[7]

The Bible and the Mesopotamian tablets agree that it was by order of the supreme deity that they were destroyed. God says to Abraham:

…the outcry regarding Sodom and Gomorrah has been great, and the accusations against them grievous…let me come down and verify. If it is as the outcry reaching me, they will be destroyed completely [8]

In Genesis we hear echoes of the Mesopotamian texts that told of the attacks by Nergal and Ninurta on the cities:

Then the Lord rained upon Sodom and upon Gomorrah
brimstone and fire from the Lord out of heaven
And he overthrew those cities and all the plain
and all the inhabitants … and that which grew upon the ground
But [Lot's] wife looked back … and became a column of salt[9]
And Abraham got up early [and] stood before the Lord
And he looked toward Sodom and Gomorrah and towards all the land of the plain and beheld and lo the smoke of the country went up as the smoke of a furnace

In his fear and rage EN.LIL didn't envision the cloud of death the assault would spawn. Killing vapors drifted east with the prevailing winds, devastating (but not destroying) the cities of southern and central Mesopotamia. The near total collapse of Šumerian culture followed, documented in many lamentation texts.

The lamentations speak of the fate of the lands that lay downwind of the explosions unleashed by the *gods*. As we pore through them, it becomes obvious that what drifted east from the Sinai was nuclear fallout (Figure 3.9.4).

One tablet bemoans the devastation of Nippur, Uruk, Ur, and Eridu, beginning with the cities closest to Sinai, reporting their deaths in an eastward sequence, the direction of the prevailing winds. Several tablets tell of the hasty departures of *anunnaki* from the cities. The texts typically speak not of destruction but of desolation, sickness, and death. The standard interpretation of the lamentations is that they reflect the results of war, though that is not consistent with their contents. In a text that is especially detailed and explicit about the nature of the catastrophe:

causing cities to be desolated…
houses to become desolate
causing stalls to be desolate
and sheepfolds to be empty
that Šumer's oxen no longer stand in their stalls
that its sheep no longer roam in its sheepfolds
that its rivers flow with water that is bitter
that its cultivated fields grow weeds
that its plains grow withering plants…
on the land fell a calamity
one unknown to man
one that had never been seen before
one which could not be withstood
It was a death…which roams the street
is let loose in the road
it stands beside a man yet none can see it
when it enters a house its appearance is not known …
There was no defending against the…evil
which has assailed the land like a ghost…
the highest wall the thickest wall
it passes as a flood
no door can shut it out

3.9 Conflict and Catastrophe

no bolt can turn it back
through the door like a snake it glides
through the hinge like a wind it blows in ...
People who stayed behind doors fell inside
Those who ran to their rooftops died there
Those who fled into the streets were struck down in the streets ...
cough and phlegm weakened the chest
the mouth was filled with spittle and foam...
dumbness and daze come upon them
an unwholesome numbness...
an evil curse, a headache..
their spirit abandoned their bodies...
the people, terrified, could hardly breathe
the evil wind clutched them
does not grant them another day
mouths were drenched in blood
heads wallowed in blood
the face was made pale by the evil wind ...
A *brown cloud* covered the land like a cloak
spread over it like a sheet...
the sun in the horizon it obliterated with darkness...
the moon at its rising it extinguished...
[the cloud] enveloped in terror
casting fear everywhere...
a wind which speeds high above an evil that overwhelms the land

The texts also are clear about the source of the pestilence. One states:

[it was] a great storm directed from An...
it came from the heart of Enlil...
in a single spawning it was spawned..
like the bitter venom of the gods
in the west it was spawned...

bearing gloom from city to city
carrying dense clouds that bring gloom from the sky
[the result of] a lightning flash...
from the plain of no pity it came...
an evil blast heralded the baleful storm
an evil blast the forerunner
of the baleful storm was
mighty offspring, valiant sons
were the heralds of the pestilence...
in a single spawning...
uprooting everything, upheaving everything

A tablet speaks of how sudden and swift was the assault:

...on that day, on that single day, on that night, on that single night...
the storm in a flash of lightning created
the people of Nippur left prostrate

The unintended devastation left the AN.UN.NA.KI <u>utterly</u> demoralized. They'd brought about horror beyond anything their warfare had ever before caused.

The prime focus of many of the tablets was, as usual, on the *gods*. The text known as *Lamentation Over the Destruction of Ur* tells of the *anunnaki* fleeing the cities before *the wind*. The text called *Lament of Uruk* states:

When An and Enlil overruled Enki and Ninki, none of the gods anticipated what would follow the attack ... the great gods paled at its immensity

The text called *Lamentation Over the Destruction of Sumer and Ur* says:

Ninḫursag wept bitter tears *escaping Isin...*
Nanče cried O my beloved city
Inanna sailed toward Africa in a [submersible craft] leaving her things

3.9 Conflict and Catastrophe

In the text referred to as *Lamentation for Uruk* it says:

[Inanna] bewailed the devastation by the evil wind against which there was no defense, which in an instant, in a blink of an eye, was created in the midst of the mountains.[10]

The text goes on to report that Ninagal weeps over the fate of Ur:

Ur has become a strange city
its temple has become a temple of tears
Ur and its people are given over to the wind

In the text called *Lamentation over Šumer*, Ninurta's wife, the healing goddess Bau, beloved in Lagaš, lingers, unable to leave her people. We do not hear her fate explicitly, yet the text ominously states:

the storm caught up with her as if she were mortal (Figure 3.9.5)

Figure 3.9.5. A stone portrait of Bau. The facial features are consistent with her Šumerian epithet, *Gula*, meaning *Big One*.

In yet another text:

thus all the gods evacuated Uruk
they kept away from it
they hid in the mountains
they escaped to the distant plains...
mob panic was brought about in Uruk...

its good sense was distorted...
Why the god's benevolent eye looks away?
the people were piled up in heaps...
a hush settled over Uruk like a cloak

    The text known as *Eridu Lament* speaks of Enki and his wife:

Ninki, its great lady, flying like a bird left her city...
its lord stayed outside his city...
Father Enki ...for the fate of his injured city wept bitter tears...
watching for a day and a night as the storm put its hand on Eridu...
the people asked where they should go.
Enki stayed out of the city as though it were an alien city
He led those who have been displaced from Eridu *into the desert
where he used his abilities to make edible* the foul tree

Next, Enki's advice to Marduk as the cloud approaches:

*Those who could, should leave [Babylon] going north, without taking
any food or drink, for they might have been* touched by the ghost
If escape was not possible, they were to get into a chamber below the
earth, into a darkness *until the evil wind had passed.*

    In another lamentation over Ur, Nannar appealed to his father:

*Enlil answered that the fate could not be changed...
Ur was granted kingship it was not granted an eternal reign
since days of yore when Šumer was founded
to the present, when people have multiplied
who has ever seen a kingship of everlasting reign? ...
Nannar and Ninagal hid in their ziggurat, in an interior* termite house
When they finally left Ur, they witnessed what had befallen the land
the people like potsherds filled the city streets
in its lofty places where they were wont to promenade

3.9 Conflict and Catastrophe

dead bodies were lying about
in boulevards where feasts were celebrated scattered they lay ...
in all of it its streets...dead bodies were lying about ...
the dead bodies, like fat placed in the sun ... melted away ...
on the banks of the Tigris and Euphrates only sickly plants grew ...
in the swamps grow sickly headed reeds that rot ...
in the orchards and gardens there is no new growth ...
the cultivated fields are not hoed
no seeds are implanted in the soil
no songs resound in the fields ...
on the plains cattle large and small become scarce
all living creatures come to an end ...
the storm has crushed the land, wiped out everything
it roared like a great wind over the land none could escape it
desolating the cities, desolating the houses ...
no one treads the highways
no one seeks out the roads

After Mesopotamia was buried deep in mud, and the population decimated, it took thousands of years before human civilization could be fully established in Šumer. It took the *anunnaki* just a few days to wipe out almost all of what they'd created.

And the AN.UN.NA.KI had another grave problem to deal with. It had become clear that the Lofty Ones who'd come to Earth were aging faster than their peers on NI.BI.RU, and that those born here were aging even faster and some had died. Why stay much longer?

In the final portion of *The Mesopotamian Tale* we deal with the last days of the rule of the gods who'd come from the heavens.

---

[1] The memory of those massacres was vivid; it gained expression in the Hebrew Bible, when God's supernatural power gave battlefield victory to His people.

[2] Canaan was in the Mesopotamian diaspora, and Enlil's son Nannar, as we've noted, had authority in its southern portion. The name of the Sinai probably incorporates his Akkadian name, Sin.

[3] In his monumental translation of the Hebrew Bible, Robert Alter discusses how Genesis 13 and 14 present a typical biblical collage, with the narrative shifting from a depiction of Abraham in a patriarchal role, to one showing him in that of a military commander of international significance. Alter explains how we can see in the text that the sources of the pasted-in passages are different than the other literary strands from which the Book of Genesis is woven.

⁴ Abraham's allegiance to the chief of the *gods* supports his existence as an historical figure, distinct from the scriptural patriarch of the Hebrew Bible: scion of a prominent family in the domain of the chief *god of heaven and Earth*, and a son of that *god's* priest. There are textual hints that Abraham was born c. 2120 BCE in Nippur, and that later his father moved the family to Ur.

Before the flood, Nippur had been a spaceflight center. The Šumerian name for the city, *Nibruki*, referred to its having been a *crossing place* from which the *anunnaki* crossed from Earth to the *planet of the crossing*. In addition, the city housed the equipment for communication with Nibiru.

The name for the Jewish people in their own language is *Ibri*. That is so like the name *Nibruki* that there must be a connection. It's as if with that name the Jews are saying: *Our origin was in Nibruki*. That fits with their using Nippur's calendar...as they have for over five millenniums. Proclaiming an origin in Nibruki would have been no small matter for the Hebrews, for the city was founded as the seat of power of Enlil, and it remained so throughout Mesopotamian history. (Those who are born and grow to maturity in a great city, like New York or London, when they settle elsewhere, refer to themselves as proud natives of their birthplace. So, too, a history-conscious people, it seems.)

⁵ The texts don't contain any mention of Abraham, but that's not surprising. Mesopotamian texts almost never mention individual humans other than kings.

⁶ Throughout time, the level of the Dead Sea has risen and fallen repeatedly. Scientists say that the water level dropped one hundred feet at a time that roughly coincides with the date of the Sinai attack, c. 2024 BCE. This supports the idea that the southern basin suddenly filled as a result of the blasts.

⁷ There were both sexual and political offenses committed by these two *gods*. The marriages of Marduk and Nabu with human women must have solidified the support for the pair of father and son *gods* among their human followers.

⁸ This passage reflects the age when the *gods* ruled and when divinity was personified and localized. The omniscient non-local Creator would not have had to make a journey of verification. Abraham's lifetime spanned a period of great transition for the Hebrews. Incompatible theological elements got mixed together as the authors of Genesis strived to deal with the events of the time.

⁹ The Hebrew word for what Lot's wife was turned into is always rendered as *salt*, but it can also mean *vapor* ... a good term for the fate of someone who lingered and was caught in a fireball. The presence near the Dead Sea of a geologic formation looking somewhat like a woman seems to have influenced the translators.

¹⁰ The most likely location of the obliterated spaceport was in the mountains at the center of the Sinai.

Finale [1]

Lying northwest of devastated Šumer, barely touched by the cloud of death, stood proud Babylon, city of MAR.DUK. He convinced the remaining nobles, reeling from the result of having opposed him, to proclaim him their supreme lord. He consolidated political power. He revised the assignments of planets, claiming and renaming NI.BI.RU for himself. He had a new creation epic written, with him as its focus.

Several of the *anunnaki* nobles were deemed personifications of the planets, but not Marduk. Now he claimed identification with one of them. Befitting his grandiosity, he chose the most magnificent, the heroic celestial lord, the awesome *Planet of the Crossing*, and he named it for himself. He commissioned a new creation epic. The Babylonian epic, known by its first words, *Enuma Eliš*, *When in the Heights*, was riddled with his propaganda.

The Šumerian creation epics had been given to humanity by the *gods* so that our race would be informed of our heritage. The Babylonian epic had a different purpose: the glorification of Marduk, the city's *god*. Unfortunately, it was the first Mesopotamian creation epic discovered. Because it focused on a deity, a *god* who shared a name with a non-existent planet, scholars could see the epic only as theologically driven fiction, which to an extent it was. That assessment affected how they approached the older creation epics they discovered later. Scholars considered those earlier accounts of the *gods* to also be pure products of human imagination.[2]

The Babylonian story misrepresented many important events. It made Marduk, not Enki, the creator of mankind. As we compare passages from the earlier epics with corresponding ones in the Babylonian tale, we realize that in the epic promulgated by Marduk we're reading an intentional fouling of recorded history … the first *big lie* from a power-mad ruler.

In the *Enuma Eliš* an event is said to have happened when the Earth colony was founded, but it could only have occurred during Marduk's ascendance. Enki and Ninki speak in a great assembly of the *gods*:

formerly Marduk was our beloved son, now he is your king
proclaim his title: king of the gods of heaven and earth…
being assembled all the [gods] bowed down
every one of the anunnaki kissed his feet
they were assembled to do obedience
they stood before him bowed and said he is our king

In the order that Marduk proclaimed, his relationships with the *gods* was based on his having given them their powers. In one tablet:

Ninurta is Marduk of the hoe
Nergal (who assaulted Tilmun) is Marduk of the attack...
Enlil is Marduk of lordship and counsel
Nannar (the Moon *god*) is Marduk of the illuminator of the night
Šamaš (whose city held the high court) is Marduk of justice
Adad is Marduk of rains

The glory that would come was proclaimed in the *Marduk Prophecy*:

in my city Babylon in its midst
my temple to heaven [the king] will raise...
in abundance he will reside
my hand he will grasp
he will lead me in processions...
to my city and my temple Esagil
for eternity I shall enter

Babylon had escaped the devastation that followed the nuclear attack, but only barely. At the start of the new dynasty, Babylonia was depopulated and demoralized. It took two centuries for the kingdom to develop some vitality, and two more for it to have the resources to build the towering ziggurat of the prophecy, the *Esagil*, meaning *House whose Head is Lofty*, the *god's* residence and temple.

Marduk predicted that his would be a glorious age, but it actually was a time of turmoil in the region, in part because of the earthquakes, volcanoes, and famines that struck the Middle East and the basin of the Mediterranean. The shift of power from Anunnaki nobles to human kings, going on for some time, accelerated. Human rulers for the first time waged war, plundering and destroying totally on their own. There was one more round of warfare directed by the few

3.10 Finale

remaining AN.UN.NA.KI lords, finally exhausting the last remaining cultures of Mesopotamia.

The time of the *anunnaki* on Earth was approaching its end, though the few remaining *gods* seem not to have considered the possibility, for the history of Mesopotamia had involved an endless cycle of resurgence after defeat. A remnant of the *lofty ones* managed to keep the old order going in northwestern Mesopotamia for 1,300 years after the nuclear attack.

Isin, in southern Šumer, rose to become the capital of the domain that once belonged to the sons of Enlil. In an indication of what was to come, its kings were not Šumerians, but Semites. They came from Mari, a city in the far northwest. (See Figures 1.4.1 and 3.10.1). The Isin dynasty rulers restored other cities too, but what was once the central region of the *lofty ones* was too badly disrupted for it to coalesce. Isin fell to Marduk's forces after 200 years.

Figure 3.10.1. An Isin dynasty statuette of a singer. The theme is Šumerian: devotion to Inanna. The pose is not.

Compared to the cultures of Šumer and Akkad, Babylon's was rather crude. For example, the rigid legal code of its first notable king, Ḥammurabi, was far less sophisticated than the elaborate legal system of Lagaš. The remaining Šumerian scribes and artisans drifted to other lands in a final diffusion of their ancestors' learning, skills, and tastes. Taking their place, Babylonian customs and art spread out over the land.

Marduk ruled proudly in Babylon.[3] He lived in the splendor of the city, taken with his own pronouncements. But his position was hollower then he knew. In fact, all the cultures of the Middle East were in disarray. The capital cities of Egypt, Assyria[4], and Hatti[5] were abandoned at times, their temples disregarded, their rites ignored. For a while the same was true even in Babylon; a chronicle from 990 BCE says that for nine years Marduk and Nabu were absent from the New Year's festivities.[6]

The importance of the *gods* was fading. Many of the tablets telling of the wars of the times don't even mention the *lofty ones*. Some conflicts were driven not by rivalries among the *anunnaki*, but by famine resulting from the region's droughts and earthquakes, or by purely human rivalries. Kings acted on their own, conquering, sacking, and displacing populations in Anatolia, the Armenian mountains, Persia, and southern and central Mesopotamia. Humanity had learned all too well.[7]

It was not, however, that the *gods* no longer had influence. Allied under Marduk, lord of Egypt and Babylon, those two states were in near constant conflict with Assyria and Hatti. The original fraternal rivalry was still being played out: two states ruled by a son of Enki in hostilities with another two, ruled by sons of Enlil.

Figure 3.10.2. Assyrian soldiers crossing a river using boats, horses, and inflated skins. From a palace of Ašurnasipal (reigned 883-859 BCE), who moved the capital of Assyria to Nimrud (Leveḫ).

3.10 Finale

In 879 BCE, the Assyrian king began a brutal expansion. (Figure 3.10.2) He conquered the coastal cities of Phoenicia, the mountain region of Lebanon and then Babylon itself, installing a viceroy there. Some time later, under king Šalmaneser V, Assyria attacked the kingdom of Israel, scattering its people ... the *Ten Lost Tribes*. He brought Babylonians, Cutheans, and Palmyrans into the depopulated northern part of Canaan and encouraged them to set up idols of their *gods*, Marduk, Nergal, and Adad, respectively. Suddenly, in 721 BCE, Merodaḫ-Baladan, a native royal in Babylon, seized power and proclaimed his city independent of Assyria. As he ascended to the throne he ...

took the hand of Marduk

That reignited conflict between Assyria and Babylon. In 689 BCE, after thirty more years of war, the victorious Assyrians took Marduk captive. In olden times it could never have been imagined that a *god* would be without a powerful weapon or that he'd be devoid of allies to protect his person ... and this was the chief of the *gods* on Earth. Clearly, power was shifting significantly from from the *lofty ones* to the kings.

The Assyrian king Sennaḫerib invaded the kingdom of Judea in southern Canaan c. 680 BCE, an event in both the Mesopotamian and Hebrew narratives. The biblical account suggests that the *gods* were not only being challenged politically, but also theologically. Sennaḫerib enraged the king of Jerusalem by comparing Yahweh to the other nations' *gods* ... who, as just noted, were being worshipped through idols in the newly colonized land to the north. The Jewish king shouted in angry denunciation that the objects of that reverence...

are not lofty ones, but man made of wood and stone

Ḫarran also carried on as if the nuclear catastrophe had not been the death knell of Mesopotamian civilization. It, too, had been unscathed by the *cloud of death*. Its *god*, Nannar, ruled his northwest remnant of Šumerian culture in the style of old. He told king Esarhaddon of Assyria to make war on Egypt, c. 675 BCE. Distant entanglements of that sort weakened Assyria; it was soon to come under Babylon's domination.

In 626 BCE Nabupolassar was crowned king of Babylon, ruling in the names of Marduk and Nabu. Assyria began to crumble. In 610 BCE its royal family and the remains of its army sought refuge in Ḫarran, but Nannar was not receptive and the Assyrians had to face the Babylonians alone. They met their final defeat. From stellae commissioned by

Addaguppi, priestess in Nannar's temple, and by Nabunaid, her son, we learn that their lord grew disgusted:

it was the sixteenth year of Nabupolassar
king of Babylon when [Nannar] lord of gods
became angry with [Harran] and his temple
and went up to heaven
and the city and the people in it went to ruin[8]

The cause of Nannar's abandonment of his city was not stated. In despair and mourning, Addaguppi attended the now empty shrines:

daily without ceasing by day and night
for months for years...
in a torn garment I was clothed
I came and went noiselessly

One day Addaguppi found a robe that had been worn by Nannar, held its hem, and prayed to him, promising that the people would worship him if he returned:

if you would return to your city
all the black headed people
would worship your divinity
If Nannar will use his powers to make Nabunaid king of Babylon and Assyria, Nabunaid would rebuild Nannar's temple in Ur and reestablish his worship wherever the people of Šumer dwelled.

The *god* appeared to his faithful servant in a vision, joining her in a messianic fantasy, as if the glory of old times could easily be revived:

[Nannar] Lord of the gods of Heaven and Earth
for my good doings looked upon me with a smile
he heard my prayers, he accepted my vow
the wrath of his heart calmed
towards [his temple] in Harran

3.10 Finale

the divine residence in which his heart rejoiced
he became reconciled...
[Nannar] Lord of the gods
looked with favor upon my words
Nabunaid my only son
issue of my womb
to the kingship he called
the kingship of Šumer and Akkad
all the lands from the border of Egypt
from the upper sea to the lower sea
in his hands he entrusted

Nabunaid was crowned king of Babylonia in Ḥarran in 555 BCE. Nannar's temple there, *the House of Double Joy*, was restored and rededicated and its rites were renewed. Other *gods* and their consorts returned. After 50 years in the heavens, the great *god* descended.[9]

this is the great miracle of [Nannar]
that has by gods and goddesses
not happened to the land
since the days of the old unknown
that the people of the land
had neither seen nor found written
on tablets since days of old
that divine [Nannar]
Lord of gods and goddesses
residing in the heavens
has come down from the heavens
in full view of Nabunaid
king of Babylon

But Nabunaid's kingdom was weak. He had a series of dreams in which Marduk blessed his reign, but they were not the good omens he took them to be. The priests of Marduk presented charges against him, including one that was especially damning: that he had placed an abomination in Marduk's temple in Babylon, the statue of a bizarre *god*. Nabunaid departed on a mission to the south, leaving his son as regent.[10]

That was Belšaruzur. In the Hebrew Bible he is *Belšazzar*, the king who was told by the prophet Daniel that *the handwriting on the wall* foretold the doom of his kingdom. Once again the Mesopotamian and biblical accounts are concordant, for that royal dynasty was soon to meet its end. When Cyrus the Great, who'd been invited to Babylon by Marduk, approached the city with his Persian army in 539 BCE, the priests and populace, chafing under Nannar, greeted him as a liberator. Cyrus entered:

[and] took the extended hands of the god

Babylonia was the last kingdom linked by history and faith with Šumer. As Marduk gave his hands to a king who was a foreigner and a monotheist, those links were broken and the political and religious transition of the Middle East accelerated. Cyrus respected the religions of the olden *gods*, yet the theology he embraced further weakened their hold on mankind.[11] According to Greek historians, during the reign of Cyrus' son, Marduk died and was buried in the great ziggurat of Babylon.

The *anunnaki* who didn't die on Earth must have returned to Nibiru. There are hardly any Mesopotamian texts relating to their departure. That's not surprising. The shame resulting from being finally disillusioned and abandoned was deep and the amnesia that developed to protect against it was dense. We'll end our exploration of The Mesopotamian Tale with a passage that seems to speak of the *gods*' final ascent, but first we'll consider a biblical passage that appears to covertly refer to their leaving.

In the Book of Genesis Jacob journeys to Ḥarran, seeking a wife among his mother's clan. That would have taken place 2,000 years before Genesis was given final form, a task that was being accomplished around the time the Jews were returning to Jerusalem from exile in Babylon, having been liberated by Cyrus. On Jacob's journey, while still in Canaan, God addressed him, saying:

[I am] the God of Abraham...and the God of Isaac...And thy seed shall be spread as dust on the ground, spreading west and east and north and south ... Behold, I am with thee. I will protect thee wherever thou goest, and <u>I shall bring thee back to this land. I shall not abandon thee until I have done that which I am saying to you</u> (emphasis added)

3.10 Finale

Analysis reveals that this is a late insertion into much older portions of text. To restate the meaning of that last sentence:

I shall not abandon thee until I have brought thee back to Canaan

The passage implies that God had warned Jacob that He would abandon the Hebrew people when, at some time in the future, He was returning them to Canaan. This is strange. There is nothing in Jewish tradition and no passage in the Hebrew Bible that suggests that the exiled Judeans, who thrived in Babylonia and significantly elaborated their culture there, ever thought of themselves as abandoned by God.

The Jews' return to Jerusalem takes place at the time when, with Cyrus' appearance, the last chapter of the rule of the *lofty ones* closes, and all mention of the *anunnaki* in the Mesopotamian tablets ceases. The editors of Genesis inserted the incongruous concept of abandonment by God just when the few remaining *gods* were leaving (or dying). Could that be coincidence? The passage makes it seem as if God warned the Jews that he would abandon them at the time of their return to Canaan ... when at the very moment of their return home, humanity's last tenuous connection with the *anunnaki* lords was being revoked by their departure.[12]

The final editors of Genesis couldn't totally exclude so huge an event occurring in their time. Yet if they were to bear witness to the final departure of the olden *gods*, they could only do so in heavily disguised terms, so as to avoid conflict with their theology.

In order to return to Nibiru the *anunnaki* would have to leave during one of its transits of the inner planets. This clarifies the tone of the biblical prophecies of the *Day of the Lord*, which began to appear in the 8th century BCE, increased in the 7th, and peaked in urgency in the 6th. As already discussed, they read much like the Šumerian descriptions of the passage of the *Lord of Heaven* that caused the flood. Those with an understanding of celestial events knew that Nibiru would come again around the middle of the 6th century BCE. The prophets were aware that terrible things might happen and they set about warning the people, though they spoke of a transcendent God, not of the planet that would be His agent.

Events in the region in the late 7th century BCE probably were connected with the expected return of Nibiru. Egypt made a military thrust at Babylon, though the two nations had always been allied under Marduk. On the way north, the pharaoh's army captured Baalbek. Possession of the spaceflight center would be critical during an approach of Nibiru, when trips between the two worlds would be feasible. Wondrous projects were undertaken in Babylon. Their purpose is not stated, but they could have been in anticipation of a visit by An.

Coordinating astronomical texts describing the position of Nibiru with the king lists, it appears that the golden orb would be visible from Earth for a few months, sometime between 610 and 550 BCE. The texts speak of an unpredicted solar eclipse in 556 BCE. The Sun's eclipses were well studied; if one occurred that was not expected, it must have been connected with Nibiru's passing. That makes 556 BCE the most likely date for humanity's last sighting of the olden *Lord of Heaven*.[13]

A passage in a copy of the *Akkadian Prophecies* touches on the *lofty ones'* abandonment of humankind. The scribe, utilizing a well-known Mesopotamian literary device, related events that he knows occurred as if they had been foretold, inserting a seemingly prophetic passage in the text he was recopying:

Roaring the gods flying
from the land will go away
from the people they will be separated
the people will the gods' abodes leave in ruins
compassion and well being will cease
Enlil in anger will lift himself off

A monotheistic king from east of Mesopotamia, Cyrus, was welcomed with his army into Babylon. From then on the tablets of Mesopotamia would make no mention of the AN.UN.NA.KI.
And so ends The Mesopotamian Tale.

3.10 Finale

[1] Tablets and carvings from this last phase of the rule of the *gods*, suffering less from the effects of time than more ancient ones, were the first to be studied by archaeologists. As a result, the period has received attention from scholars and space in museums out of proportion to its role in the human story. As we will soon discuss, the tragic human condition is a consequence of the long rule of the *annunaki*. The contribution of this short period to our sad reality is insignificant.

[2] The gods of Greece and Rome were obviously human inventions; it seemed evident to the scholars that the same was true of the Mesopotamian deities.

[3] Marduk's rise in Babylon coincided with his absence in Egypt. He'd been known along the Nile as Ra; he now became Amon-Ra, *Unseen Ra*. As we've discussed, the astrologic Age of the Ram was the basis for Marduk's claim to primacy. In Egypt the zodiac was revised, and the Ram was made the first of the twelve signs, as it still is in western astrology.

[4] Ninurta was the city's ruling *god*. His name in Akkadian was Ašur, the source of the term Assyria.

[5] Hatti was the realm of the Hittites who came to Anatolia from the north. They adopted as their chief *god* Enlil's son Iškur, whom they called Tešub.

[6] The history of resurgent Babylon in the period following the devastation of Šumer reflects the turmoil in the Middle East. In the 1300 years that elapsed from the founding of the city's first new dynasty to the end of its ninth, Babylon's kings fought more than twenty wars against over half a dozen nations, experiencing defeat more often than victory. In fact, the city was twice sacked and rebuilt.

⁷ Human civilization was to closely follow the model established by the *anunnaki*. The explorer with whom Thomas More converses at the start of his *Utopia* puts it this way: *Practically all princes ... take greater delight in spending their time in military matters than on the good arts of peace ... They are much more concerned how to get new kingdoms...by fair means or foul, than to administer well what they already have.*

⁸ In another convergence of biblical and Mesopotamian texts, the prophet Ezekiel gave an eyewitness account of the ascent of a *divine chariot* from Ḥarran. (Ezekiel also reported traveling to Jerusalem as a passenger in such a craft.)

⁹ At this time, Nibiru was passing through the inner Solar System. Fifty years earlier, it would have been close enough for Nannar to journey there easily.

¹⁰ During Nabunaid's ten year sojourn, he subdued northern Arabia, making Teima his principal base. He founded six towns, five of which are mentioned in later Arab texts as Jewish Arab settlements. According to Mesopotamian texts Jews exiled from Jerusalem were prominent in the king's retinue. Since Nabunaid worshipped Nannar, *god* of the moon, his symbol, the crescent, would have become familiar in the region. Islam's taking the crescent moon as its insignia made it easier for the adherents of the old faith to adopt the new one.

¹¹ The Persians were Zoroastrians, early worshippers of the One. Remnants of that faith survive in Iran, and an offshoot, the Yazidis, in Iraq.

¹² There's another hint connecting Jacob's biblical journey with the historical world of the *anunnaki*. He has a dream in which divine beings are famously journeying up to heaven and back down to Earth. What they are traveling upon is ordinarily said to be a ladder, but the word for it would be more accurately translated as *ramp*, suggesting that the dream depicts a scene at the foot of a ramp. In Mesopotamia, stepped ramps led to the tops of the ziggurats, where the residences of the *gods* were built. That adds meaning to Jacob's exclamation, after God speaks to him from above: "[Surely] this [place] is the house of God."

¹³ To block the Sun itself, Nibiru would have to be in the plane of the ecliptic. It's briefly in that plane as it crosses the Asteroid Belt, but at that moment it is well outside Earth's orbit. Nibiru, therefore, couldn't have cast a shadow on Earth. Its gravity, however, might have altered the Moon's motion, causing a solar eclipse. A tablet describing the event hints at this:

the solar disc became darkened and stood in the radiance of the great planet

In a total solar eclipse, the Moon covers the disc of the Sun, which appears dark. At the same time, in the scene described in the text, the golden shell surrounding Nibiru would have been basking in full sunlight, radiant.

Part Four

Unanswered Questions

Scientists and scholars have difficulty dealing with facts that upend accepted theories and violate established principles. They pretend those inconvenient realities do not exist, dismiss them as insignificant, or inaccurately claim that they've already been examined and therefore don't warrant further consideration. The questions those bothersome facts raise, some of them profound and troubling, are left unanswered.

We shall now consider several of these matters, and find that the seemingly insoluble puzzles they present are readily resolved when The Mesopotamian Tale is taken to be a compilation of essentially factual, historical accounts of humanity's origins and early times.

The first of these mysteries lies in the elaborate burials found in one of the cities of Šumer. They've rarely been publicized and are virtually unknown ... understandably.

Burials in Ur

The restoration of Mesopotamia had been in progress for over a thousand years when the *anunnaki* turned their gaze to the site of Ur, a major city still buried deep in mud. A greater Ur began to rise, one that would have unprecedented commercial, cultural, and religious importance ... and it would contain burial sites of a kind found nowhere else on Earth. These burials, in what archaeologists call the royal cemetery, predate the earliest tombs of the Egyptian kings by a millennium.

In each of these burials a ramp led down to a subterranean plaza roofed with a vaulted ceiling supporting the soil overhead. In each of these underground courts stood a small tomb, built of stone brought from afar. Beautiful, opulent artifacts were placed in the tombs. Inside one was a gorgeous golden helmet, a silver-sheathed dagger of gold, a delicate silver belt, golden jewelry, and other objects made of precious materials. The tomb artifacts were crafted with superb skill and exquisite taste; they included musical instruments built with rare woods, a silver lyre, and intricate stone carvings. Some of the tombs held implements and vessels that would have served well in everyday use ... were they not made of gold, silver, and alabaster. (Figures 4.1.0 through 4.1.2 and 3.6.3) We're told that these were royal burials, but when that idea is examined, it doesn't hold up.

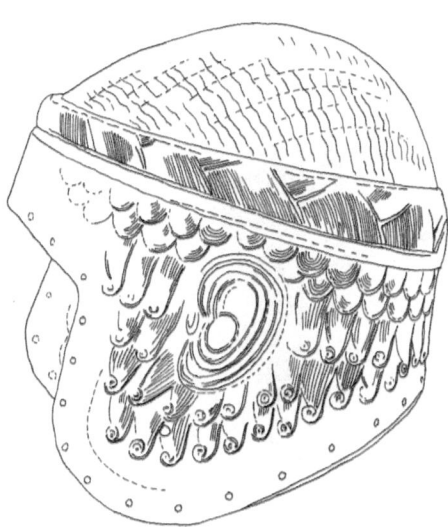

Figure 4.1.0. A golden helmet from one of the tombs.

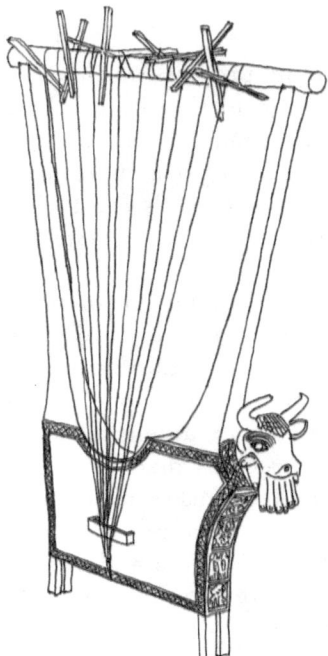

Figure 4.1.1. A wooden lyre from a tomb, c. 2400 BCE. Restored.

Figure 4.1.2. A portion of the inlaid front of the instrument shown in the preceding figure.

4.1 Burials in Ur

On the ramps leading into the chambers and on the plazas below are processions of people and animals, joined in death with the one laid to rest inside the stone tomb. A few of the funerals involved several dozen people, all dying willingly, lying together in good, calm order, free of any marks of violence. In some, suicide by poison is evident from cups lying by the bones. Could human rulers have inspired the devotion or exercise the influence that had dozens of their subjects willing to die soon after they did?[1] The tablets lauded the kings of Šumer in many ways. If these were royal funerals wouldn't they have been celebrated in writing? The Mesopotamian Tale helps us to make sense of these funerals and of the silence surrounding them. (Figures 4.1.3 through 4.1.5)

Riches of the sort found in the burial chambers were possessed by the *lofty ones*, but not by their servants, the kings. Indeed, it was notable for a king to have a single silver bowl to present as a gift to his *god*. Tablets tell of the ruling *anunnaki* owning ceremonial implements of the kind found inside the tombs. A hymn sang that when Enlil broke ground for the *Heaven Earth Bond* in Nippur, he used a hoe with a gold handle, a gold-silver blade, and a lapis lazuli tip. Another sang of Inanna playing an instrument of silver. In one text Ninmaḫ takes up a gold chisel and a silver hammer. In another, when An and his queen visited Earth, everything

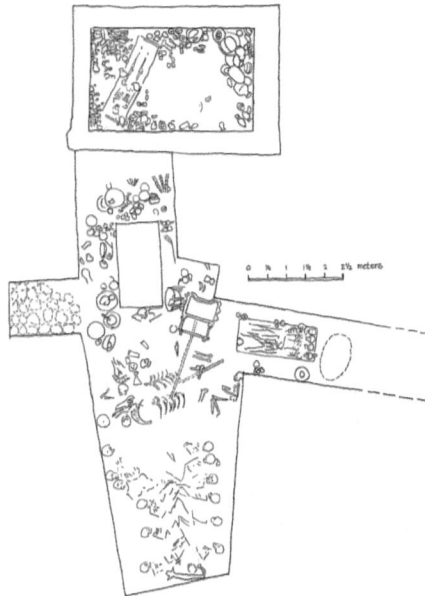

Figure 4.1.3. One of the burials in the cemetery of Ur. In the outer space there are 24 humans and 2 draft animals (near a chariot). In the tomb chamber there are many precious artifacts. If the archaeologist's drawing is accurate, the one for whom the funeral was conducted was over 7'4" tall.

Figure 4.1.4. An archaeologist's conception of a funeral in Ur ... before the mass suicide.

Figure 4.1.5. Looking up from the shadows of the burial plaza: a stepped ramp, a broken-through seal at the entrance, and an excavated stepped ramp outside.

utilized to cook and serve their food was of gold and alabaster. Clearly, the objects in the burial chambers were the possessions of *anunnaki* nobles. The bodies must be theirs, too; it was the *gods* who inspired the extreme devotion manifested in these burials, not the kings.[2]

But did those of the *long life* ever die? They may have visibly aged, but none of the *gods of heaven and earth* were ever said to have died. Texts tell, however, that *anunnaki* born here, the *gods of earth*, died after lives that

4.1 Burials in Ur

were short by *anunnaki* standards. Apparently for them, the *bread of life* and the *water of life* from Nibiru did not produce the longevity they would have on the home planet. The bones in the underground stone tombs of Ur could only have belonged to Earth-born *anunnaki* nobles.[3]

The funeral processions in the burial plazas are consistent with the fundamental reality for the peoples of Mesopotamia: their deep attachment to the *gods* around whom their communities were organized. When the one who'd been a society's supreme authority for many human generations died, it shook that society to its core. We can see how those who'd been close to a *lofty one* could have felt that life was no longer worth living after he was gone. To be buried with one's *god* was a statement of devotion, a confirmation of status, a high honor, and a means of soothing and abbreviating grief. In Šumer the life of humans had always counted for so little; what mattered most were the *gods*. So it was when one of them died.

An artifact found in one of the small stone tombs provides additional evidence that the central figures in the funerals were not human. In that chamber, a central female body was surrounded by several others, all adorned with gorgeous, delicate golden headdresses. The one worn by the central figure, incorporating fine leaves, ribbons, and other accouterments, all of gold, is truly remarkable ... not solely on account of its being the most elaborate, which it is, but also because of its size.

The pieces of this headdress, found in disarray, have been assembled in half a dozen different ways since it was first put on display in the archaeological museum of the University of Pennsylvania in the late 1920's. In each of the reconstructions, great mounds representing hair were used because, no matter how its pieces were combined, the assembled headdress was huge. But those displays are problematic. In all the history of the ancient Middle East, many styles of coiffure appear in carvings and paintings, but virtually none involved masses of hair. It is as if the curators transported back in time the techniques and products of modern hairdressers. (See Figs. 4.1.6 and 4.1.7)

Had they instead crafted a display with the headdress resting on one of the hairstyles common in Mesopotamian images, the skull of their mannequin would have had to be unusually large. Curiously, a head like that would have been consistent with the report of the anthropologist who first examined the skeleton. He said that its cranium had a capacity at least 250 cubic centimeters, greater than the mean for modern Caucasian women. That impressive head could only have been that of a member of the race the King James Bible called *giants in the Earth*.[4]

Figure 4.1.6. One of the earliest reconstructions of the headdress, including the tall comb and large hoop earrings found with it.

4.1 Burials in Ur

Figure 4.1.7. Two later reconfigurations of the headdress.

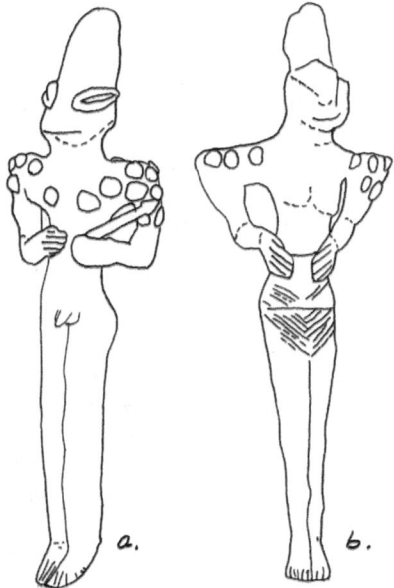

Figure 4.1.8. Gods?

---

¹ In fact, the person in the lead in one of the processions is the king of the city.

² There's a telling detail to consider. Several of the honored dead were female, but as far as we know, no city in Mesopotamia was ever ruled by a queen.

³ The whole truth may be a bit more complicated, for there are some burials in Ur somewhat similar to the grand ones we've been discussing, yet much less elaborate. Perhaps the bodies in these minor tombs were those of royal *demigods*, given funerals modeled on those of the *gods* ... just as the lifestyles of the human kings were modeled on the lives of the *gods* they worshipped and obeyed.

⁴ To be fair, there was something else besides the restrictions of conventional thinking that kept the curators from making a huge mannequin skull: the rest of the skeleton was small and delicate. We know, though, that some *anunnaki* females were not tall. There are images of Inanna depicting her as much shorter than the male *gods* with whom she is standing. Did she, too, have a cranium out of proportion to her frame, as did the *goddess* in this tomb?

Two curious figurines from this period, a female found in Ur and a male from Eridu, provoke a question about the heads of the great *gods*. All depictions of the ruling *anunnaki* show them wearing peaked tiaras. They never are seen bareheaded or wearing the round, flat crowns of the human kings. Did the tall headgear of the noble *gods* cover heads that were disproportionately large? Could that be what these small carvings are telling us? (Figure 4.1.8)

The figurines' heads resemble the Paracus skulls exhibited in a museum in Peru. Anatomic features (e.g., the absence of cranial sutures) make it clear that they are not *Homo sapiens* skulls. One implication: human cranial deformation began in emulation of annunaki nobles.

Desert Lines

The Nazca is a high-altitude desert in Peru. Its soil is barren. Its air is cold, dry, thin, and still. No remains of human habitation have been found in the Nazca; living in that forbidding place would involve hauling supplies long distances over harsh terrain. Ordinarily, nothing disturbs the isolation and stillness there...except for the small planes flying above, carrying tourists looking down in amazement, visitors from around the world, come to gaze at the mysteries on the desert floor.

They see stylized animals and precisely traced geometric forms spread over an area of 200 square miles. Some of the figures are hundreds of feet across, drawn much as you'd make lines on the ground with a stick, by plowing up soil. With the play of sunlight and shadow, the shallow troughs in the earth with which the figures are made become visible from the air...but only from the air. The furrows in the ground are so gentle, the scale of the drawings so great, and the landscape so flat, that an uninitiated person standing by one of the figures would have no idea it existed, let alone what it looked like. (See Figures 4.2.1 & 4.2.2)

Figure 4.2.1. The gigantic creatures of the Nazca, drawn to the same scale. The salamander measures 600' from tip of nose to tip of tail.

Maybe, just maybe, the figures were made by humans long ago, using scale drawings, hand tools, and measuring ropes, subsisting on food and water brought with enormous effort. The struggle inherent in that scenario makes it extremely unlikely.

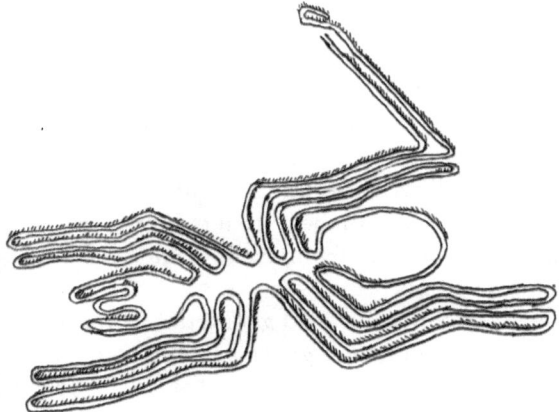

Figure 4.2.2. The spider as seen obliquely from an airplane. The distance from the ends of the hind legs to the ends of the forelegs is 150'.

Another type of mark on the desert floor that the tourists marvel at is just as puzzling, perhaps more so: a tangle of over 700 lines, straight as laser beams, going in every direction, varying in length from a few hundred yards to almost a mile, some narrow, some wide. Without points of elevation for sighting and without surveying instruments, it's not possible to carve long, perfectly straight lines on this terrain. Yet there they are. And in utter chaos. Laborious studies have failed to disclose any relationships among them...geometric, numeric, or astronomic. How could these lines have been made with an incomprehensible level of skill, yet lack any communicative, practical, or esthetic purpose? (See Fig. 4.2.3)

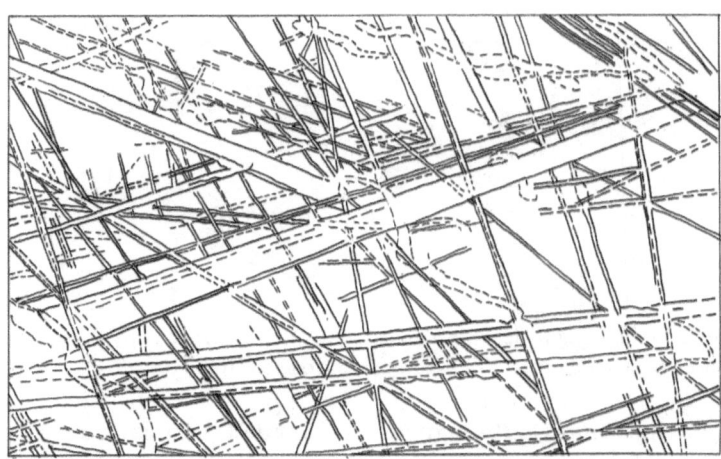

Figure 4.2.3. A few of the Nazca Lines. The curved shapes are natural features.

4.2 Desert Lines

The two mysteries drawn in the soil of the Nazca must somehow be connected. The Mesopotamian Tale, with a bit of extrapolation, lets us solve them both. Gold for Nibiru was not the only substance the *lofty ones* mined. They needed minerals in their cities in mineral-poor Mesopotamia, and mineral-rich Peru evidently drew their attention. Around Lake Titicaca, high in the Peruvian Andes, are ruins and artifacts that can only be those of an *anunnaki* colony. A stone bowl found there is covered with carved characters in imitation of the cuneiform tablets of Mesopotamia. Blocks of stone are dressed and carved with a precision that hand tools could not have yielded. Channels cut in stones found lying on the ground could easily have served in a smelting operation. The settlements are grand, with masonry structures of impressive size and quality. (See Figure 4.2.4) The soil and climate of the region, though, could not have supported much of a population; many of the necessities of life had to be brought in. Pondering how that was done and how minerals were shipped out, we can answer the riddle of the straight lines.

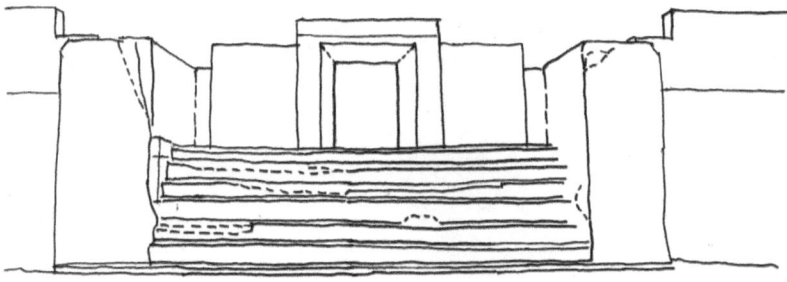

Figure 4.2.4. The magnificent entrance to a temple in Tiwanaku, a port city on Lake Titicaca.

Shipments to and from Mesopotamia by sea were feasible for places such as eastern Africa, but not from high in the Andes. From there, the logical means was air transport. We know from carvings and texts that *anunnaki* aircraft used thrust engines, as do ours. They flew to some extent like our own and, like our aircraft, they needed level ground to land and take off. The flat surface of the Nazca desert was a natural choice as the transportation base for the region's mining operations.

That explains the straight lines. They were not intentionally carved; they were etched by the exhaust gases of aircraft taking off and landing. Their lengths varied because different payloads and different types of craft meant there'd be different lengths of travel along the ground; different engine configurations left marks of different widths. The lines pointed in all directions because, with no nearby obstructions and no winds, the pilots could land and take off in whatever was the most convenient orientation at that moment. The lines are a graphic operations log, unintentionally recorded by pilots with the exhausts of their engines. On ground that knows neither wind nor rain, they've lasted thousands of years.[1]

When we accept that *anunnaki* craft flew to and from the Nazca, it becomes evident for whom the animals and geometric shapes were made: for the *lofty ones* to enjoy from their aircraft. And, obviously, they were the artists. The single long snaking lines with which the drawings were made might have been plowed with an energy beam from the air or with a remote-controlled rover. For the *gods*, it wasn't hard.

Next, we investigate two other mysteries, similar to each other, also involving things on the ground. One is also in Peru; the other is much closer to Mesopotamia.

---

[1] When two of the Nazca lines overlap, the way they do supports this explanation. There are no four-cornered intersections; the track left by one craft simply covers a portion of the other that it happens to cross. (See again Fig. 4.2.3)

The same sort of straight lines, whose lengths total 10,000 miles, are located on another desert plateau, the Altiplano, in another mineral-rich region, Bolivia. Unaccompanied by beautiful, fanciful figures like those drawn on the floor of the Nazca, the Altiplano lines are not so well known.

Great Stones

The cultures in and around Cuzco, Peru, date from as far back as 8,000 BCE. They built walls containing astounding stones ... astounding more for their complex and unique shapes than for their weights of up to 200 tons, or for their having been transported over 20 miles of steep terrain. While masonry walls are ordinarily made of rectilinear blocks laid together with horizontal and vertical joints, these stones are more like pieces of giant jigsaw puzzles. Their joint surfaces seem to have been carved with the ease with which a knife cuts butter. The remarkable shape of one huge boulder earned it a name, *The Stone of Twelve Angles*. (Figure 4.3.1) Some lesser stones have up to thirty angles. The walls of Cuzco were made so well that despite the passage of time they are perfectly intact, joints so tight that not even a thin blade can be slipped between the stones. The tallest walls, at a site called Sacsahuaman, are said to be the ramparts of a fortress, though the true function of the structure is unknown. (Figures 4.3.2 and 4.3.3).

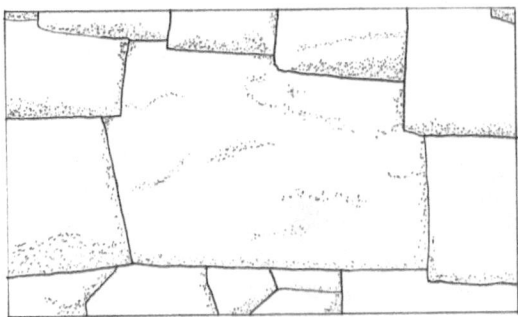

Figure 4.3.1. The Stone of the Twelve Angles.

With computer graphics, laser-guided tools, and powerful cranes, we could build walls like these, though it would be challenging. However, there is no way these massive rocks could be shaped with tools guided only by eyes and placed with hoists powered only by muscles ... by us or any humans before us. No engineer, architect, or mason would think it even remotely possible. Yet archaeologists and historians blithely assume that a primitive culture (that didn't even possess the wheel) erected these walls. To their way of thinking, there's no alternative: the pre-Inca peoples did the work, period. But we mean to solve this puzzle in a way that respects physical reality. Also, there's a secondary question: however this feat was accomplished, what was its purpose? But before we go further into this conundrum, there's a mystery in stone to ponder in the Middle East.

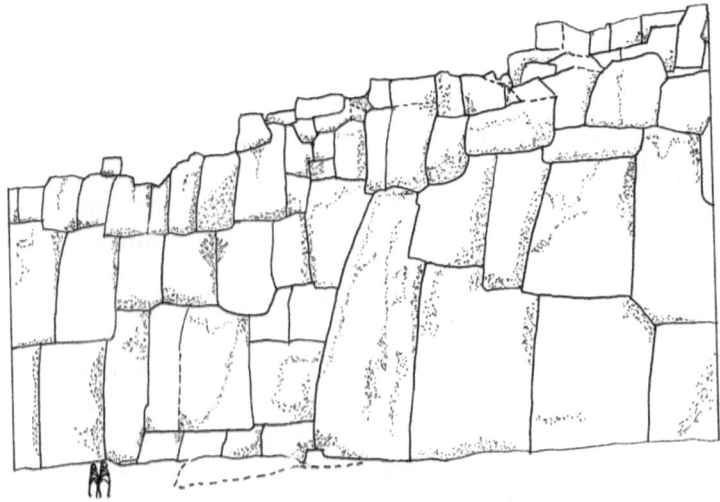

Figure 4.3.2. A section of the walls of Sacsahuaman. The largest stones are up to 27 feet tall, 14 feet wide, and 12 feet thick.

Figure 4.3.3. Sacsahuaman. There are extensive stone designs embedded in the level platforms created by the walls.

In Lebanon there's a high valley called Baalbek, *Cleft of the Lord*, lying between two mountain ranges. No one ever settled in or near this remote place, yet it's the site of one of the largest structures ever built in ancient times: a raised, paved platform with sides up to half a mile in length. On that plaza stand the ruins of the largest temples the Romans ever built, dedicated to Jupiter and Venus. Earlier, the Greeks raised temples there to Zeus and Aphrodite, the corresponding gods in their religion. Earlier still, the Assyrians erected temples on the platform to Baal and Aštarte, their corresponding deities. Under the Assyrian ruins archaeologists have found

4.3 Great Stones

others. In all, there are nine successive layers of temple ruins on this huge table of stone, and deep below its surface there's a vast tunnel network.

Figure 4.3.4. A portion of the wall containing The Trilith of Baalbek. From an early drawing by an archaeologist, showing one and a half of the stones.

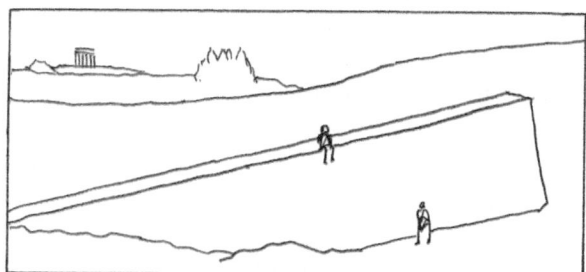

Figure 4.3.5. A fourth stone, quarried but not transported to the platform — which is seen in the distance with the ruins of the Temple of Jupiter, also visible in Figure 4.3.4.

One after another, cultures came to this isolated valley and built temples. What drew them? Who built the platform? What are we to make of its labyrinthine underworld? And how are we to deal with Baalbek's most stubborn mystery? Lodged in one of the walls bordering the platform are three stones that dwarf every stone ever quarried, measuring over 15' high by 80' long, weighing nearly 2,000 tons each. When scholars came upon these Gargantuan stones, they gave them a name: *The Trilith of Baalbek*. (Figures 4.3.4 and 4.3.5) [1]

How could these giants have been quarried, transported over hilly ground, and lifted into place? That question has never been seriously pursued. Scholars simply assume that it was all done with equipment of wood and rope powered by humans and draft animals. Impossible. No mechanical engineer given the facts about *The Trilith of Baalbek* would think for a moment that what was evidently done in antiquity could be accomplished now without specially designed powerful equipment.[2]

And there's another question, as at Cuzco. What was the purpose? The three great stones are within a wall that merely retains the soil and rock on which the platform's pavement rests. What possessed the builders to go to such effort? The other stones with which the wall is built are massive, in the range of 50 tons each. Couldn't around 120 of them have done as well as the three giants? Relying heavily on The Mesopotamian Tale, we can develop answers to these questions.

We've reasoned that after the Deluge, with their spaceflight centers buried in mud, the *lofty ones* needed new ones. Several lines of documentary evidence suggest that the platform of Baalbek was an *anunnaki* launch site. For example, ancient Arab texts quoting earlier sources say that the platform was built shortly after the Flood by a race of giants. The Hebrew Bible calls the place the *House of Šemeš*. That name is Hebrew for Šamaš, the Šumerian *god* of rocketry. And Šamaš was identified with the Sun, and the Greek name for the site was *Sun City, Heliopolis*.

The most compelling documentary evidence for Baalbek's being a spaceport is in the Epic of Gilgameš, in which that *demigod* king of Uruk goes on a quest to win the long life of the *gods*. Gilgameš and his android companion head west, the direction one would take from Uruk if going toward Lebanon. He means to find *the landing place* in the dominion of Šamaš, for he hoped that if he reached the *abode of An* he'd have his wish granted. On the way they enter a forest. He and his friend are awestruck.

their words were silenced...they stood still and gazed at the forest they looked at the height of the cedars...beheld the cedar mountain

4.3 Great Stones

Only one such forest existed in the Middle East, the famous *Cedars of Lebanon*. Gilgameš and his companion are searching for what sounds very much like a buried launch bunker.

> who my friends can scale heaven only the gods
> by going to the underground place of Šamaš…

They attempt to enter a tunnel, but are repelled by its fierce guardian. Exhausted, they lie down to rest. Gilgameš is startled out of his sleep:

> the high ground toppled
> it laid me low, trapped by feet
> the glare was overpowering

After he and his friend fall back asleep, it happens again. Clearly Gilgameš is near the *anunnaki* launch facility.

> what I saw was totally awesome
> the heavens shrieked, the earth boomed
> though daylight was dawning, darkness came
> lightning flashed, a flame shot up
> the clouds swelled it rained death
> then the glow vanished the fire went out
> furthermore, all that had fallen was turned to ashes [3]

There are also physical facts suggesting that Baalbek was a base for spaceflight. The platform certainly was not made just to support buildings. The surface consists of blocks up to 6 feet thick and from 12 to 30 feet in length. They are far stronger than what would be needed for the foundations of buildings. Strength like theirs, though, would withstand the force and heat of rockets lifting off. If the control and supply chambers for a spaceflight base are underground, they're protected from the exhausts of engines and from mishaps … hence the tunnel complex.

The giant stones? They solved a structural problem. The adhesion between adjacent stones in a wall is nil. Vibration causes them to move slightly in relation to each other; repeated heavy vibration will gradually compromise the integrity of a wall. The fewer the vertical joints, the less the structure is at risk. The solution to the structural threat from the vibration of rocket launches was to place stupendous stones in a critical section of wall. We don't know the specifics of *anunnaki* technology, though from what the *lofty ones* accomplished with the *Trilith of Baalbek*, clearly they possessed equipment that could move enormous weights.

The platform at Baalbek was a place of the *lofty ones*; from there they ascended to the heavens. Because it was built by the *gods* and connected them with their home above, after they were gone it remained holy for successive cultures in the region. (Figures 4.3.6 and 4.3.7)

Figure 4.3.6. Šamaš at work in a high valley. On his left, his great-uncle Enki, Lord of all construction projects. On his right, his twin sister Inanna. The *god* of rocketry is building the spaceflight facility in the mountains. From a finely crafted cylinder seal.

Figure 4.3.7. Šamaš, in the mountain valley, opens the gates of the heavens ... on a less carefully made cylinder seal. Since the flood closed the access to orbit and to Nibiru by burying the spaceports on the Mesopotamian plain, in building the facility at Baalbek, Šamaš did indeed open the way.

It's safe to assume the *anunnaki* had also been in Cuzco, where local legends say the walls were built by a giant race. Peru is a rich source of ores, and the *gods* needed to have mining operations outside Mesopotamia.[4] Given the advanced technology of the *gods*, there's no mystery about how

4.3 Great Stones

the Cuzco stones were shaped and placed. We can picture the *anunnaki* working with ease, quarrying and transporting the stones, then carving and placing them with precision and creativity.

As their kind intended with the giant stones at Baalbek, they meant to achieve stability in the face of vibration. In the Andes the source of vibration is earthquakes. Think of what earthquakes have done to ordinary stone buildings in the region. The solution for the *anunnaki* was to minimize the number of joints by using the full size of the boulders they found, and to shape the joints so that they locked together.

As we next shall see, The Mesopotamian Tale resolves questions about other astounding accomplishments.

---

[1] Let's try to grasp what 2,000 tons means. A railroad locomotive is a familiar heavy object. Imagine one of the largest ever built, a steam behemoth from the 1950s. Then imagine two of them side by side. Then picture four more pairs of these giants stacked atop the bottom two. Lastly, imagine these ten locomotives lashed together with cables. That mass of iron and steel would weigh about the same as one of the three monster stones in the wall at Baalbek.

[2] A waterway project on the Ohio River in Illinois involved moving concrete blocks weighing 2,500 tons, heavier than the stones of the Trilith, but by only 25%. This feat, never before attempted, involved the construction of a giant crane. Primarily because of the difficulty of moving the blocks, as of 2014 the project was more than 2.5 billion USD over budget and its completion was clearly going to take 20 years more than had been expected at the start.

[3] In the standard translations of the Epic of Gilgameš, the hero is repeatedly roused by powerful dreams. In Sitchin's translation, which I find trustworthy, what Gilgameš sees, he sees with open eyes after being woken from sleep by great noise and vibration. Given the challenges of translation from cuneiform, Sitchin's outlier version is plausible. Those who went to the Kennedy Space Center to witness space shuttle launches felt the power that had apparently startled Gilgameš at the Baalbek launch site. Miles from the rockets lifting off, the ground under their feet shook. Just like an earthquake.

[4] There were immense copper mines in northern Michigan, for example, of a scale far beyond what the region's indigenous people could have operated.

Impossible Skill and Knowledge

Human abilities have progressed, with both incremental advances and daring leaps, generally in a logical sequence. Yet artifacts survive whose creation seems to have required knowledge far in advance of their times. In this chapter, we'll discuss three of them.

• In Šumer, cylinder seals were one way to create multiple copies of images. The scenes were incised in reverse on tiny stone cylinders, at most slightly more than an inch in length. The seals were rolled, making impressions on soft clay tablets that were then dried.

One such seal, carved in Akkad c. 2500 BCE, now in the Vorderasiatisches Museum in Berlin, is way out of step with how its time is generally understood. The image it produces includes a depiction of the Solar System in the sky above two *gods*. The planets are in a line circling the Sun; they are represented in the correct order and with accurate size relationships. There is a little circle for tiny Mercury, a larger one for Venus, one of the same size for Earth (which is as big as Venus), a little circle close to Earth (the Moon), one smaller than Earth but larger than Mercury, for Mars (also correct), a big one for giant Jupiter, one almost as big for Saturn (which is not quite so gigantic), then large circles for Uranus and Neptune (also in scale), and a small one for miniscule Pluto. (Figures 4.4.1 and 4.4.2)

Figure 4.4.1. The cylinder seal showing the Solar System in the sky above two *gods* standing before Enlil, who holds a plow.

In this image the Sun is at the center of the Solar System, though it's widely believed that Copernicus was the first one to propose that it is. Uranus, Neptune, and Pluto are shown, though to the naked eye they're not visible. [1] The Šumerians had no telescopes; various scientific instruments are mentioned in their tablets, but never the telescope.

Supporting the idea that the seal contains facts actually known by the Šumerians, they called Earth the seventh planet, showing it in carvings as a celestial body with seven points. While we speak of our home as the *third rock from the sun*, it also is the seventh when counting in from Pluto.[2]

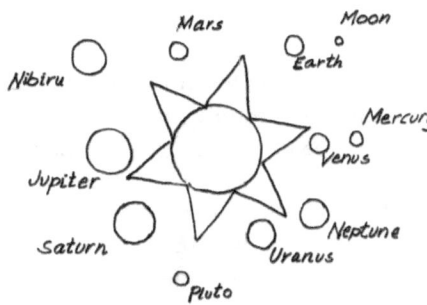

Figure 4.4.2. The representation of the Solar System on the seal. (It is not clear why Venus appears below Mercury in the circle of planets. Perhaps this shows that Venus once had an eccentric orbit, as hypothesized by Velikovsky.)

How could the Šumerians have known the relative sizes of the planets in our system? Some can't be seen and the visible ones are just points of light. And what are we to make of the seal's seemingly incongruous elements? Outside the circle of known planets, between Mars and Jupiter, sits an extra planet, a bit larger than Earth. And Pluto sits between Saturn and Uranus, instead of beyond Neptune.

The mysteries of the seal begin to dissolve if we grant that the *anunnaki* gave astronomy to the Šumerians along with all their other gifts after the Flood. In fact, all the Mesopotamian cultures were conversant with the Solar System's workings, as well as with the complexities of spherical astronomy: the ecliptic, the zodiac, solstices, zenith, equinoxes, rising and setting times, and even precession.

In the diagram on the seal, the body outside the circle of the known planets is Nibiru which, most of the time, is outside the rest of the system. It's shown between Jupiter and Mars because as it crosses the ecliptic on its way toward the Sun it passes between them. Regarding what seems like an error in the position of Pluto: its placement illustrates a bit of Šumerian Solar System history. Texts tell that on the passage of Nibiru that involved the collision with Tiamat, it pulled a moon of Saturn out of its orbit, making it a planet. Pluto's strange path, taking it briefly inside the orbit of Uranus and close to Saturn, confounds our astronomers. This diagram of the system, showing Pluto in a place it only rarely occupies, reflects its weird orbit and its extraordinary history. (Figure 4.4.3)

Confirming that the Šumerians knew the Solar System inside and out, we have their ephemerides, tables of the positions of the planets, past and future. Our own ephemerides are based on observational data, but the ones of Šumer, as accurate as ours, were based on complex formulas and computational rules, not data. Astronomers haven't been able to figure out how to use them.

Figure 4.4.3. As in this cylinder seal, Enki is sometimes accompanied by a god facing both toward him and away. Enki's planet was Neptune. The accompanying god is identified with Pluto. Since Pluto's can pass inside Uranus's orbit, it is a planetary god who can look at Enki's planet in two ways, from inside and outside Neptune's orbit. The Greeks misinterpreted this visual metaphor as the image of two-faced deity.

There's a secondary mystery in the *anunnaki's* gift of planetary astronomy. It's the one thing granted to humanity that appears to have had no practical value. The farmers of Šumer didn't need astronomy to time their planting and harvesting. Its sailors may have relied on celestial navigation, but that involves the stars, not the planets. The puzzle presented by the cylinder seal isn't fully solved until we grasp why the *lofty ones* gave humankind so much information about planetary motion.

To the *anunnaki*, planetary astronomy had great practical value because it's the working basis of astrology, and for them astrology was an essential science. Astrologers conceive of the planets not simply as physical objects, but as powerful bodies of consciousness. To astrologers each planet has a personality, and the shifting spatial relationships between planets, and between the planets and the zodiacal signs, generate a shifting dynamic in the heavens ... akin to the shifting emotional relationships within a family. Studying those relationships was vital, for the *lofty ones* apparently believed that the interactions in the heavens deeply affected life on Earth. Therefore, for civilization to thrive, it needed astrology, and to apply astrology, humans would have to master planetary astronomy.[3]

When the *anunnaki* left Earth, they took the knowledge of the heavens, kept on small devices called ME's, with them. A great deal of learning was lost. With no way to observe the planets beyond Saturn, they were eventually forgotten.[4] Centuries later, as astronomy grew through patient observation, a vast body of lost learning was rediscovered. But no one knew that. The significance of the diagram on the cylinder seal from Akkad couldn't possibly be appreciated when it was unearthed.

• Our second mysterious artifact is a map drawn in Turkey in 1513, commissioned by an admiral known as Piri Reis. Its maker was not a cartographer, but a copyist who said that his sources were very old maps.

The map shows the entire coast of Antarctica and the lower west coasts of Africa and South America with a high degree of accuracy.

Yet Antarctica was not discovered until 1818, Europeans did not visit the western coast of South America until 1830, and the coast of Antarctica has been totally obscured since c. 4000 BCE, covered by thick shelves of ice extending far out over the ocean.

There is no way human beings could have gathered the information on this map. But it's easy to imagine the *anunnaki* mapping Earth from orbit just as we do. The Piri Reis map is a sample of the geographic data the *gods* must have accumulated as they surveyed the planet.[5]

- The third artifact we'll consider is the Great Pyramid of Giza. We won't focus on methods of construction, or esoteric mathematics, or its relation to the other pyramids, subjects about which much has been written, but on simpler questions of its measurements and orientation.

The Great Pyramid has a square base. In geometry a square has four equal sides and four right angles and lies in a plane. But no physical object meant to conform to a geometric formula ever does so exactly. There is perfection in mathematics, but not in manufacturing or in construction. When something is meant to be square, there are always some differences in the lengths of its sides, some deviations from right angles at its corners, and some warping of its surface. When an object is to be made with great precision, the tolerable deviations from its desired measurements are decided upon in advance. These are the *tolerances*, allowable deviations, based on the purpose to which the object will be put and by the resources available to produce it. The smaller the tolerances, the greater is the care that must be taken in achieving them, and the greater the cost of doing so.

One of the astounding realities of the Great Pyramid is how infinitesimal are the tolerances achieved in making its base. The lengths of the four sides are so close to equal, the corner angles so close to 90°, and the corners so close to the same elevation, that civil engineers and surveyors conversant with the numbers are amazed by them. The average length of the sides is 755'. The difference between the shortest side and the longest is 8", a tolerance of 0.088%, less than one tenth of one percent. The average variation between the corner angles is 0°1'47" of arc, less than 1/30th of a degree. (One corner is within an unbelievable 0° 0' 2" of a perfect right angle.) The bedrock base was leveled to within 0.1" of perfection, a variance of 0.0001%, between the elevations of the corners. These are tolerances typically met with things made in precision machine shops and optical laboratories, not vast construction sites.

The orientation of the pyramid's base with Earth's poles is as remarkable as the perfection of its shape. Its sides are out of alignment with Earth's axis an average of 0° 3' of arc, a deviation of 0.015%. If the sides had been off by 3° instead of 3' their divergence from the cardinal points of the compass would still not be noticeable.

With lasers for measurement and GPS for orientation, we could, with great effort and at outrageous expense, match the tolerances achieved by the builders of the pyramid. But the ancient Egyptians did not even have basic optics; they had ropes and sticks for measuring lengths and angles. Builders with means such as those could not even imagine the perfection of the base of the Great Pyramid. Yet there it stands. It can only have been the work of the *lofty ones*. Ancient Egyptian writings tell of the age before the pharaohs, when the land was ruled and populated by *gods*. At Giza the Great Pyramid confirms those texts, one of which calls a son of Ptah/Enki *god of the cord that measures the earth*.[6]

Not only are there striking examples such as these of knowledge and skill possessed too early, the totality of the arts and sciences of civilization appeared too suddenly, as we discuss in the next chapter.

---

[1] Under ideal conditions, Uranus is just barely visible. Before the invention of the telescope, it could not be tracked well and was thought to be a faint star.

² That's how space travelers would count the planets as they passed them on the way toward the center of the system. Those who travel the deeps note landmarks as they approach their landing place. I once had to return four totally intoxicated foreign sailors in my taxi to their ship berthed in the port of Philadelphia, on the Delaware River. It was located, they kept saying, at a place I'd never heard of: *Fortbridge*. Finally, I got it. Their vessel was docked near the *fourth bridge* they'd sailed under on their way upriver from the sea.

³ The *anunnaki* thought of some scientific disciplines as paired fields of learning, with objective and subjective dimensions. They paired astronomy with astrology, chemistry with alchemy, and physics with metaphysics.

⁴ The knowledge was lost gradually. The Solar System of Hipparchus and Aristarchus, c. 200 BCE, was heliocentric, based on information thousands of years old, they said. Three hundred fifty years later, in the time of Ptolemy, complicated geocentric concepts achieved dominance.

⁵ Lest we think of the Piri Reis map as a singular anomaly, a 1507 map (the one crediting Amerigo Vespucci with discoveries in the New World) shows the Pacific Ocean six years before it was first seen by a European, as well as the western coast of South America. The clerics who published it knew that what they drew was out of step with the learning of their times by writing: *Do not be afraid of what it is you see on this map, for it is how you will come to see your world in the future.*

⁶ The puzzle posed by the perfection of the Great Pyramid won't be fully solved until we know its purpose. We can speculate, though. Was it ...

- Structural? For the pyramid to remain intact, while lesser ones became piles of rubble, its stones had to be cut and placed with utmost precision. The single most critical element in this regard was the foundation. It had to be absolutely level to insure that the mass wouldn't be pulled apart by lateral forces generated by courses above that were not perfectly level. Otherwise, gravity and weather would long ago have brought down this artificial mountain.
- Functional? The pyramid may have had a purpose related to navigation, communication, astronomy, or mapping. In Mesopotamian texts about a structure that is almost certainly the Great Pyramid, the terms *radiance* and *brilliance* appear. Whatever unknown functions the pyramid may have served, the precision of its shape and orientation may have been critical to its operation.
- Esthetic? The *gods* gave great attention to their personal possessions. It would be consistent with their standards to build with utmost perfection.
- Religious? If the pyramid was linked to *anunnaki* spiritual beliefs, its physical perfection could have been a manifestation of devotion.
- Didactic? The *anunnaki* could have meant the pyramid's precision to serve as a message to those who would someday be able to read it. It could have been meant to be a clue to our origins, in case our origins had been forgotten.

The Origin of Civilization

Everything that constitutes civilized life appeared c. 4000 BCE, with a speed that anthropologists and archaeologists can't explain. In fact, they don't even try. Over several hundred years, the blink of an eye in the long course of human history, all the arts and sciences of civilization came into being in one place: Šumer. For tens of thousands of years before, weapons, tools, and pottery had been very gradually evolving in settlements everywhere. Yet there was nothing gradual about the advance in Šumer; all of a sudden there was writing, literature, science, mathematics, civic organization, architecture, agriculture, vehicles ... and more.

Neighboring cultures were static. In Anatolia, at a well-studied site settled c. 7000 BCE called Çatalhöyük, the people had ovens, pottery, and carved implements. They stored food, painted murals, and kept goats. Their culture was thoughtful, organized, and artistic ... but not evolving. In the 1,400 years of the town's existence, their way of life didn't change; the artifacts found at its earliest levels and those at its latest were identical. If the human cultures of the Middle East had been moving toward what was achieved in Šumer, we ought to see some signs of innovation in Çatalhöyük. What we find, though, fits what archaeology teaches: in prehistoric cultures, the development of tools, implements, and techniques was very slow. The contrast with what unfolded in Šumer is striking. (Figures 4.5.1 and 4.5.2) [1]

Figure 4.5.1. A hook and eye fastener for a belt, made of bone.

Figure 4.5.2. A flint dagger with a bone handle in the form of a snake. The items in this Figure and the preceding one are typical of the Çatalhöyük artifacts: well conceived and carefully crafted, but not beginning to approach the level of artistry achieved in Šumer. (See Figures 4.1.0 through 4.1.2.)

Let's start with one aspect of Šumerian culture: its rich, complex script. Dozens of representational pictographs were suddenly in use in Šumer. Carved on stone and drawn with realistic orientation, the images were later turned 90°, and later still, abstracted into symbols incised on clay tablets. This is *cuneiform*, named for the wedge-like strokes of the styli. (See Figures 1.4.1 and 1.4.2) The Šumerian script of syllables led to the Semitic scripts of consonants, and from those the Greek, Roman, and Cyrillic alphabets arose. But the script of Šumer that led the way to so many others had no precursor. Before the *god*-focused Šumerian scribes recorded their spoken language, no humans had ever written anything. (Figure 4.5.3)

Figure 4.5.3. A votive statuette of a scribe, carved in stone.

We know the Šumerians through their cuneiform tablets. We can read their love poems, absorb passages of their philosophy, reflect on a king's exploits, hum their tunes ... and realize that we live in a world akin to theirs and that they were people with whom we could converse. There's a tablet on which an alumnus complains of having been beaten in school for truancy, sloppiness, and verbosity. He and his school seem so real.[2]

As previously reported in *The Mesopotamian Tale*, the scribes wrote about all that Šumer accomplished and possessed: wheeled vehicles and

4.5 The Origin of Civilization

draft animals; boats of all kinds; canals for irrigation and transportation; baked bricks and paved streets; libraries, temples, granaries, schools, and multistory buildings; textiles and metals; domesticated stock, grains, and fruits; a musical scale and instruments; board games (Figure 4.5.4); customs duties; judges and juries; civic administration and a bicameral house of deputies; money, weights, and measures; and organized commerce. Their tablets held royal chronologies; essays on philosophy, geography, botany, zoology, and education; texts of advanced mathematics, astronomy, medicine, surgery, and pharmacology; epics, proverbs, and memoirs; guides for grammar and vocabulary; business contracts and records; and legal codes, with family, labor, and tax laws.[3]

Figure 4.5.4. A board game found in a tomb in Ur. Texts with its rules were also unearthed.

To appreciate the depth of their accomplishment let's consider just one area: the domestication of animals and plants. From the creatures of the wild the Šumerians developed beasts of burden, cattle, sheep, goats, swine, fowl, and pets. What was achieved was so complete that in the intervening millennia virtually no wild species have been domesticated.[4] Within a short span of time, improved grains, fruits, and vegetables were developed from wild plants. With plant genetics, archaeology, and linguistics, we can trace how the plant foods of Šumer were further developed into European and Asian varieties.

It's not only a matter of scope; there's the quality of what the Šumerians accomplished. The formulas they used for predicting eclipses are as accurate as our computer applications. Commercial documents and letters recently discovered in a trade outpost reveal extraordinary sophistication in business, especially in finance. The surviving pieces of Šumerian artwork show impeccable taste and superior craftsmanship. Their textiles were magnificent.[5] In short, all the areas of skill and learning that constitute civilization suddenly flashed into existence in Šumer, fully formed. In a testament to the power of our psychological defenses, scholars document what happened, yet show no concern for the mystery it presents.

There's also a lesser mystery within the greater one. The first agricultural advances of Šumer did not take place on the broad plain of Mesopotamia, but in the foothills of the mountains standing to the north and west. It took many hundred of years for agriculture to spread to the flatlands. The soil in those hills was considerably thinner than the soil of the alluvial plain, and slopes are always less convenient to farm than level fields, so why did agriculture first appear in the hills?

The texts reveal why precursors of the high culture of Šumer have not been found. Because they never existed. The tablets tell that the advanced culture built by the *anunnaki* was obliterated by the flood and, as the *anunnaki* rebuilt, they taught the arts and sciences of civilization to humanity. A clear explanation. The lesser puzzle about the first sites of food production? They were in the hills because the deep mud covering the plains needed time to dry before it could be farmed.

We tend to think that when the Šumerians spoke of the arts and sciences of civilization not as human achievements but as *gifts of the gods*, they were revealing idiosyncratic religiosity as well as unusual modesty. Though it hurts our pride to think that humans didn't develop civilization, the Šumerian texts and carvings should be taken at their word; human civilization[6] began as a collection of gifts from the *anunnaki*.

Regarding the early pre-flood times, long before the granting of civilization to humankind, texts tell about the very first plants and animals the *gods* tended on Earth. The *Myth of Cattle and Grain* says:

When from the heights of heaven to earth
An had caused the anunnaki to come forth
Grains had not yet been brought forth had not yet vegetated
There was no ewe a lamb had not yet been dropped
There was no she goat a kid had not yet been dropped
Weaving [of wool] had not yet been brought forth ...
In those days in the creation chamber of the gods
In the house of fashioning in the pure mound
wooly cattle and grains were ... fashioned

4.5 The Origin of Civilization

The level of production was not sufficient. The new race was given basic instruction so their lords would have their needs met.

> The anunnaki in their holy mound eat but are not satisfied
> The good milk from the sheepfold
> The anunnaki in their holy mound drink but are not satisfied ...
> After An Enlil Enki and [Ninmaḫ] fashioned the black headed people
> ... in the Edin they placed them ...
> [Servant] humans [were taught] tilling of the land ...
> Keeping of sheep...for the sake of the gods ...
> That which by planting multiplies had not been fashioned ...
> terraces had not been set up
> The triple grain of thirty days did not exist...

The humans were later to learn a great deal about raising crops and livestock. The development of agriculture after the deluge was directed by Enlil, facilitated by seeds sent from Nibiru to Earth.

> An provided [cereals] from heaven to Enlil ...
> Enlil went up the peak ...
> He looked down where the waters filled as a sea (the flood waters)
> He looked up there was the mountain of aromatic cedars
> He hauled up the barley terraced it on the mountain
> That which vegetates he hauled up
> Terraced the grain cereals on the mountain

Texts tell of progress after the deluge, Enlil involved in farming, Enki involved with scientific and technical projects, their respective areas of interest in the age before the deluge.[7]

Next we take up the puzzle presented by the timing of our appearance on Earth.

¹ There are structures outside Mesopotamia built before the flood that show advanced technique and learning. These include the ceremonial buildings of fine masonry found in Anatolia. These structures have been seen as proof of advanced human abilities, yet the people dwelling in those places at those times were living in primitive conditions. Such works were erected by the *anunnaki* in the widely distributed sites of Mesopotamian involvement.

² His may be the first documented case of Attention Deficit/Hyperactivity Disorder. An even more poignant text is one that reveals that mothers in Mesopotamia, like mothers ever since, sang lullabies to their babies. From a Babylonian tablet, c. 3000 BCE: *little baby in the dark house / You have seen the sun rise / Why are you crying? / Why are you screaming? / You have disturbed the house god // Who has disturbed me? says the house god / The baby has disturbed you, the baby has scared you / Making noises like a drunkard who cannot sit still on his stool / He has disturbed your sleep // Call the baby now, says the house god.*

³ Šumerian arithmetic involved the concepts of place, using the base 60, a highly meaningful number for the *anunnaki*. (Sixty signified the highest rank in their society, that of Nibiru's king, and 60 x 60 is the orbital period of Niburu in Earth years.) The Šumerian base 60 is still with us: there are 60 minutes in an hour and 60 minutes in a degree. And those minutes are each divided into 60 seconds. Also, there are 6 times 60 degrees in a circle. A simpler Mesopotamian system using a base 20 developed in parallel. There are linguistic remnants of both bases. In French, for example, to denote 70 one says *sixty-ten*, for 80 one says *four-twenty*, and for 90, *four-twenty-ten*. From the system with base 20, the Assyrians developed a simpler one with a base 10. This was later adopted by the Arabs.

⁴ The camel is the only Old World exception.

⁵ In one of those tales that give parts of the Hebrew Bible such an authentic feel, after the fall of Jericho, one of Joshua's soldier risked the death penalty for looting in order to have a fine Šumerian coat.

⁶ In the human civilization of Mesopotamia, human beings served in all disciplines and at all levels of authority, up to and including kings. In the the pre-flood civilization of the *anunnaki*, humans served only at lower levels

⁷ An account of the gift of civilization appears in an apocryphal Jewish text, the Book of Enoḫ. In it some of the *watchers*, i.e., *gods*, defect. As they procreate with humans, they give instruction in the arts and technologies of civilization. The text notes in obvious fantasy which of the *watchers* gave which set of skills to humanity, and relocates the gift of civilization from after the Flood to an earlier time.

The Origin of Our Species

Scientists have been arguing about the significance of particular findings in homonin[1] fossils for more than a hundred years. Yet there's one thing they agree on: from the earliest species onward, the bodily form of the homonins has changed at a constant rate.[2] This consensus is the source of a puzzle that is sometimes mentioned but never pursued: with the birth of humankind, the pace of change increased dramatically.

When we consider the skeletal differences between ourselves and *Homo erectus*, the homonin species immediately preceding us, and consider the fixed rate of change leading up to *H. erectus*, it's obvious that we shouldn't be here yet. There's so much difference between *Homo erectus* and *Homo sapiens* that if the pace of evolution had stayed constant, we wouldn't have come into existence until at least a million years from now.

Could the rate of change of skeletal form really have sharply increased just as we were emerging? There's no way to understand a sudden acceleration in the pace of evolution, especially if it involves only one species. The time of our emergence and the rate of homonin development leading up to *H. erectus* are not in dispute. The scientific consensus about *H. sapiens'* evolution must be wrong in some basic way.

The matter of *missing links* is a closely related puzzle. As evolution proceeds, changes in anatomical form occur through small, discrete steps. This was true for the homonin skeleton all through the line's development, until the appearance of *H. sapiens*. The forehead, for instance, went from markedly sloped to almost vertical in a series of minor increments. Yet with the emergence of humans, two major leaps in morphology occurred.

One was the volume of the skull; suddenly it grew much larger. A fully intact *Homo erectus* skull, unearthed in the Caucasus in 2005, provided the most precise ever measurement of the creature's brain. It was no more than one third the volume of the ours.[3] A three-fold increase from one homonin species to the next was utterly unprecedented.[4]

The other radical change in morphology with humanity's birth was our fully upright posture. All earlier homonins leaned forward to some extent, a remnant of knuckle-walking. Suddenly the human pelvis developed an anterior tilt, the disc between the last lumbar vertebrae and the sacrum became wedge-like, and several bones changed shape. A vertical alignment of pelvis, torso, and head was achieved for the first time.

The cranial and postural *missing links* are a significant issue, but they don't confound conventional thinking as definitively as does our too early birth. Though it's unlikely, fossils may someday be found that provide the links ... but a million missing years can never be found. The Mesopotamian Tale solves the puzzle. We don't need to explain how evolution brought us forth too soon if we acknowledge that it wasn't through natural process alone that we came to exist. The tablets and carvings, taken at face value, tell how Enki and Enmaḫ spliced *anunnaki* and *Homo erectus* genes to fashion us in their laboratory.

The combat between Reason and Faith over humanity's origin would end were the accounts of the *gods* in the Mesopotamian tablets widely accepted as factual. The scientific and religious camps both insist they're right because to an extent they both are. We really did evolve naturally, up to *Homo erectus*; and we really were made in our makers' *image* and *likeness*, the terms in Genesis that denote *form* and *function*.

Positing an achievement in genetic manipulation of this magnitude raises many questions, but the idea that the *anunnaki* found compatibility between themselves and a less developed species is not so startling as it once would have been. Biotechnology is advancing so fast that we can barely imagine the feats that will soon be commonplace. Furthermore, it's clear that the two worlds on which our two parent species evolved have much in common. The *anunnaki* quickly made themselves at home here, breathing the air, drinking the water, and raising their crops, thus demonstrating that Earth and Nibiru are very much alike. Their similarity also makes it easier to accept the genetic compatibility of our two parents.

It's evident, in addition, that we don't know nearly enough about how evolution works. The scientific and philosophical discussion is wide open. Concepts based exclusively on random mutation and natural selection no longer dominate. An idea gaining adherents is that some sort of template influences the emergence of new forms. One of the better known concepts is Rupert Sheldrake's *morphogenetic field*, an energy continuum holding coded information that somehow manifests itself in anatomy, physiology, and ecology. How two advanced life forms on different planets could have enough genetic compatibility that they could successfully be hybridized in a laboratory is something that surely needs to be explored, but it isn't justified to dismiss the proposition out of hand.[5]

Scientists struggle to find a story of human development on which they can agree.[6] We can see why that is. How can they develop a coherent chronology if they're blind to the artifice involved in our birth? The picture would be even more confusing if several human variants were produced in the *gods'* laboratory and made their way into the world, as seems likely. It could be that the Neanderthals, a not quite perfected version of human, were the last of such work-in-progress variants.

The Mesopotamian Tale agrees with a central theme of the conventional story of human development: our African origin. The tablets say that the gold mines of the *gods* were in Africa, that Enki saw primitive homonins near the mining operations, and that the new species was born in

4.6 The Origin of Our Species

his compound. It's logical that human migrations began with some of the new creatures leaving his domain, either encouraged to go or slipping away, some eventually finding their way out of Africa.

The new field of genographics says that the first humans leaving Africa passed through the Levant. Our reading of The Mesopotamian Tale tells us that the tracks of the first migrants from Africa were later crossed by those of the people leaving the cities of the *gods*. DNA studies show that the first hunter-gatherer humans in Europe were of African origin, short and dark-skinned, and that the next wave to populate Europe, taller and lighter-skinned, brought farming from the Middle East. That means that the wave that left the Middle East did so well after the flood, carrying skills and learning they'd developed under the tutelage of the *anunnaki*.

Genographic studies reveal that a third wave entered Europe from the Russian steppes c. 2,500 BCE. They were the descendants of human beings who headed north from the Middle East and later went west.

We next address the most confounding and most important mystery about *Homo sapiens sapiens*.

¹ The species of the genus *Homo*, previously called *hominids* in the literature.

² A constant rate of change means, for example, that if a certain bone gets longer as the line evolves from species to species, its increase is in proportion to the span of time. In 10,000 years it lengthens a certain amount, in 20,000 years, twice as much, in 30,000 years, three times as much ... and so on.

³ The specimen was an early version of *H. erectus*. The skull volume of the species did increase with time. However, the increase from the earliest version to the latest was minimal.

⁴ The functional leap of the brain from *H. erectus* to *H. sapiens* was enormous. The neuronal density in the human brain is 3 times that of all other mammals. With the appearance of humans, with a brain 3 times the volume of their predecessors, the number of neurons in the brain of the genus *Homo* jumped by a factor of 9. The number of neurons, however, is not a good indicator of intelligence; the number of connections between them is a much better one. A human neuron is linked to thousands of others; a fair average is 7,000 such links. The increase in neurons by a factor of 9, then, increased the density of the homonin neural network by a factor approaching 9 x 7,000. The functional capacity of the brain, therefore, from *H. erectus* to *H. sapiens* increased by a factor in the range of 60,000.

⁵ It's not logical to state that a race with millions of years of development beyond our own could not have accomplished what's described in the Mesopotamian texts just because we can't imagine it being done. Consider this: the passages telling of Enki and Enmaḫ repeating incantations during the combination procedure may be a reference to their using mental intention to influence a physical process.

⁶ At a major convocation of paleoanthropologists in 2014, the recent finding of a homonin species in southern Africa with features both more advanced and more primitive than other species led a prominent participant to state that it may seem that the overall picture is getting clearer, but that it really isn't.

The Human Condition

In bringing forth the most advanced species on Earth, could Nature have produced such a misfit, shredding the web of life and bringing destruction upon itself? Everything we know about the process of evolution tells us that mistakes of such magnitude don't occur. We began this book's journey with that question. It's not just an intellectual challenge; it resonates in the life or death dilemma we face.

If positing an entirely natural origin for ourselves runs counter to reason, no wonder so many people posit the opposite, a supernatural origin, including adherents of Asian traditions, members of indigenous tribes, and those who embrace the Book of Genesis as revealed truth. What they believe is as plausible as what mainstream science asks us to believe ... which is to say, not plausible at all. If we choose a third option, taking The Mesopotamian Tale to be essentially factual, not only can we reconcile the two opposing views, we can explain how we became trapped in tragedy — and in doing so light a path toward our liberation.

As each species appears and takes its place, it manifests life's paired drives: to prosper through reproduction and to diversify through evolution. Each species invents its own way of being and fits itself into its unique niche, every one but *Homo sapiens*. The tablets and images from Mesopotamia teach that we were invented to serve creatures from another world and made to fit circumstances they controlled. The laws of nature, which assign to each life form its purpose and place, did not apply to us when we were born. That's how our trouble began. Genetic manipulation could not match the perfection attained through natural evolution.

In primates, evolved patterns of behavior are the basis for orderly societies. Instinct, aided by instruction, keeps strife between group members within limits. The first *H. sapiens*, however, didn't receive clear instinctual directives from *H. erectus*, genetic engineering having interfered; furthermore, no community of their kind existed to provide guidance. With instinct compromised and communal teaching lacking, the first humans entered the world without knowing how to behave in it.

Had we evolved naturally, we would intuitively have grasped who we were and where we belonged. Imagine our confusion when we looked at our genetic parents and saw beings different from us and from each other: small, dark, hairy earthlings, and tall, light, smooth-skinned beings from the sky. The disparities between them made it seem as if within ourselves we had a lower self and a higher self. Could we feel sure about who we were? Could we identify with one parent without rejecting the other?[1]

The situation strained the thinking portion of our mental apparatus, located in the *neo-cortex*. This part of the brain assesses our physical and social environments; solves problems; maintains attention; and monitors emotions, impulses, and thoughts. Overwhelmed by the unnatural circumstances of our birth, operating without an orienting framework, the neo-cortex went into an unproductive focus on our identity and purpose. Mass amnesia for our origin preserved this state, so we've never fully emerged from a gnawing uncertainty about our nature. Blocked from knowing how we arose, are haunted by the question, *Who are we?*

This uncertainty is problematic to be sure, yet its contribution to the human tragedy is nowhere near as obvious as the disruptions we suffered early in our existence in two other domains of our mental apparatus: the threat responses and the emotions. We'll discuss the latter soon. First, the threat responses. They appeared with the reptiles: a system that reacts to threats to life (and also facilitates life-sustaining behavior when conditions are favorable). It generates the three patterned reactions to danger, Flight, Fight, and Freeze, programmed in a division of the nervous system known as the *autonomic system*, centered in the *brain stem*.

A threat is perceived and one of the three automatic reaction patterns is triggered. When the threat passes, the reaction spontaneously shuts off unless de-activation is prevented. When that occurs, the person enters an arrested state of physiologic and mental alarm known as *trauma*.[2]

Trauma doesn't exist in the natural world. Having survived a threat, an animal discharges any persisting neuromuscular activation with movement, usually shaking or jumping, as humans can also do.[3] We frequently don't, though, out of obedience to cultural norms. As a result, we too often remain in autonomic activation. When severe and overt, trauma manifests as Post-Traumatic Stress Disorder, with an elevated startle response, hyper-vigilance, emotional numbing, flashbacks, and nightmares. When less frankly expressed, it contributes to depression, alcoholism, recurrent anxiety, and personality disorders, as well as to a wide range of medical illnesses. And it's contagious; the emotion, ideation, and behavior of a person in trauma can traumatize others.

Humanity, observed as a unified entity, functions like a person in trauma: we're violent, impulsive, self-destructive, amnesic, and both unresponsive and over-reactive. We are a species in trauma; trauma-shaped behaviors are central to the human tragedy. In Fight, nations plunge into war. In Flight, cultures escape reality with diversions. In Freeze, societies stay inactive in the face of approaching crises. Humankind has been operating in trauma for the entire time for which we have records. What could have taken a neural system evolved to protect life, as it does so well, and made it also a source of suffering?

When a person is in trauma, yet has no knowledge of its cause, clinicians watch his behavior for clues pointing to the traumatizing events,

4.7 The Human Condition

since someone in trauma often reenacts those events. A girl who was sexually abused may marry an abuser or become a prostitute. In looking for clues about the source of humanity's condition, we start with our most self-destructive behavior: war. Could it be that war is reenacting early traumatic experience? Of course it is: our service in the *wars of the gods*.

Battling with swords, spears, and arrows, our ancestor warriors experienced the highest possible level of autonomic activation. Endless warfare kept returning the soldiers to that intense state. Through contagion, trauma spread from the warriors to their families and their communities. The nervous system activation of trauma moved from the battlefields of the *anunnaki* lords into all spheres of human life.[4]

People who together have been through terrifying trials form intense, lasting bonds. Comrades in the hell of organized war develop powerful attachments: to each other, to their units, to their branch of the military ... and to war itself. This is the *trauma bond*, subjectively positive, but terribly problematic, for when its rewarding feelings are roused, the autonomic threat responses are also activated. As a form of attachment, it has an addictive quality, both re-traumatizing and soothing.

Fighting for the *lofty ones* produced an especially intense trauma bond. A warrior's killing rage was fused with his love for his *god*. Emotional circuits that were never meant to operate together became connected. Soldiers entered battle with a loving, awed attachment to their lord. They didn't have to be coerced. Risking their lives for their *god* was an exalted opportunity, and killing the followers of his rival was a powerful reward. A soldier's death in service to his *god* was a high honor.[5]

Glorious sanctified sacrifice in battle became a virtue. In the artificial battles in Rome, gladiators would cry out: *Hail, Caesar! We who are about to die salute you!* These warped values are still strong in the Middle East, the region where they were first formed.[6] The pattern has never been broken since we first fell in love with war. Civilized mankind continued to seek battle after the *gods* were forgotten; war is a way of continuing to worship them, an attempt to re-experience the service that once gave meaning to human life. A modern warrior is subjugated to unyielding military rule, reenacting subjugation to the *gods* of our early times.[7]

We developed a love of war and a longing for the kinship of battle. The strong feelings of love and rapture arising in the context of war have been extensively written about. No one really knows what those emotional states were like except those who've experienced them. Our bond with war is addressed by the clinical psychologist Edward Tick in his book *War and the Soul*. After telling how war and divinity were intertwined in antiquity for Hebrews and Greeks, and later for Norsemen, he shows that we never fully turn away from war because we believe the divine is at the center of it ... which is exactly what The Mesopotamian Tale teaches.

Dr. Tick observes that war is never solely about its alleged specific causes; there's a force that draws us into its cosmic arena. In an altered state of awareness, we serve the Lord of Hosts, Krishna, Ares, or a transcendent principle. All sides claim that they are fulfilling divine will or an elevated cause such as racial purity or the rights of man. Dr. Tick says that war is not the last resort of sane people ... not the exception, but the rule, with 14,600 wars in the 6,000 years of written history.[8]

War continues to traumatize. On the national mall in Washington, standing before the memorial Wall, seeing the names of the more than 55,000 Americans who died in the Vietnam War, one is overcome by the tragedy of it all, so useless and avoidable. Yet it would take another wall, twice as large, to hold the names of the traumatized veterans of Vietnam who have killed themselves since the combat ended, for that number is over 110,000 and climbing. Conflicts since then have produced fresh waves of traumatized warriors. In 2013 the United States government reported that on the average twenty-two veterans were killing themselves every day.

Trauma spreads outward from war, starting with the warriors and their loved ones as the broken and the dead return home. The activation of the visceral system by a threat is easily transmitted. A traumatized person can induce trauma in those with whom he is in contact. Television and films facilitate the dissemination of trauma all too well. It spreads down through time, from parent to child and from one warrior generation to the next. Activation in the autonomic nervous system from one cause is essentially the same as from another; warfare compounds natural disasters, disease outbreaks, and deadly accidents, perpetuating a maelstrom of trauma, making it a fixed aspect of human life and a major contributor to the human tragedy. The texts and images of Mesopotamia tell us how civilized humanity entered a life colored by trauma.

Now for the second of the neural systems that evolved to protect life and also can do us great harm. With the rise of the mammals, the emotions appeared. Emotions have biological cores, nine innate neural responses called *affects*, centered in the brain's *limbic system*. The affects assist survival by selecting the most relevant data from the incoming flood of sensations and highlighting the most critical information.

The affect *fear* fixes attention on the bear glimpsed through the trees. The affect *distress* facilitates a reaction to the flame beginning to touch the hand. The affect *enjoyment* enhances awareness of a gentle stroke on the shoulder. By making selected perceptions prominent, the affects focus us on what's most significant. They also produce bodily and facial displays, rapidly transmitting information about the immediate environment between group members ... another aspect of their survival value.[9]

When a significant event occurs (bear appears, skin gets warm, shoulder is stroked), an affect is engaged. A *script* is then created in which affect, circumstance, and meaning are recorded. This speeds responses to similar episodes: their evaluations will benefit from head starts. An emotion combines three elements: affect, bodily feelings, and scripts from past events, both recent and remote. Thus, a few neural patterns, the nine affects, are the cores of a vast range of states, the emotions. An affect is physiologic. The emotion it engenders is, in addition, biographic. When an affect is engaged, it can potentially recruit any of the scripts with which it's linked. Trouble can enter the scene if the script recruited is not fully appropriate to present circumstances, as sometimes occurs.

The affect *shame* claims the focus of our concern in the system of the emotions because of its role in the human tragedy. The term *shame* refers to a neurophysiologic pattern, not the state of feeling ashamed for having done something. (*Being ashamed* is one of many emotions derived from the affect *shame*.) *Shame* is an auxiliary affect, arising only when one of the positive affects, *interest* or *enjoyment*, is suddenly interrupted. Subjectively, *shame* is highly aversive. Its bodily sensations, including cringing feelings and muscle weakness, are markedly unpleasant.

This affect makes good evolutionary sense. The positive affects have momentum. When we're feeling good, we like to keep feeling good, so if circumstances suddenly make a positive affect inappropriate, it needs to be extinguished quickly, lest there be a delay in taking action. We might stay so engaged with the pleasures of lunch and companionship in a sunny clearing that we fail for a moment to respond to that glimpse of the bear in the trees ... and become his lunch. Shame's aversive feelings make sure that pleasure is shut down quickly, facilitating a fitting response to the changed reality. Also, by insuring a complete shutdown of interest and enjoyment, shame helps motivate a return to a positive state.

With the infinity of ways positive affects can be interrupted, the range of scripts associated with shame is huge. The shame reaction can result in any of these emotions: embarrassed, ashamed, hurt, rejected, unattractive, inadequate, unworthy, stupid, worthless, hopeless, doomed, humiliated, unlovable, sad, mortified, despairing, lonely, shy, frustrated, inferior, alienated. That's quite a list.

Though shame evolved to alert us and then quickly die out, it can get caught up with a script it has roused and form a continuous loop, making the emotion persist. If a relatively benign event recruits a potent yet poorly matched script, this affect can lead to real difficulty.

Scripts have power in the system of affects and emotions because their function is mostly unconscious. In fact, for emotions to function efficiently, scripts need to be mostly out of awareness. In many situations, the time required for thinking could be fatal. Imagine if you had to *think about it* before hitting the brake in a road emergency. Evolution chose to err on the side of safety: speed of a reaction over a guarantee of its appropriateness. The trouble is that a script may determine how one feels, and therefore how one acts, without any realization of what has just happened within. We may respond with negative emotion and unwarranted behavior more on the basis of a recruited script than on present reality. The psychotherapies that involve *making the unconscious conscious* cultivate awareness of scripts that operate insidiously.

Largely through the operation of unconscious scripts, shame wreaks havoc in people and societies. All forms of addiction are attempts to escape intolerable levels of the shame emotions. Narcissism, a toxic form of pride, is a reaction to emotions based in shame (and fear). When shame emotions sustained by scripts become unbearable, some people get angry to escape their feelings of weakness; attacking others to keep from feeling shame takes many forms, from road rage to racism. In some people, the escape from shame leads to hostility against the self, that is, depression. Poorly managed shame is an unrecognized causal factor in many psychological conditions and interpersonal problems. Destructive ways of defending against shame emotions get embedded in societies and passed on through generations. There are cultures drenched in misogyny, xenophobia, alcoholism, and arrogance, all of which serve to defend against shame.

Via the negative affects, emotions help us to survive danger; and via the positive ones, they help us to have a life worth living. Yet they also cause immense suffering, principally via one affect, shame. Could natural evolution have gone so far awry? Once again the answer is, *No, it didn't*. The Mesopotamian Tale teaches that the *gods* deeply embedded shame scripts in our ancestors through conditions that caused frequent impediments to their positive experiences of life. We can discern several categories of shame-related scripts in the The Tale.

• *Unrequited love.* We adored the *gods*. As dependent beings, we longed for them to care for us. Not having love returned impedes the positive feelings one has for the other and for oneself, producing shame. The tablets reveal that between us and the *anunnaki*, devotion went only one way. We were slaves, soldiers to be sacrificed, valued solely for our service. Scripts of unworthiness were carved deeply within us.[10]

• *Abandonment.* The tales of the deluge were the most captivating of the Mesopotamian sagas — and an unparalleled source of shame.

4.7 The Human Condition

Whenever a person recalled how the *gods* let so many perish, it generated a fresh wave of shame (and fear), reinforcing scripts of insignificance. In the devastation of Šumer by nuclear fallout, most of the *gods* abandoned their cities, adding to the survivors' misery; and a thousand years later, the few remaining ones abandoned humanity entirely.

• *Inadequacy.* We were small, ignorant, and unskilled compared with the *gods*, and as a result we developed negative self-concept scripts. Murals from Mesopotamia (and Egypt) depict humans, small, naked, and bowing, carrying food to the great enthroned ones ... stark images of the realities of human life. (See Figures 3.7.1 and 3.7.2)

Figure 4.7.1. A metal figurine of a man presenting a box, wearing only a belt. The *gods* were shown elegantly robed. Ordinary humans were depicted unclothed.

• *Enslavement.* Slavery severely interferes with the positive experience of life. The shame it causes is powerful. Among the scripts it established in us are ones of hopelessness, entrapment, and impotence.[11]

• *Mortality.* Being alive tends to generate positive affect. We live with a baseline level of bodily enjoyment and are drawn to things that stir our interest, unless circumstances stand in the way. The very presence of the *anunnaki* stood in the way of enjoyment and interest, generating shame. The reality of death at the end of a short life hit us whenever we thought about our *gods*. Contact with those whose lifetimes spanned tens of thousands of years sharply interrupted our pleasure in living. The fear and dread of dying that plague so many people are largely the products of the scripts resulting from living with the *gods*.[12]

Figure 4.7.2. A shell inlay from an object, probably wooden, that has not survived. Even a priest could be naked.

Shame, a protective mammalian affect, acquired a destructive role for humanity through the scripts that became fused to it by life under the *anunnaki*. Those shame-bonded scripts passed from generation to generation, making oversensitivity to shame a central component of the human condition. The transmission via scripts is multi-layered: conscious, through society's valued precepts; semi-conscious, via tales; and totally out of awareness, through the workings of the Collective Unconscious. The shame-emotions have the potential to cause immense suffering, mostly through the behaviors with which we try to escape them.[13]

In this chapter we've discussed how the manner in which we were crafted and treated by our makers and rulers resulted in dysfunction in three domains of our mental apparatus: confusion and doubt about our identity, role, and purpose; entrapment in reenactments that perpetuate trauma; and entanglement in shame emotions and defenses against them. How the three domains achieve integration is not yet well understood, though obviously they do. In combat, for example, thinking provides tactics, emotions produce anger, and from the visceral system the fight reflex emerges ... all three, simultaneously.

By now you may be wondering, *How can we use this information to turn things around for humanity?* There's a great deal yet to cover before we can address that question in depth, as we do in Part Five. We can take a first glance, though, at how The Mesopotamian Tale can empower us.

4.7 The Human Condition

- A truism shared by wisdom traditions, philosophies, and modern psychology: If you don't know your origins, you can't know yourself, and as a result you'll be unable to solve your problems. As it is for a person, so too for our species. Mass amnesia keeps us in the dark about the source of our troubles. New possibilities will spontaneously appear with the spread of knowledge about how we were made and what we first endured. The truth, all by itself, will begin to set us free.

- We are great problem-solvers, proud of our abilities to fix things. Yet our optimism and confidence are fading. Can we hope to fix the most critical problem we've ever faced, our degradation of the world? We are trying to stop the mayhem, but we've barely been able to slow it down. Until now we haven't had a clue as to why our efforts are failing. The Mesopotamian Tale reveals that we've been blind to the source of our destructive behavior; neuropsychology explains how we've been hobbled in our attempts to escape our destructiveness. Once we understand that we've been working blindfolded and hobbled, and learn that there are ways to free up our innate powers, we'll experience a new surge of optimism, an *Aha!* that will reinvigorate our efforts.

In the three chapters to follow we confront theological conundra.

---

[1] The problem of *higher* and *lower* parts within has been noted over the ages. Henry Wadsworth Longfellow wrote: *Human hearts are tossed and drifted / Midway between earth and heaven.* In Eugene O'Neil's *The Hairy Ape* Yank voices his plight in the final scene: *I ain't on oith, and I ain't in heaven, get me? I'm in de middle tryin' to separate 'em, takin' all de woist punches from bot' of 'em. Maybe dat's what dey call hell, huh?*

² We'll use the word *trauma* to mean a persisting state resulting from a traumatizing event, and not extend it to mean the event itself, though that is a common usage.

³ The touchdown dance and ball-spike in American football is an example.

⁴ Destructive warfare is not a universal human reality. It's only the wars of civilized nations, modeled on the wars of the *gods*, that are fought for glory, power, and enrichment through plunder and subjugation. For indigenous nations war is intended to insure the resources available to sustain the group or to defend it against another group's trying to insure theirs. In contrast, wars begun by the rulers of nations for the acquisition of power and prestige may be touted as benefiting their people's welfare, but that is always a ruse. Political rulers are rewarded with riches and power for their armies' victories; indigenous warriors are rewarded with honor for their personal bravery. Tribal chiefs fight for the community, not the other way around. The warfare of civilized nations is a force utterly in opposition to life, the ultimate anathema. It involves a chaotic disruption of the natural order. Indigenous combat is the opposite: an orderly enterprise in the service of life as it is manifesting in two competing groups. Through restraint, tribal warfare usually avoids excessive loss. Furthermore, tribes use ritual to help warriors deactivate their autonomic nervous systems after returning from battle, thus preventing the perpetuation and dissemination of trauma.

⁵ Those who battled Japanese forces in World War II were initially in disbelief over the ferocity and self-sacrifice of their enemy. The source of the fervor of the Japanese warriors was their absolute devotion to the Emperor, whom they took to be a living god, the embodiment of a lineage of over two thousand years. Hitler and Mussolini were able to inspire utter devotion in some of their followers and form battalions of fanatics. The resurgence of extreme loyalty in the mid-twentieth century should be understood as a cautionary tale.

⁶ In 2013, as it became clear that Egypt's Islamist president was about to be removed from power, one of his followers spoke words to a journalist that were flashed to the world: *Dying for the sake of God is more sublime than anything!* In the 21st century, suicidal fanatics act on the basis of this belief.

⁷ In the American Revolution, George Washington faced the task of building an army, which must be run by obedience, by enlisting the men of an emerging nation whose guiding principle was personal freedom. To achieve the necessary subjugation, he presented himself as taking command solely to deliver freedom for all, an ideal for which the men were willing to risk sacrificing their lives, so that their families and communities could enjoy its fruits. By his manner with his officers, Washington modeled the principles of freedom. And he made it clear that he had no wish to retain control after victory. For the first time, men in a war of civilization were subjugated to a principle, a relative advance over subjugation to a

ruler or a *god*. Still, the loyalty Washington inspired derived in part from his being a lot like the *gods* of old, a giant in his time, huge and powerful, the most accomplished equestrian in the army, a wealthy man served by slaves (including his ever-present personal attendant), a warrior of raw courage who frankly loved battle. The people most likely would have succeeded in making Washington ruler for life, had he let them. In a time of great uncertainty, the king having been dispensed with, the ancient desire to look up to a *god* had been stirred.

[8] He was not thinking about living *gods* fomenting real wars with our ancestors as pawns; he was speaking of mythical wars between mythical gods existing only in our ancestors' minds, fictional wars that somehow fused with real wars. Dr. Tick journeyed back to the time when warfare and worship operated in unison, and intuited that our fatal bonding to war was rooted in our attachment to a violent Divine. His intuition told him that for the first civilized humans the gods were quite real, emotionally and spiritually. The Mesopotamian Tale reveals that, in addition, they were quite real physically.

Isaiah Berlin also sensed the connection between war and the *gods*. In a 1959 essay on European unity he explained that war appears to be the only solution to differences between nations because *[One nation's] gods are in conflict with those of others ... and [there's no authority] by which the claims of these rival divinities can be adjudicated*. He used the words *gods* and *divinities* to stand metaphorically for nations' values, traditions, and interests. In an essay on the origins of fascism, he said, *Wars will not cease, however hateful, because wars are not a human invention: they are divinely instituted*. Intuition led Professor Berlin to the very edge of knowledge of our forgotten origins, just as it did for Dr. Tick.

[9] There's a second positive affect, *interest*, and one neutral one, *surprise*. The other negative affects are *anger*, *shame*, *disgust*, and *dissmell* ... an unfamiliar term. Dissmell is to inhaling as disgust is to swallowing.

[10] Shakespeare remembered the *lofty ones*' basic attitude toward us. He has King Lear say: *As flies to wanton boys are we to the gods / They kill us for their sport*.

[11] In the United States, members of families recently emerged from slavery felt such humiliation from the bondage of their parents and grandparents that they would refuse to speak of it, no matter how compassionately they were approached.

[12] The most popular epic in Mesopotamia was that of Gilgameš, the king who tried to reach the planet of the *lofty ones*, where he hoped to petition for the long life they enjoyed. The epic was translated and copied repeatedly, for it spoke to the pain felt by every human who lived in the presence of seemingly immortal *gods*.

[13] Those behaviors are described in Appendix A, where the psychologies of chronic trauma and chronic shame are discussed in detail.

Words of the Bible

After World War I, Zionists began settling in Palestine, the Jews' Promised Land. They taught themselves to speak Hebrew, a language in use for over two thousand years for prayer, scholarship, communal documentation, and literature, but not for daily discourse. Developing a modern version of their ancient language paralleled the development of a modern society on their ancient land.[1] They made use of a traditional way of mastering the language: translating from the Hebrew Bible.

The Acknowledgment, a page in this book's front papers, mentioned an incident in a classroom of immigrant youngsters in Palestine. They were translating a passage in Genesis, the one that refers to the age before the Flood as a time of *giants in the Earth* ... the standard rendition. A pupil, perplexed, raised his hand. Why was a word translated as *giants* when that was not what it meant at all? The Hebrew word, transliterated *nefilim*, was NFLM.[2] The root *nefil*, NFL, means to descend, to go down. The suffice M turns a singular Hebrew word into a plural word, so NFLM means *those who came down*, or *were sent down*, or something similar, but in no way can it mean *giants*. The young scholar asked why a noun vital to the sentence was being so grossly misrepresented.

It's curious that NFLM is mistranslated as it always is, but that's a minor puzzle compared with the consistent misrepresentation of a word in the Hebrew Bible that's said to mean *God*. The word, transliterated *elohim*, is ELHM. The root EL, originally meaning *one on high*, refers in the Scriptures to the One.[3] With the suffix M (the H serves for pronunciation), the actual meaning of *elohim* is *ones on high* ... that is, *gods*, not *God*. Though *elohim* is treated in most biblical sentences as a masculine singular noun, it clearly is a plural word. Prophets, scholars, and rabbis have always fixed their attention on how the word is grammatically framed in most cases and have ignored its true meaning, insisting that when the Bible says *gods* it is almost always meaning *God*.[4]

How can this be? The sacred Scriptures of the people who led the world to worship the One, clouding the central tenet of their faith? The struggle between the monotheism of the Israelites and the polytheism of their time resounds throughout the Hebrew Bible. So fierce is Jewish devotion to the One that, when facing an imminent threat of violent death, through the ages observant Jews have shouted a fervent affirmation: *Hear, O Israel! The Lord is our God! The Lord is One!* Yet again and again in their Scriptures, God is referred to in the plural. An astounding disparity.

To make matters worse, there are other biblical plurals connected with the One. In the Garden of Eden, while speaking aloud about what to do now that Adam and Eve had eaten of the Tree of Knowing, God voices concern that humans will become *like us*. The pronoun is plural. There's no ambiguity in the sentence, or about the context: God is speaking with peers. Who are they? The *people of the Book* have reverence for its every letter, so they're forced to impose their beliefs on inconvenient words. Jewish scholars philosophize, seeking to make the matter a non-issue, but we'd prefer to discover what this puzzle can teach us.

During the centuries when the books of the Bible were being written, edited, and codified, the Mesopotamian texts were held in great esteem. The then ancient tales, copied from generation to generation, translated from one tongue to the next, contained the knowledge of the societies from which Hebrew culture had sprung, as well as the world's early history as conveyed to those cultures by the *gods*. But with the *anunnaki* no longer the overwhelming power on Earth, the tales involving them had to be recast. The *lofty ones* had imposed themselves between mankind and the One; without their dominating presence the Jews were finding their way to a direct relationship with Source. A new world view was being developed out of the only one humankind had ever known.

Naturally, there'd be some contradictions in thought and expression among people in the midst of so profound a change. Humanity's attachment to the great beings who'd always been loved and feared was too strong to suddenly disappear. The bond had to be retained in some way; language provided a means. In Mesopotamia, to speak of the living *gods* collectively people had naturally used a plural noun...just as the Greeks and Romans later would refer collectively to *the gods*. When the Hebrew scribes wanted to refer to the One who'd replaced all the *gods*, they felt an irresistible pull from the archaic plurals of Mesopotamia and pressed a plural word of their own into service to signify God: *elohim*. In so doing the scribes made a gesture of remembrance toward the olden *gods*, the focus of the traditions from which their own culture had emerged.[5]

The authors of the Hebrew Bible had to patch together contrasting elements. In Genesis, for example, God reveals Himself to Abraham, while a few chapters earlier, the *gods'* account of the history of Earth had been infused into the account of the creation of the Universe. The scribes' devotion to the One is beyond question, yet with the word *elohim*, they made a deliberate bow to the *anunnaki* pantheon.[6]

Jews do something similar in their religious practice today, unconsciously. In prayers they call on *elohainu, our God*, a word that combines the root *el* with the suffix *ainu, our*. But in those same prayers, when they say *elohim*, they ignore the fact that they are using the suffix that turns *one on high* into *ones on high*. They say *gods* while thinking *God*. The teachings of their faith fill their hearts and minds while their mouths form a word befitting the religion that was the historic source of their own.[7]

Concerning the word *nefilim*: the poets composing Genesis chose to include this word as a reference to the tales of their ancestors. In fact, the meaning in Hebrew of NFLM, *those who came down,* is close to the meaning in Šumerian of AN.UN.NA.KI, *those who came from heaven to earth.* When the word *nefilim* was first written, it reflected the recollections of the *anunnaki.* Later, mistranslation prevented the stirring of those memories.[8]

Next, we consider another theological system, developing roughly at the same time as the Jews' and just as important to the western world. It, too, presents an arresting puzzle.

---

[1] Most Jews were familiar with the Hebrew alphabet. In Europe, they used it when writing their dialects of German, Spanish, French, and Italian; in the Middle East, they used it to write their dialect of Arabic, Arabic itself, and Aramaic.

[2] The Hebrew alphabet consists solely of consonants. When needed, subscripts and superscripts are added to indicate vowels.

[3] The root word *el* can retain its association with height, as in the phrase *el elyon*, ordinarily translated *God on high*, while literally meaning *loftiest lofty one*. The

Hebrew root derives from the Akkadian root *ilu*, which referred to the many aspects of height associated with the *anunnaki*: they were tall, sat on thrones, resided atop ziggurats, flew in aircraft, journeyed in space, and came from a celestial body. In Mesopotamia, *ilu* referred exclusively to the *anunnaki*. Since they presented themselves as divinities, *ilu* came to signify *divine being*. (It is also the source of the Arabic *Allah*.) The Hebrew root has had staying power. In English, for example, it's in words conveying physical or social height, such as elevation, election, elite, elegy, and elegant. Names of Hebrew origin ending in *el* denote a relationship with the divine, for instance, Ariel, *lion of God*, and Daniel, *God's judge*.

[4] The fluidity of the concept of divinity is reflected in those places in the Hebrew Bible where the word *elohim* is treated grammatically not as a singular word, but as a plural...in some of them, seeming to mean lesser celestial entities and in others, apparently meaning idols representing those entities, and in still others, eminent humans. The word *elohim*, conveying so many meanings, illustrates the transition from the world-view from which the Jews were emerging, to their new one.

[5] The Hebrew scribes and prophets took to their tasks with utmost devotion. They were the spiritual descendants of the scribes and priests of the *gods* of Šumer. From the way they wove the Mesopotamian stories into their writings, it's evident they considered the then ancient accounts to be precious keepsakes. This was noted by the first century CE Roman-Jewish historian Josephus in his apologia for his faith: *[Our] prophets alone had the privilege [of writing the records] ... obtaining the knowledge of the most remote and ancient history through inspiration ... Our books, those which are justly accredited ... contain the record of all time.* The evolution of the Bible reflects a process of liberation and reorientation taking place in a context of awe, gratitude, and reverence for what had been recorded by the Šumerian forebears of the Hebrews. The Jewish scribes weren't just dealing with old stories; they were dealing with historic reality, partly lost to conscious memory and partly remembered. Theirs was an enterprise of writing, layering, and incorporating.

[6] The authors of Genesis linked the age of the patriarchs with the time of the *Lofty Ones* not just with language, but also with imagery. When the biblical Abraham found himself face to face with a flesh and blood deity, God having chosen to take the form of a man, the scene recreates the period in which humanoid olden *gods* walked the Earth ... the days the historic Abraham actually lived.

[7] A parallel in Islam: Moḥammed and his followers suppressed the worship of idols of the departed *gods*, yet when dictating the Holy Q'ran, the Prophet always quoted Allah referring to Himself in the plural.

[8] The first humans were much smaller than their makers, so *those who came down* actually were *giants*, in a sense. As they entered Canaan, on several occasions the Israelites met and marveled at the stature of men they encountered ... apparently descendants of the *nefilim*. The standard translation of *nefilim* as giants is a linguistic misrepresentation that nevertheless conveys a physical truth.

The Gods of Greece

The biblical Jews and the classical Greeks at about the same time were laying the foundation of western civilization, each in their own manner. Turning our attention from the first to the second, we encounter another theological quandary. The literature and philosophy of the Greeks tell us that their gods, along with supernatural powers and immortality, had moral failings. We have to wonder how beings who could be jealous, cruel, lustful, and arrogant could have been considered divine.

For anyone schooled in the institutions of the West, that's a troubling question. We strongly identify with the Greeks of classical times. Our forms of government, art, science, and philosophy descend directly from theirs. It wasn't that long ago that a man unable to read ancient Greek wasn't considered fully educated. How could the Greeks, ardent seekers of truth and keen observers of themselves, have revered the deeply flawed gods depicted in their drama and poetry?

The explanation often given is that, unable to deal with their personal failings, the Greeks created imaginary beings onto whom they could project their shortcomings. The centrality of the gods in Greek life, however, does not allow such neat psychologizing to suffice. Another suggestion is that the Greeks called up their gods in order to explain the miseries of human existence. That's closer to the truth. The Grecian deities were surely derived from the Mesopotamian *gods*, and they were the ones who actually had set humanity on a tragic path.

There'd been a broad flow of culture into Greece from the Middle East. The styles and images of the pre-Hellenic Minoan and Mycenaen cultures were adaptations of the styles and images of lands to the east. The first Hellenic cities were not on the Greek mainland, but in western Anatolia. There the Hellenes met the Hittites, a people from the north who were deeply influenced by Mesopotamian culture; among the *gods* they worshipped was Iškur, a son of Enlil. (Figure 4.9.1) When Greek texts speak of where the gods came from, it's not from the sky, it's from across the eastern sea. The Anatolian Greek cities (and the cities of Phoenicia) served as conduits for the westward flow of Middle East culture.

When the Greeks imported and adapted the Mesopotamian deities, the flaws of the *anunnaki* nobles, so vital to their identities, were included, hence the troubling attributes of the Greek gods. Yet two questions remain: the relationship between the Greek and Mesopotamian pantheons, and the tension between faith and reason in Greece.[1]

After the nuclear disaster of the 20th century BCE, the *gods'* influence was waning, politically and spiritually; by the mid-6th century, they were gone. The classical Greeks knew them only through oral transmission and translations of Mesopotamian texts. In this transitional time, they, like the

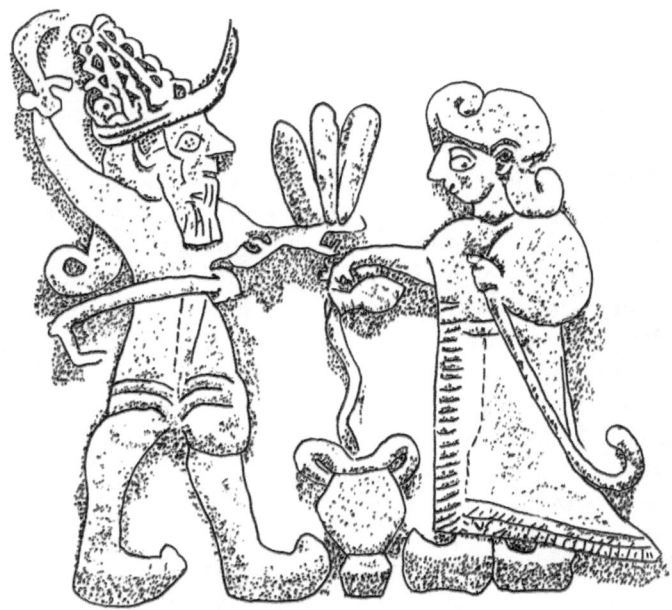

Figure 4.9.1. A Hitte king pouring a libation for Iškur. A stone carving.

Jews, needed to develop a new faith free of the living presence of the *anunnaki* nobles. Their choice was to remake the *gods* of old into gods of their own. The deities of Greek culture are analogous to characters in the historical novels of our time, both factual and fictional in nature.

To an extent, the Greek gods reflected historical reality, manifesting the roles, traits, and behaviors of the *lofty ones*. And yet, to fit the times, new deities and invented and elaborated incidents were inserted. The *Iliad* depicts a world evolving from the one that existed before. When the *anunnaki* ruled human life, armies of men were set against each other for the glory of their *gods*, who sometimes decided the outcome with airborne weapons. The battles of the *Iliad*, however, are fought for the honor of kings and warriors, not for the glory of gods. The deities have a role in the epic, but a lesser one than the *lofty ones* often had in the Mesopotamian wars. Homer's gods intervene for the benefit of warriors they favor, not for their own personal gain. The *Iliad's* gods were concerned with the actions, thoughts, and passions of men, which is telling, for to the olden *gods* the lives of men were of no matter.

The Greeks were free to invent new gods, since they'd never known physically present deities. They felt drawn to personify primal energies. They saw war, for instance, as a seminal force in human affairs.[2] The Sea could easily be represented by an updated Enki, one of whose roles had been Lord of the Deep; he was recast as Poseidon. But how to represent war? Many of the *anunnaki* nobles were war *gods* at one time or another. There was no sound basis for choosing one of them as the model for the new god of war. Ares was introducd as the personification of the terrible, irresistible force they knew to be a core activity of man.[3]

Ares, Eros, Nike, and the other invented deities tend to obscure the strong connection between the Greek and Mesopotamian faiths, as does the deconstruction of a central figure of the Mesopotamian pantheon. Inanna, indomitable warrior and irresistible seductress, must have been too much for the Greeks to imagine, never having seen her in action. They distributed her attributes among their goddesses, especially Athena and Aphrodite (Figures 4.9.2 and 4.9.3, and see Figures 7.3.1 through 7.3.7.).

Figure 4.9.2. Inanna as a pilot, with helmet, goggles, and bared breasts. A carved wall panel.

As the only religion civilized humans had ever known was fading, Jews and Greeks chose opposite directions. The Hebrews denied that the old religion ever had been valid, claiming that the one true religion had been revealed to them. The Greeks embraced an updated version of the old faith. Neither path would be smooth. The Bible reveals the conflict in Hebrew society over the *gods*. Conflict arose in Greece, too.

Greek philosophers were developing concepts of a non-deistic Spirit. When Plato wrote about the One, grammar made it seem as if he was speaking of a person, but he was really conceiving of a principle, an immaterial intelligence ... not all that different from the non-personified aspects of the Hebrews' God.[4] Yet while Greece's intellectual leaders were creating a humanistic culture drawing from the well of human nature, its religious authorities were leading the populace in practices connected with the earlier enchantment with the *lofty ones*. The *gods* of old, in their altered personas and accompanied by newcomers, could not be so easily dismissed; the people's rituals were a form of devotion that stretched far back in time.

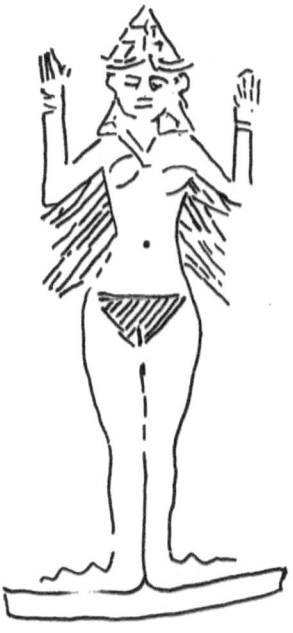

Figure 4.9.3. An image of Inanna incised on a clay vase, making clear her interest in flying and sex.

In Joan Connelly's book *The Parthenon Enigma*, she states: *Theirs was a spirit-saturated, anxious world dominated by ... an overwhelming urgency to keep things right with the gods*. The identity and cohesiveness of each city state depended on a focus on its gods. Ritual and ceremony were important, as they'd been in ancient times, yet how could the priests know for sure that they had made things pleasing enough to the gods?

Life under the *anunnaki* had bred shame and fear emotions that became chronic. Attachment to the gods who so closely resembled the departed *lofty ones* recharged those troublesome emotions ... without giving the comfort that the presence of the living *gods* had provided. That was what left the Greeks insecure, spiritually and psychologically.

Maintaining the devotion they so badly needed involved a suspension of reality that ran counter to the ascendance of reason in their society. The conflict was epitomized with the execution of Socrates, yet his was not the only voice undermining beliefs rooted in antiquity. A character in a play by Euripides said to Zeus: *You are a stupid kind of god, or by nature you are unjust*. In a play by Aristophanes one man disdains another for prostrating himself before an idol: *Do you really believe in gods? What's your proof?* The philosopher Xenophanes ridiculed the idea that the gods had human form.

4.9 The Gods of Greece

The tension in Greek society over the existence of the *gods* was in part relieved in Hellenistic times, with the god-like radiance of Alexander the Great. More complete relief came as the land was swept by the faith focused on Jesus, whose followers used the language of Greece to spread the Word. Moving from the religion of many gods to the religion of the One took time. In Rome a back and forth process lasted generations before the Christian offshoot of Judaism became the state religion.[5]

A merging of the two world views was achieved in the Renaissance, when the gods of Greece and Rome were given a place in the culture of Christianity as the elemental forces of the Universe. The faith of the One God had finally become secure enough so that, in their altered Greek and Roman versions, the *gods* of Mesopotamia could be acknowledged.

Next we address our third and last theological puzzle.

---

[1] When Hesiod compiled his *Theogony* c. 700 BCE, giving the origins and genealogies of the Greek gods, the only great *lofty ones* still on Earth were Marduk and Nannar, ruling in Mesopotamia's northwest rump.

[2] According to the philosopher Herakleitos of Ephesos: *War is the father of all and the king of all and some he has made gods and some men, some bond and some free.*

[3] Their choice of the red planet Mars to represent the war god had a visual basis and an historical one, too. Its name in Šumerian, Laḫmu, meant *makes war*.

[4] Plato's concept of soul versus body, the eternal immaterial world versus the transient physical one, led to the idea of the Holy Spirit, so vital to Christianity that Nietzsche called the faith's spiritual core *Platonism for the masses*.

[5] In a parallel development, a monotheism over a thousand years old, Zoroastrianism, eventually became the state religion of the Persian Empire, successor to the states of Mesopotamia.

The Cross

In the early days of Christianity four symbols came into common use to represent Jesus: the fish, the chi-rho, the alpha-omega, and the cross of equal arms, known as the Greek cross. It's easy to understand how the first three were chosen. Not so, the fourth.

The fish: This simple, elegant graphic involves two arcs. At one end they come together at a point, forming the head, and at the other they cross, becoming a tail. (Figure 4.10.1) The symbol has had staying power; the fish now appears on bumper stickers and car magnets all over the United States. (Figure 4.10.2)[1] It was adopted primarily because the word for fish in the language of the Gospels, *icthys*, is an acrostic. Its five letters are the initial letters of the Greek words *Jesus Anointed God's Son Savior*.[2] And in the Gospels fish and fishing are prominent.

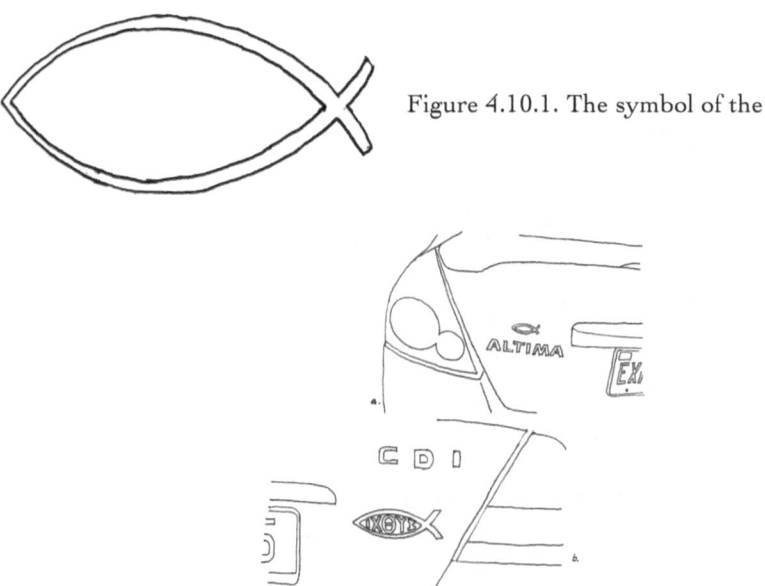

Figure 4.10.1. The symbol of the fish.

Figure 4.10.2. Fish magnets on the trunks of two cars.

The chi-rho: The superimposed Greek capitals *chi* and *rho*, form a Christogram. They are the first letters of the Greek word *christos, anointed*, so the monogram stands for *the anointed one*. It was repurposed for this use by the new faith, already serving as a scholarly margin note for a passage worth remembering, *chi* and *rho* also being the first letters of the word *chreston, good*.[3] (Figures 4.10.3 through 4.10.6)

The alpha-omega: The first and last letters of the Greek alphabet. Their use to represent Jesus derives from the statement *I am the alpha and omega* in Revelations. (Figures 4.10.5 through 4.10.8)[4]

Figure 4.10.3. The Chi Rho symbol.

Figure 4.10.4. The Chi Rho on a 4th century altar in Algeria.

Figure 4.10.5. The obverse of a 4th century Roman coin.

Figure 4.10.6. Fragment of an inscription in the Catacombs of Domitilla in Rome.

Figure 4.10.7. The Alpha Omega symbol.

Figure 4.10.8. A fifth century fresco of Jesus with the Alpha Omega.

The Greek cross: When the first churches were being organized, the new Lord was represented by the cross of four equal arms. The Eastern traditions, the churches that descend directly from the first Christian communities, remain attached to the symmetric cross. It's the basis for the favored floor plan of their houses of worship. (Figures 4.10.9 through 4.10.12) Unlike the three symbols just discussed, the fish, the chi-rho, and the alpha-omega, the symmetric cross doesn't relate to anything in the Bible. Yet before the Roman cross, with its major role in the Gospels, replaced it, the Greek cross was Christianity's only cross. But why?

210   Part Four: Unanswered Questions

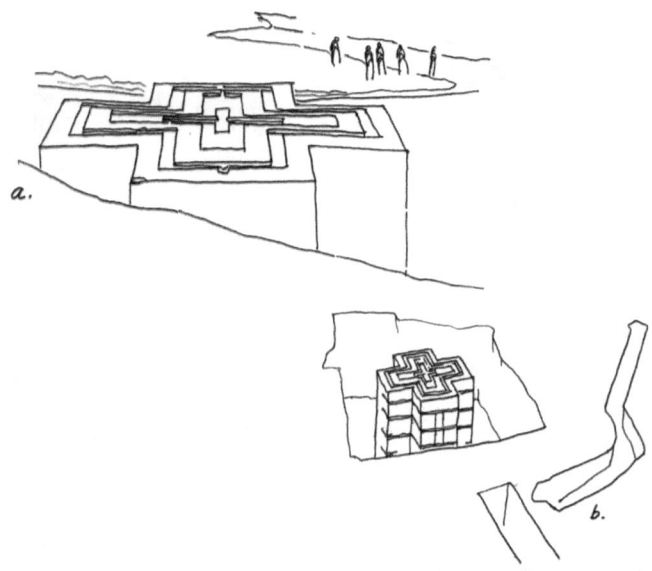

Figure 4.10.9. Ethiopian Orthodox churches in the form of the Greek cross hewn from solid rock.

Figure 4.10.10. S. Hrip'sime Armenian Orthodox Church near Vagharshapat, built c. 618. Floor plan and exterior view.

4.10 The Sign of the Cross

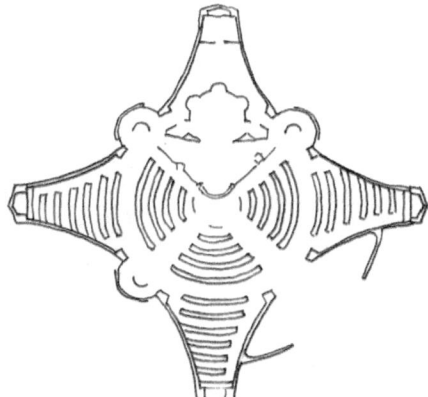

Figure 4.10.11. Floor plan of Annunciation Greek Orthodox Church near Milwaukee, Wisconsin built 1958, F. L. Wright, architect.

Figure 4.10.12. A jeweled cross, several centuries old, the treasure of a family in Armenia.

Thousands of years earlier, in carvings and seals, the symmetric cross had been sacred. It was one of the two symbols for the *Planet of the Crossing*. The cross of equal arms appeared in Mesopotamia in three versions: by itself, contained within a circle, and accompanied by radiations. (Figures 4.10.13 through 4.10.16) It was an abstract statement referring to the path Nibiru takes as it moves through the inner Solar System, crossing the ecliptic plane. The Šumerians knew about its two fateful passages, the one causing the collision with Tiamat and the other causing the flood. The new faith took the symbol of the original *Ruler of Heaven*, Nibiru, and used it to designate the new *Ruler of Heaven*.

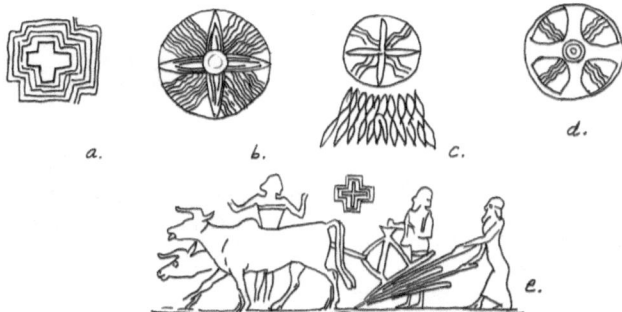

Figure 4.10.13. Depictions of Nibiru.

Figure 4.10.14. A Šumerian cylinder seal showing a *god* and two images of Nibiru, illustrating its positions above and below the plane of the ecliptic, which it crossed twice as it traversed the inner Solar System.

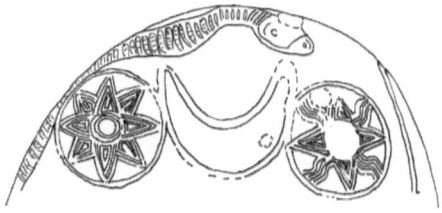

Figure 4.10.15. The upper portion of a stone from Babylonia, with the radiating cross of Nibiru and its king, AN; the crescent Moon, symbol of Nannar; the eight-pointed star, representing Inanna; and the snake, for Enki.

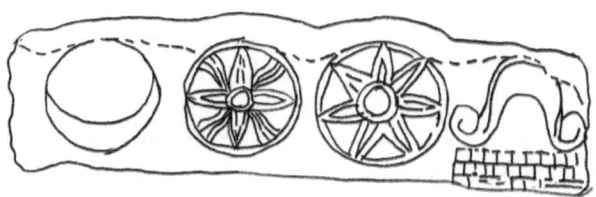

Figure 4.10.16. AN represented by the planet he rules, the radiating cross, and his three children on Earth: Enki, represented by the Moon; Enlil, by the seven pointed star of Earth; and Ninmaḫ, by the umbilical cord cutter.

It seems curious at first that the early Christians would adopt a symbol appearing in Mesopotamian artifacts thousands of years earlier. Actually, the cross had been in use in locations and times closer to their own. Starting in the 9th century BCE, it appeared increasingly in images of kings of Babylon, Assyria, and Egypt, on their persons and in the sky above them. (Figures 4.10.17 and 4.10.18). The increasing frequency of its appearance in Middle Eastern images corresponded to the mounting urgency with which the Hebrew prophets spoke of the coming Day of the Lord, which actually were warnings of the anticipated return of Nibiru, conveyed in the language of Jewish theology.

Figure 4.10.17. A king wearing a cross accepting an enemy's surrender in an Assyrian carving.

The approach of Nibiru had to be prominent in the minds of educated people in the 6th century BCE; it was to pass through the inner Solar System around mid-century. As it turned out, that transit was benign and left no mark in history. The prophecies of the Day of the Lord lost their immediacy, yet they remained useful as reminders of God's power and were retained when the Hebrew canon was established. Approaches of the old *Ruler of Heaven* had always raised expectations of a momentous occurrence; with Nibiru's 6th century BCE passage, the symmetric cross renewed its prominence, eventually leading to its use to represent a momentous occurrence of another kind: the arrival of the Savior.[5]

Figure 4.10.18. An Assyrian stella showing a king wearing a cross.

The Greek cross was in time replaced by the Roman one.[6] Yet long after the Roman cross became dominant, Christianity's first cross reappeared in a way that illustrates the power it still held. The most magnificent structure of the early Renaissance, the dome of the cathedral of Florence, is so wondrous that, although the church is named for a saint, everyone calls the building *il Duomo, the Dome.* On the peak of the dome stands a structure known as a lantern, and at its apex two golden shapes float above the city.

Figure 4.10.22. The cross of equal arms and the golden globe atop the Duomo.

4.10 The Sign of the Cross

On the point of the lantern sits a gilded sphere. On the sphere, connected by a small truncated pyramid, stands a gilded Greek cross. (Figure 4.10.22) Atop the most magnificent creation in Christendom were placed two of the symbols that once represented the planet Nibiru, humanity's first Lord of Heaven: one abstract, the cross of equal arms, and one realistic, the golden globe. We would expect the visual climax of Christianity's most impressive structure to be the cross that had for centuries been its primary symbol: the one telling of the Son of God sacrificed and risen. But instead there stands the faith's original cross.[7]

The architect of the dome, Brunelleschi, placed at the pinnacle of his creation a familiar composite form symbolizing Christ's dominion over the world: the orb bearing the cross. The orb and cross had long been used in the regalia, crowns, and coats of arms of Christian kings to represent their authority. (See Figs 4.10.23 through 4.10.25) Since the kings ruled in Christ's name, their displaying a symbol of His dominion was fitting. Like the cross on the globe high over Florence, the crosses on royal orbs generally weren't the Roman crosses with which the Savior was ordinarily identified. They were almost always Greek crosses.

Figure 4.10.23. An Orb and Cross, to be held in ceremonies by a king.

Figure 4.10.24. An Orb and Cross on a crown.

Figure 4.10.25. A portrait of Henry VIII of England by Hans Holbein the Younger. A ruler on Earth is wearing a symbol of humanity's original Ruler of Heaven, Nibiru, the cross within a circle.

The Collective Unconscious was at work in the royal use of the cross and orb. Nibiru, the planet that appeared at the times of its crossing through the inner Solar System as a golden sphere, had been depicted in two dimensions as a disc containing a symmetric cross. The cross had also served to represent An, Nibiru's king. Since An had authorized kingship for humanity he was the original source of secular and spiritual authority on Earth. The reasons the disc and symmetric cross had been revered in ancient times were forgotten, yet the reverence for the two forms survived. The planet that was once the ruling celestial *god of heaven*, and the royal flesh and blood *god of heaven* (whose name meant *heaven*), had not been totally obliterated from human consciousness.

Using the orb and Greek cross as Brunelleschi did was an extraordinary act. He could have used the Roman cross and could have omitted the sphere. Yet the more ancient symbols called to him and were accepted by the religious authorities who approved his design.[8]

The next pair of enigmas we consider involves the actual astronomical crossing to which we've been referring.

4.10 The Sign of the Cross 217

Figure 4.10.19. A carved Cross of St. John.

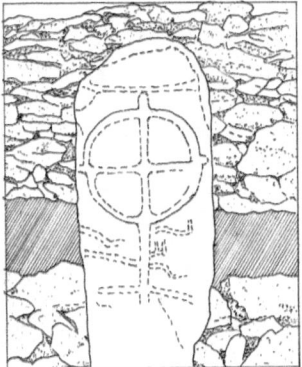

Figure 4.10.20. An early Celtic cross on a stone pillar in County Kerry, Ireland. Within the circle the Greek cross can easily be discerned.

Figure 4.10.21. A typical Celtic cross standing in northern Wales. The cross of equal arms within the circle is not so obvious, leading to the standard interpretation of the circle as a remnant of Sun worship.

[1] It even has been used in email tag lines: <><

[2] The letters of the Greek word *icthys* appear within the graphic fish in the lower image in Figure 4.10.2. The names of the Greek letters, the corresponding Roman letters, the words of the acrostic, and their meanings are as follows:

Iota	I	Iesous	Jesus
Chi	C	Christos	Anointed
Theta	TH	Theou	God
Upsilon	Y	Huios	Son
Sigma	S	Soter	Savior

[3] The letter chi could also convey deeper meaning. Instead of the pure form of the letter, its arms in the Christogram could be shown crossing at a more narrow angle, approximating the angle of the crossing of the plane of the ecliptic with the celestial equator. (As in Figure 4.10.5) To Plato, the intersection of those two heavenly planes formed the Soul of the World. To early Christian theologians, this celestial cross represented the pre-existing Christ of the Universe.

[4] There were two other early symbols, used less often: the lamb, for its innocence, and the date palm, for sprouting new leaves as its dying ones hung down.

[5] The Star of Bethlehem provides a celestial link between the narratives of the return of Nibiru and the coming of Jesus.

[6] The Greek cross did not totally succumb to the Roman cross. It was the cross of the Knights Templar and the Knights of St. John. (Figure 4.10.19) Six Greek crosses were placed on one of the vestments of the Pope. In Medieval and Renaissance works of painting and sculpture, behind Christ's head the Greek cross fills His halo. In a version of the Roman cross used by several churches, we glimpse a Greek cross within a circle. The best known of these is the Celtic cross. (Figures 4.11.20 and 4.11.21)

[7] The presence of the Greek cross atop the cathedral of Florence is such an historical anomaly that in twenty editions of the massive, authoritative, *Sir Bannister Fletcher's A History of Architecture*, no editor has noticed a glaring error in two drawings of *il duomo*. They clearly show a Roman cross.

[8] Nibiru's cross seems to be stirring in the Collective Unconscious once again. To explain aberrations in the outermost members of the Solar System, as we've discussed, astronomers posit the existence of a planet in deep space. Astronomy buffs call it *Planet X*. A cross whose arms are equal – the letter X – is again being used to designate the *Planet of the Crossing*.

Planetary Anomalies

There's a well-founded scientific consensus about how the Sun, planets, and moons came into existence. Before using the Mesopotamian Tale to resolve the next pair of puzzles, let's summarize that consensus.

Diffuse hydrogen in space begins to concentrate around a point, the center of a star that's beginning to form. As more hydrogen is drawn in, solar processes begin. Pressure develops within the growing mass, and heat, light, and other forms of energy are produced, along with the chemical elements. Most stars, when they eventually die, release into space the matter they created over their working lifetimes.

Early in our Sun's life, it drew material released by stars that had died into a *solar nebula*, a disc of dust, rocks, ice, and gas swirling around itself. Within that wide disk, lesser accretion discs formed, each one centered on a growing spherical mass. Gravitational coalescence continued until almost all the material in the solar nebula was pulled into the spheres.

Physical formuli named for Newton and Kepler describe the motion of the planets; they tell how the dimensions of a planet's orbit relate to its movement around the Sun. Their equations, however, fail to address one aspect of the orbits. They imply that there's no particular relationships among the orbits other than the obvious ... that they be far enough apart so that the planets don't bother each other. The formuli imply that a planet could be a bit farther from the Sun than it actually is if it orbited more slowly and that it could be a bit closer if it circled a little faster. In the language of physics, the equations of Newton and Kepler imply that the planetary orbits are not *quantitized*.

A mathematical relationship, however, exists among the orbits, revealing that they indeed are quantitized. It was expressed in a formula announced by a series of less renowned 18th century astronomers. A simple algebraic equation, it is usually called Bode's Rule. In its updated versions, when the integers 1 through 10, standing for the nine known planets and the Asteroid Belt, are entered for one of the terms of the formula, and the corresponding orbital periods are entered for another term, the formula gives the distance from the Sun for all the members of the system. The results are within 5% of the actual orbital dimensions, a remarkable level of accuracy for a simple equation. In addition, for the giant planets and their families of moons, Bode's Rule gives the distances between planet and moon with the same level of accuracy.[1] (Figure 4.11.0)

If there's a simple equation giving the dimensions of the orbits of the planets, there must be a physical function determining the orbits; when a correlation between a formula and physical reality is strong, the math has a material basis. In other words, there's an aspect of gravity, not yet understood, that locates the orbits of the planets. Bode's Rule implies that as the planets coalesced, their orbits were predetermined.[2]

Bode's Rule was developed by observing the motions of the six planets that then were known. The rule attracted attention because of what it predicted. In 1768, when it first was widely published, the seventh planet, Uranus, barely at the limit of unaided vision, was thought to be a dim star. In 1781 it was recognized as a planet by Herschel. Bode was delighted to announce that Uranus dwelled exactly where the formula predicted that a planet lying beyond Saturn would be located.

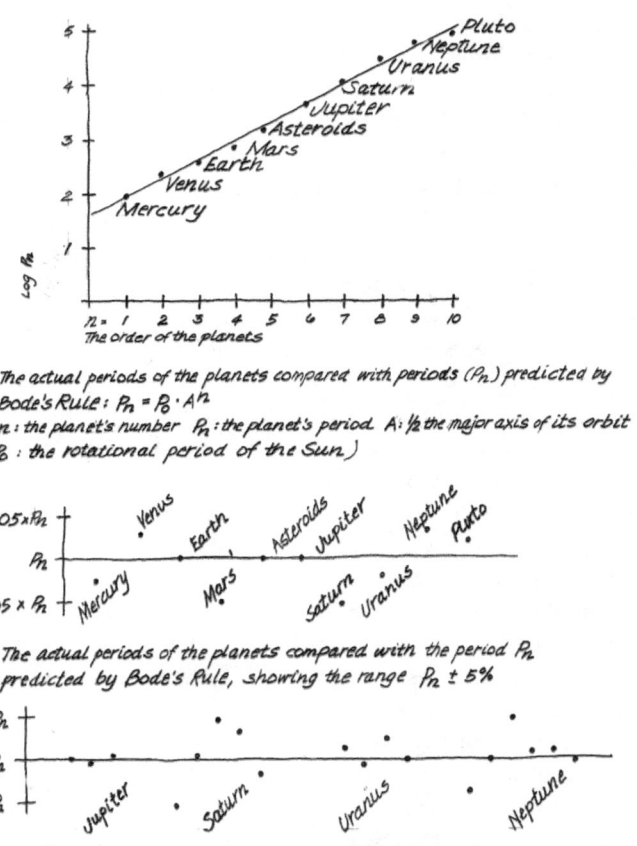

a. The actual periods of the planets compared with periods (P_n) predicted by Bode's Rule: $P_n = P_0 \cdot A^n$
(n : the planet's number P_n : the planet's period A: ½ the major axis of its orbit P_0 : the rotational period of the Sun)

b. The actual periods of the planets compared with the period P_n predicted by Bode's Rule, showing the range $P_n \pm 5\%$

c. The actual periods of the principal moons of the giant planets compared with the predicted period P_n, showing the range $P_n \pm 5\%$ (Not shown, a moon of Uranus at $P_n +18\%$)

Figure 4.11.0. Bode's Rule Illustrated.

When Neptune was discovered, though, the planet's position did not correspond as well with what the rule predicted, and it fell out of favor. However, the disparity resulted from a peculiarity in the way the formula was expressed at the time.[3] The rule, which has long been discredited as a limited, coincidental finding, is being revisited. Not only do its current

4.11 Planetary Anomalies

iterations give good fits for the orbits of Neptune and Pluto, it has recently been shown to be the organizing principle for the planetary systems of numerous other stars in our galaxy.

Before the rule lost respect because of its poor showing with Neptune's orbit, astronomers took it quite seriously. At the turn of the 19th century they used it to search for the planet that the rule suggested would be in an orbit between Mars and Jupiter. They found a small object in the orbit predicted. Then they found another at the same distance, and then another. A horde of small bodies was later located there. By now more than a million asteroids with a diameter over one kilometer have been found in the predicted fifth planetary orbit.[4]

But why didn't all that material coalesce into a planet? Actually, when the asteroids were first studied, astronomers speculated that they were the remnants of a planet that had broken up. But their profession was shying away from hypotheses involving catastrophic events in the Solar System, so they postulated that conditions between Mars and Jupiter must have prevented matter from coalescing. The explanation they developed involves complex arguments related to points of resonance in Jupiter's gravitational field. A critique of that theory would be beyond the scope of this work. We'll restrict our complaint about the consensus explanation to one telling fact conventional astronomy ignores.

All the major asteroids are aligned in axial rotation; they spin on parallel north-south axes. If those thousands of bodies had no historical relationship to each other they'd be spinning chaotically, every which way. There is only one known process that could bring a band of big rocks into such remarkable rotational alignment: bodies created by the disintegration of a much larger one retain the rotation of the parent body.

The Mesopotamian Tale resolves the puzzle of the belt of asteroids. In the account we've discussed, it was between Mars and Jupiter that the planet Tiamat once dwelled. Nibiru's elongated path always passed through Tiamat's orbit. On a fateful transit, Tiamat was too near the point where Nibiru crossed its orbit, and one of the visitor's moons crashed into her. The wounded planet found a new orbit, while the material torn away remained in her old orbit, spread out, and formed the ring of asteroids. That means that when the 19th century astronomers found small bodies where Bode's Rule said a planet would be, they couldn't see the planet ... because they were standing on it. (Figure 4.11.1)

But how could there have been an empty Bode's Rule orbit? We deduce from the Mesopotamian creation epics that the third orbit from the Sun had once belonged to Nibiru, and that its ejection from the inner Solar System created a vacancy that later would be available to the wounded Tiamat. Where else in the Solar System could there have been a place for Nibiru to take form and to serve as a platform for the evolution of advanced life? Therefore, when the *anunnaki* left Nibiru for Earth they were voyaging to their planet's original place in the Solar System.

Proposing that Earth started out in an orbit beyond Mars and that life flourished there, raises questions in evolutionary biology, geology, and climatology. One of the obvious issues to resolve is how at that time Tiamat could have been warm enough, since the present consensus is that the zone of habitability in the Solar System does not extend beyond Mars. That conclusion, though, is based on questionable assumptions.

Tens of millions of years ago the level of carbon dioxide in the atmosphere of our planet was higher than now. That could have resulted in substantial greenhouse warming. Other factors, such as volcanic activity, may have heated the atmosphere. Also, it's now evident that Mars once had surface water and an atmosphere much denser than its present one. These facts suggest a scenario in which there was a phase in the life of the Solar System when the 3rd, 4th, and 5th planets, Nibiru, Laḫmu (the Šumerian name for Mars), and Tiamat, circled the Sun in a zone that was friendly to life.[5]

Figure 4.11.1. Someone drinking beer through a hollow reed was a common theme in Mesopotamian carvings. The reed in this image is a visual pun, representing the Asteroid Belt between Venus (the 8-pointed body), Earth-and-Moon, and Mars, on one side, and Jupiter and Saturn on the other.

The second puzzle to address in this chapter has to do with Earth's asymmetry. The equations of physics suggest that as material accrues to form a planet or a moon, it arranges itself symmetrically around the body's rotational axis. For the planets and moons we've observed from Earth and to which we've sent surveying instruments, axial symmetry of the mass does appear to be the rule. Our planet's continental crust, however, is far from evenly distributed; the deep basin of the Pacific Ocean occupies nearly half the surface of the globe.

If Earth achieved its present form solely through accretion, the process would have somehow had to result in the rocky elevated masses of the continents, 15 to 40 miles thick, gathering in a supercontinent (as we know they once were) covering less than half of the surface of the planet,

4.11 Planetary Anomalies

while all the rest was ocean basin. Not only that, but the floor of that ocean, without the crust that volcanic flow has since built up, would have been on average 12 miles below present sea level.

That scenario is inconsistent with a process of gradual coalescence. This puzzle, too, is resolved by The Mesopotamian Tale, with a bit of extrapolation. Let us assume that Tiamat was originally symmetrical around its axis of rotation. The collision with Nibiru's moon, tearing away a large sector of its outer layers, produced substantial assymetry. Missing a portion of its surface, our planet began to heal by closing in around the void, contracting into a slightly smaller sphere. In the process, the areas of rocky crust on the face opposite the wound were pulled apart, their separation defining most of the ocean basins ... but not that of the Pacific. That great basin is the scar remaining from the collision. The Ring of Fire, the volcanoes and earthquakes that surround the Pacific, testify to the violence of its birth and to the effort our planet is still exerting to achieve stability around her great wound. The trenches on the floor of the Pacific, the deepest openings in Earth's surface, extending most of the way through the oceanic crust, also speak to a violent origin.[6]

The last mystery we'll ponder is placed at the end of this part because it isn't fully resolved by the sources of The Mesopotamian Tale that we possess. A resolution is possible, but it relies on an extrapolation from the known texts.

[1] One updated version of the formula (illustrated by Fig. 4.10.1a) says that the time it takes for the Nth planet to complete its circuit around the Sun (e.g., 365.25 days for the 3rd planet) equals the time it takes for the Sun, spinning on its axis, to complete one rotation, multiplied by a factor that yields one-half the major axis of its orbit, to the Nth power. That is, when the number N and the length of the Nth planet's year are entered, the formula yields the major axis of the planet's orbit. (The orbits are not circles, but ellipses. An ellipse is defined by two lines at right angles to each other, its major and minor axes. All the aspects of an orbit can be derived when one of the axes has been determined)

[2] Bode's Rule implies that the orbits are fixed, like the notes of a musical scale. The iteration cited in Note 1 says that the function that defines them is physically linked to the Sun's rotation, a phenomenon with no known relationship to the gravitational operation of the Solar System. Such a connection is reminiscent of Descartes' concept of the Universe. Before Newton, he envisioned the heavenly bodies carried along on fluid spiral vortices. The idea is also concordant with the radical cosmology proposed by Wilhelm Reich. Acknowledging that there is a physical principle underlying Bode's Rule requires admitting that there's a major gap in our understanding of gravity. The issues here are substantial and their resolution may require revising Einstein's General Theory of Relativity.

[3] The early form of Bode's Rule, first announced in 1715 by David Gregory, utilized an obsolete term, the Astronomical Unit, the average Sun-to-Earth distance. The A.U. can help one visualize the distances between the planets but it has no relationship to the system's dynamics. Organizing the equation around the A.U. compromised the rule's applicability.

[4] Though the asteroids are spread over a wide band, the orbit given by Bode's Rule is home to over 90% of the mass of the Asteroid Belt.

[5] This means that not only are Nibiru and Earth quite similar chemically, as we've reasoned, but they both at different times offered the third orbit from the Sun as a platform for the evolution of their homonin lines. This makes it a bit easier to give credence to the idea that our two parent species were genetically compatible.

[6] The cataclysm had to have been the trigger for one of Earth's mass extinctions and a major determining factor in our planet's plate tectonics.

The Aquatic Ape

In 1930 a renegade theory of human evolution was proposed, the Aquatic Ape Hypothesis, our final puzzle. Hardly any scientists give it credibility, yet if approached with an open mind, it has great appeal. The theory states that at one point in time, our line migrated from dry land to a wet environment, such as a marshy delta at the edge of a warm sea; and that the line lived long enough in water to evolve adaptations to marine life; and that later it returned to land, retaining its marine adaptations. Many facts support these ideas.

* **Primates avoid water; we love it and are adapted to it.** With one revealing exception (discussed below) the primates, including our closest relatives, the great apes, avoid bodies of water and lack any adaption to it.[1] We, in contrast, have great affinity for water, as seen at our beaches in summer and in all our water-based activities.

Our bodies are well suited to being in water. (1) Our fully upright skeletal configuration on land renders us streamlined in water and the exceptional range of motion of our shoulder joints, evolved at the cost of easy dislocation, allows a variety of effective swimming strokes. In contrast, the apes' bent-over posture and limited range of shoulder motion would restrict them to a doggie paddle, were they ever to attempt to swim. (2) The human nose is shaped so that water can easily be kept out of the nostrils, especially when swimming. Not so for the apes. (3) We have a subcutaneous fat layer, a body-sheath that provides thermal insulation and buoyancy, important features for any animal spending long periods of time in water. All mammals adapted to aquatic life have this layer, but none of the great apes do. (4) All primate species have a furry skin that would cause frictional drag if they swam. The smooth skin of the *naked ape*, as we've been called, glides through the water.[2] (5) When we're fully submerged, we undergo a physiologic shift. Our *diving reflex* is not the state of alert we'd expect in an animal that takes frequent breaths, but the opposite. The changes are all in the direction of greater calm, including a dropping blood pressure and heart rate; we respond to full immersion as if water is a friendly and safe environment.

* **Babies and Mothers.** Infants are at home in water. When submerged, newborns hold their breath and make spontaneous swimming motions. Given the right learning environment, babies teach themselves to swim earlier than they can learn to walk. *Baby fat* gives them buoyancy as well as thermal insulation; newborn great apes, in contrast, are skinny.[3]

- **Tears**. Marine animals, all shed salty tears. Ridding their bodies of salt is important because they're constantly bathed in it. Species who live on land or in fresh water do not shed tears ... with just two exceptions. One is the elephant, whose evolutionary path went from land, to living in the ocean, then back to land. We are the other one.

- **Nutrients**. The human brain, for full development and functioning, requires two substances that are hard to obtain in sufficient quantities except by eating seafood (or taking supplements): iodine and essential fatty acids. If a species has a need for a type of food, that food was readily available at some point in that species' evolutionary history.

- **Sex**. Humans share a trait with the mammals that mate in water, the whales, dolphins, and manatees: face-to-face coitus. No other land mammal does ... with one telling exception, the bonobo. The bonobo is also the only great ape that enjoys playing with water and being in it. It's interesting that the ape that likes being in water is also the only other land animal that has frontal coitus. What they have in common with us structurally is a configuration of the pelvic bones that gives our two species a fully upright posture, facilitating both swimming, and frontal coitus.

There's an issue, however, that makes serious consideration of the Aquatic Ape Hypothesis impossible for most scientists. There is good evidence for the theory in anatomy, physiology, and behavior, yet if we had an aquatic ancestor, his fossils and artifacts should by now have been found in areas that once were estuaries or shallow bays. A developing line of hominin species going from land to water and back to land would have left its story to be discovered, as the ancestors of the elephant and hippo did. The total absence of fossil evidence blocks acceptance of the theory. The Mesopotamian Tale doesn't provide a simple solution to this puzzle, as it did for the ones we've so far considered, yet it does hint at one.

What if the ancestors of our kind who adapted to marine life left their bones not on Earth but on Nibiru? What if *H. sapiens'* marine adaptations didn't come from *H. erectus* but through the *anunnaki*? Mesopotamian texts and images tell nothing concerning the remote history of the *lofty ones*, yet they suggest that the *anunnaki* had a strong affinity for water.

The first place on Earth where the *gods* settled would have been attractive to beings who recalled a remote aquatic past. While practical factors, such as the nearby presence of petroleum, can explain the *lofty ones'* settling where they did, the great marsh where the waters of the Tigris and Euphrates meet the Persian Gulf may have had another kind of appeal. It is one of those areas on the planet where an aquatic ape would be entirely at home. Its dry land, wet land, and open water are intimately intermixed.[4]

4.12.6 The Aquatic Ape

Besides the practical reasons for setttling there, Enki and his followers may have had deeper, perhaps unconscious, ancestral ones.

Carvings showing the earliest days of settlement depict buildings and boats made of the reeds that still grow in the marsh, to heights of twenty feet. Those images make it look as if the *anunnaki* took to the marshland with ease and comfort. (Figures 4.12.0 through 4.12.5) They could have placed their first settlement farther northwest, on the dry plain of the rivers, and still have had good access to the gulf, yet they chose to be close to the marsh ... and it was 45,000 years before they built an inland city.

In the vicinity of the marsh, the *lofty ones* may have found a home that felt like home, as implied by its name, *Eridu, home far away*. Though the *anunnaki* eventually settled well inland, they never abandoned the great marsh near Eridu. (Figure 4.12.6) Carvings of *lofty ones* in fish costumes and with mermen, though as yet unexplained, suggest the *gods* had a strong interest in aquatic life. (Figures 4.12.7 and 4.12.8)

We're at the end of a series of puzzles that conventional thinking is powerless to solve and that conventional thinkers avoid. We easily found solutions because we took The Mesopotamian Tale to be essentially factual. In the next part of the book we look at other matters through the lens of The Mesopotamian Tale.

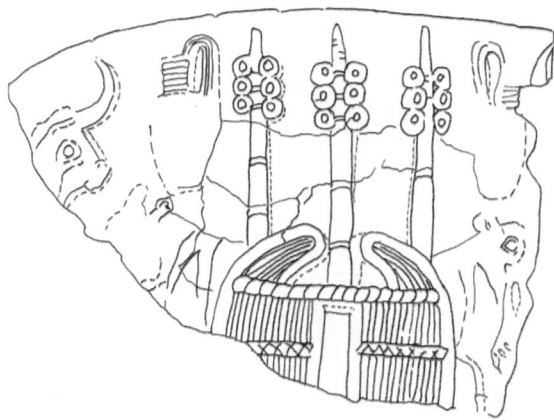

Figure 4.12.0. An image in clay of a reed structure. The function of the masts is unknown.

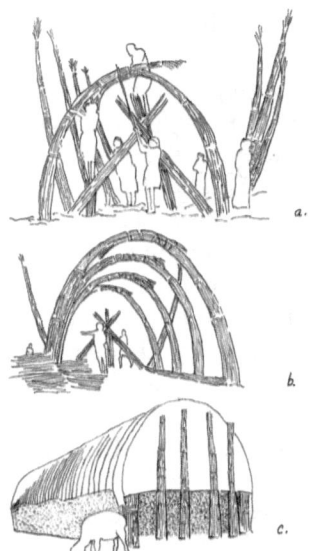

Figure 4.12.1. A traditional reed building of the southern Iraqi marshes, in construction and completed.

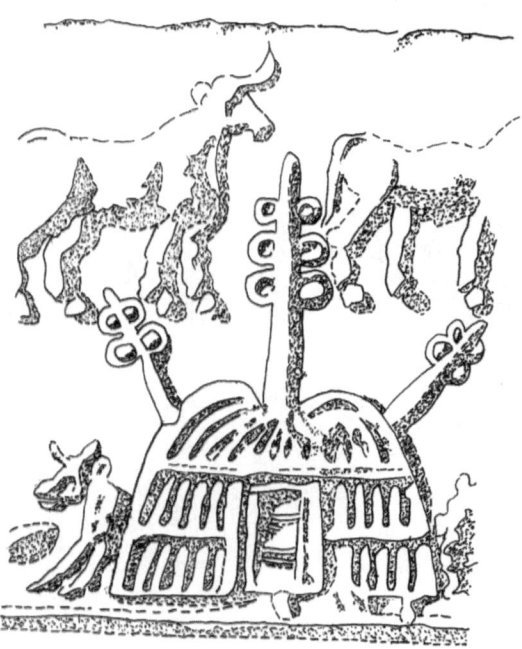

Figure 4.12.2. A reed structure on an early Šumerian cylinder seal.

4.12.6 The Aquatic Ape

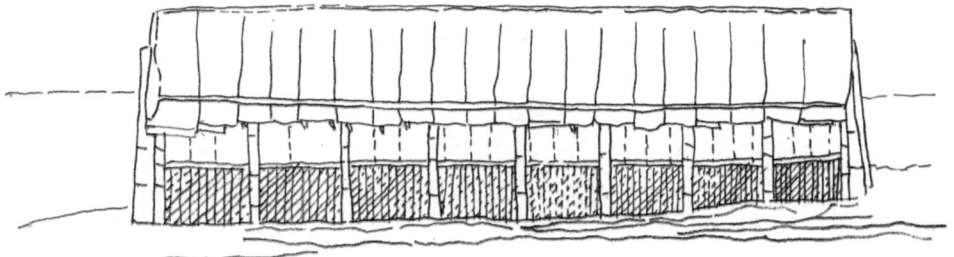

Figure 4.12.3. A traditional Iraqi reed stucture at the edge of a waterway. From an early 20th century photograph.

Figure 4.12.4. From an early Šumerian cylinder seal: Enki travelling through the reeds in a reed boat.

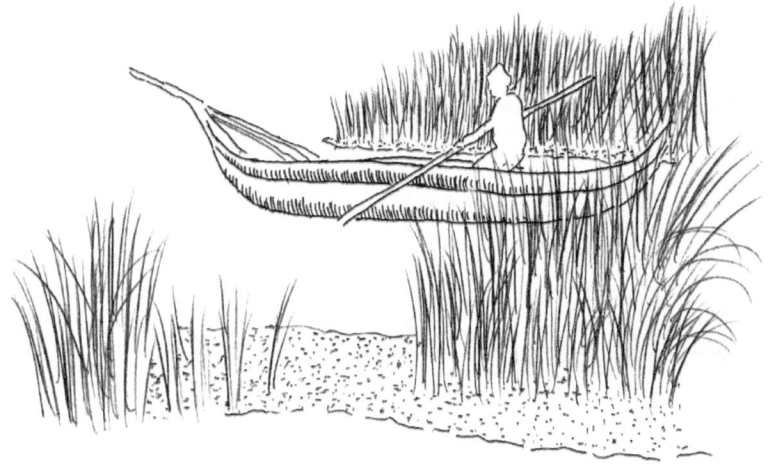

Figure 4.12.5. A traditional reed boat in use on Lake Titicaca, once the watery center of an *anunnaki* mining colony in the Andes.

Figure 4.12.6. An alabaster relief from Nineveh c. 650 BCE. The army of Sennaḫerib in battle in the great marsh. (An enemy cavalryman raises his arm in surrender to an Assyrian warrior.)

4.12.6 The Aquatic Ape   231

Figure 4.12.7. An early cylinder seal with two mermen.

Figure 4.12.18. A carving of a man in fish costume, from Nineveh.

---

[1] There have been rare sightings of gorillas cooling off and wading in shallow pools...but never in deeper water.

[2] The only other hairless land mammals, the hippopotamus and the elephant, evolved from land animals that adapted to aquatic life and later returned to land.

[3] When a pregnant woman goes under water, her baby's heart slows along with hers. Mothers who labor and deliver in birthing tubs generally have a gentler and less painful experience. The summertime births that Russian midwives attend in the shallows of the Black Sea are spellbinding.

[4] They are less so now than they were naturally...before Saddam Hussein altered the local hydrology, in his campaign to further disempower the Marsh Arabs.

Part Five

The Rest of the Picture

What's accomplished when a theory is applied is one measure of its validity. In Part Four we applied to several troublesome mysteries, the thesis that The Mesopotamian Tale is essentially a factual historical account. Simply by assuming the thesis to be valid, we were able to easily resolve those quandaries. In Part Five we'll aim to solidify the credibility of the thesis, as we use it to deepen our understanding of several aspects of our functioning.

Sexuality

Among the great apes, our nearest relatives, each species has its own manner of forming mating pairs. A species' approach to reproduction defines the structure of its society. The sexual and social rules by which an ape species lives are dictated by its genes. Between two species, how similar they are in their sexual behavior and societal organization correlates strongly with how similar their genomes are.

We can't know anything about the sexuality of *Homo erectus*, the homonin employed by the *gods* in the crafting of humankind, yet we can posit that, as with the living great apes, its sexual behavior was defined by genetically encoded instinct. We can also posit that the *anunnaki*, having existed as a species for millions of years and living in a highly structured society, had sexual mores vastly different from those of *H. erectus*.

The two parent species were so different from each other, that neither of their two sets of genetically encoded sexual instincts could provide a template for their hybrid offspring's sexuality. In addition, the earliest humans were deprived of the augmentation of instinct primate societies provide; *Homo erectus* wasn't available, and the *lofty ones* weren't interested. Having begun life without clear guidance about sexuality from either instinct or culture, humankind wasn't able to develop a standard for sexual behavior … and became the only animal on Earth without one. No wonder we're plagued with so much sexual dysfunction.[1]

Logic says that there's one aspect of our sexuality that could only have come to us through the *anunnaki's* genes. In mammals, female sexual receptivity is governed by the estrous cycle, which in turn is coordinated with the seasons … so that newborns get the best possible chance to survive.[2] With us, however, neither the menstrual cycle nor the season determines the time for sexual activity. It's the state of the relationship between the partners that must be right, and if it is, a woman can be sexually receptive at any time of year or point in her cycle.

We're virtually the only mammal for whom sex is a year-round activity. Since we're the only species carrying genes from the *anunnaki*, our celestial parent species must be the source of the freedom from season and ovulation that characterizes a woman's sexuality. If the *lofty ones'* sexuality had originally been seasonally linked when their planet was in its original orbit, then after it was ejected into season-less darkness, the link would have been eventually lost. That loss would have been reflected in their genes. That would have made it easier for Enki and Enmaḫ to craft us to be, as the *anunnaki* must have been, free of seasonal fertility.[3]

In the next three chapters The Mesopotamian Tale links biblical times with present reality.

[1] Unhappiness related to sexuality takes many forms: shame, guilt, inhibition, infidelity, chronic sexual tension, and thoughts of inadequacy. Life-negative sexual behaviors are also numerous: rape, honor killing, genital mutilation, sexual sadism and masochism, fetishism, exhibitionism, pedophilia, pornography, prostitution, homophobia, misogyny, and sex addiction.

[2] There are only two other exceptions to the connection between mammals' sexuality and the cycles of seasons and estrous. One is the Eurasian badger, which mates year round; the interval between conception and implantation in that animal can be extended so that birth can be well timed, no matter when mating occurs. Dolphins are the other ... one more aspect of their mysterious connection with us.

[3] Perhaps in order to expand the human population more rapidly.

Brother Against Brother

One brother favored over another is a repeating theme in the Book of Genesis. Cain, first son of Adam and Eve, jealous that his younger brother has found more favor with God, kills him. Išmael, first son of Abraham, born to his wife's servant, is driven into the desert after Abraham's wife gives birth to Isaac, so that the legitimate son's birthright could never be challenged. Jacob, the younger of Isaac's twins, tricks his father into giving to him his older brother's birthright. Jacob so openly favors Joseph that his jealous brothers sell him into slavery. Later in the Joseph narrative, Jacob dismisses Joseph's objections and blesses Judah, Joseph's fourth son, not his first, Reuben. When twins are born to Judah, Zerah is the first to begin to emerge, with his arm, but Perez overtakes him and is born first...and becomes the progenitor of the kings of the Nation of Judah, in southern Canaan. How come this theme is so important?

Its source is revealed by The Mesopotamian Tale. The biblical theme reflects the rivalry between the two sons of An, king of Nibiru, which proved so costly to humankind. We recall that Enki, An's first son, born to a concubine, was replaced as leader of the *anunnaki* when Enlil, the king's second son, born to his wife, was given supreme power on Earth. Rivalries between the clans of the two brothers fueled the never-ending wars of the *gods*, the prime source of humanity's traumatized state. The shadow cast on humanity by the clan warfare of the *gods* was too dark to be ignored. The *lofty ones'* fraternal conflict became embedded in the Jews' communal narrative in the form of the brother versus brother theme.[1]

As the Zionists worked toward founding a Jewish state, they were cautioned against treating the Palestinian Arabs with contempt. Since Arabs claim descent from Išmael, and Jews from Isaac, nothing was more critical for their shared future. Jewish tradition never having said much about Abraham's cruelty toward his firstborn son in Genesis, it is understandable that the settlers' leaders wouldn't recognize the importance of that advice.[2] When the Israelis got the upper hand, they treated the Arabs much as Abraham was said to have treated Išmael, and for a similar reason. They meant to insure rights that they claimed were theirs, as Abraham and his wife meant to protect Isaac's.[3]

Even though there were men of ill will among their Arab neighbors, the European Jews, with their long history of oppression, might have known better. But those who recently arrived had been horrendously traumatized. As war loomed, the population learned that there was little assistance coming their way and that they were facing vastly outnumbering forces and explicit threats of annihilation. No way could they avoid the pattern of victim becoming perpetrator.

The Palestinian Arabs have seen Išmael's expulsion repeated in Israel's War of Independence, in the Six Day War, and in Jewish settlements on the West Bank. The settlers and their supporters claim rights on biblical grounds, while denying the rights of the people who'd been living there for centuries. Arabs identifying with the son who was sent away to die, Jews identifying with the son who was granted privileges and blessings ... that's an explosive narrative.

As of this writing, for over sixty years the two sides have been unable to reconcile. The stakes in their struggle are high; at times it engages the entire region as well as world powers. How can it be that so many people, working so hard for so long to put an end to the hatred and violence, have achieved so little? Of course, geography gives proximate causes for the trouble, such as the scarcity of water. Furthermore, Palestine has never been free for very long from conflicts over land. Yet after so many failed attempts, it's clear that a deep force is driving this enmity.

That force is the process of reenactment. In distant antiquity the sands of the Middle East were repeatedly soaked in human blood. Endless warfare was fueled by rivalry between the clans of the two royal brothers from Nibiru. No longer consciously remembered, that rivalry is recalled viscerally and is amplified by the tales of brother against brother in the Hebrew Bible, sacred text for both Jews and Muslims. Palestinians and Israelis, living where the *lofty ones* fought, are repeatedly re-enacting the rivalries of the royal *anunnaki clans*.

All the violence in the Middle East, in fact, has qualities of the wars of the *lofty ones*. Both sides tend to be dominated by factions that seek victory through brutality, never relying on moderation, compromise, or reconciliation. Since victory is rarely total and permanent, it's followed eventually by more violence. The cycle will continue until the peoples of the region wake to the fact that they are caught in an endless restaging of the clan rivalry that shaped life for their ancestors in Mesopotamia and extract themselves from the drama that has been their fate.[4]

Next, we turn our attention to the geographic focal point of the conflicts between the cultures of the Middle East, the Temple Mount of Jerusalem.

[1] Genesis keeps repeating a story element that reverses the principle of primogeniture, which was a foundational rule in the ancient Middle East. Starting with the Cain and Abel tale, again and again the younger brother is favored over the first born. This supports the proposition that the origin of this biblical theme can be found in the way the rule of Earth was divided between the royal brothers from Nibiru...the superior position given to the second-born.

[2] In the Book of Genesis and in the Holy Q'ran, God treats Išmael and Ḥagar well, but Abraham most assuredly does not.

[3] The biblical narrative offers another painful twist. Esau's brother tricked him out of the birthright of sovereignty over land in Canaan. Esau is said to have gone east from Canaan, and to have become progenitor of a nation. East of Israel was where many Palestinians wound up after the 1948 war.

[4] As if the inheritance of fraternal enmity isn't the source of enough trouble, there's another biblical theme feeding entitlement in the Israelis and despair in the Palestinians. In the Hebrew Bible, God explicity promises Abraham, Isaac, Jacob, Moses, and Joshua that the wandering Jews would have a home in Canaan. The Jews must have felt that their claim to the land was shaky. Why else would the authors of the books of the Hebrew Bible keep repeating that possession of Canaan was granted to them by the Creator of the Universe?

Holding a scriptural deed that they claimed was beyond questioning, the Zionists were inclined to dismiss the rights of the people already living there. When Lord Balfour, the Foreign Minister of Great Britain (which held the League of Nations mandate for Palestine), assured the Zionists that the Jewish people would have a home in Palestine, a restaging of the biblical promises was set in motion. Once again, a powerful authority was granting rights in the land of Canaan to Jewish outsiders. The legal instrument, a Foreign Office white paper, became known as the Balfour Declaration, a document the Zionists fervently, though selectively, cited. How ironic that its author bore the title *Lord*.

Jerusalem

Jerusalem's first buildings stood on three hills. At the peak of one of them, Mount Moriah, the Temple Mount, there's a rock outcropping Muslims call the Foundation Stone. Until Moḥammed captured Mecca and directed his followers to pray facing in its direction, he had them bow in their devotions toward this rock. Some Islamic scholars hold that Moḥammed ascended to Heaven from the Stone. It's housed in the Dome of the Rock, one of the oldest of Islam's buildings. To Muslims this is a sacred place, their second most holy site.

For the Jews their most holy place lies just below this Muslim compound, the sole surviving fragment of what was once the focal point of the Hebrew religion. Known as the Western Wall, it defines and supports one edge of the plaza above. Jewish scripture holds that on an earlier platform there Solomon built his temple to God, housing the Holy of Holies, the Ark with the Tablets of The Law, inscribed by the very hand of God. Many think that the Ark sat upon the rock outcropping now sacred to the Muslims. On a plaza at the base of the Wall, as they have for centuries, Jews stand in prayer, facing the stones of a wall that once was the edge of their Temple precinct.[1]

If the enmity between Muslims and Jews has a geographic center, it is this hill. The spatial convergence of the two faiths cannot be coincidental; surely it did not become a holy place to the Muslims simply because the Jews had made it holy with the Temple. Whatever made it sacred to one made it sacred to the other. What was that?

Tradition holds that on Abraham's journey into Canaan, he and God conversed, and Judaism was born. When he'd set out from Ḥarran with his family and his band of followers, among the things he'd left behind was the institution of kingship. In the centuries between his departure and his people's approach to Jerusalem, the Hebrews had leaders, priests, and prophets, but no kings. They conquered cities in Canaan after their escape from slavery in Egypt, yet appointed no kings. They may have called for Saul, David's predecessor, to be king, and he may have been anointed, yet he remained the tribal chief of a seminomadic people. The term used to refer to him signified not *king*, but *military leader*.

Things changed as the Jews drew close to Jerusalem. David was anointed king of Israel in Hebron, and ruled there before traveling north to the city on the three hills. After defeating the forces of the priest king of Jerusalem, he began development by fortifying a promontory south of Mount Moriah c. 1,000 BCE. In time he became the ruler of a realm extending south and north from Jerusalem, even to Damascus, a true king, the first one the Israelites ever had. Textual evidence and the physical realities of the Temple Mount suggest that the power that drew the Hebrews to Jerusalem also led them to elevate their leader to kingship.

First, the physical realities. In the body of the Western Wall, buried below the present level of the ground, yet exposed by a tunnel, are immense masonry blocks. Three of them are of the same scale as the monster stones known as the *Trilith of Baalbek* at the *anunnaki* space facility in the Lebanese mountains. Weighing between 350 and 600 tons, these stones are 14 feet tall and from 25 to 40 feet long. They are not quite so massive as the ones at Baalbek, yet the greatest of them weighs as much as nine modern battle tanks. Historians say that Herod the Great, king of Judea, built the Western Wall when he improved the Temple compound. Tour guides in the tunnel have been known to say that no one has yet figured out how Herod moved such gargantuan stones. No one ever will. While there's no reason to doubt that Herod rebuilt the upper portion of the wall, the immense blocks near its base could not have been the work of human beings in antiquity. Their weight is far beyond what can be moved with any imaginable mechanism of timber and rope powered by muscle. They could only have been quarried and placed with the advanced technology of the *anunnaki* ... as were the giant stones in Lebanon.

But why the immense stones at the base of what's only a retaining wall? The same question, when raised about the *Trilith of Baalbek*, confirmed the function of the platform in Lebanon, since the only logical reason for using stones of that scale was to keep a wall secure against the vibration of rocket launches. As we shall see, the same must have been true for the giant stones in the Western Wall.

Obviously, the Hebrew Bible couldn't report that the platform stood when David and his people came to Jerusalem, yet what it says, and what it ignores, reveals that indeed the structure was already there. The books 1 Samuel and 2 Kings report that a low-lying area between two of the three hills was filled in on David's orders. The passages read as if the builders were proud of their work, though the volume of fill was not all that great. Nothing is said, however, about the fill involved in the creation of the plaza atop Mount Moriah. Building up from the natural contours of the hill to create the platform took 60 million cubic feet of stone and soil, a feat dwarfing the infill that the books do mention.

The books also tell that tens of thousands of men labored seven years to erect God's temple, describing every aspect of the building and its furnishings in meticulous detail, so their silence on the creation of the platform is telling. If David or Solomon, before the temple could be built, had moved so immense a quantity of material and erected great walls to contain it, the Bible would have lauded the accomplishment. By omission, the scribes confirm the true history of the Mount.

Enlil gave rule of Jerusalem, *Ur Šulim* in Šumerian, *City of Supreme Place*, to the *god* with responsibility for all *anunnaki* rocketry.

5.3 Jerusalem

He called in Šamaš the grandchild of Ninlil [his wife]
He took him [by the hand] in Šulim he placed him

Jewish sources subtly hint at Jerusalem's role in spaceflight. In the book of Genesis God directs Abraham to

the land of Moriah

for the sacrifice of his son, saying that once he was nearing the site he'd be directed to a mount. Tradition holds that as Abraham approached the mount, he saw

a pillar of fire reaching from Earth to Heaven

That's a good description of a rocket launch.

It's curious, though, that the *annuanki* chose an isolated site almost devoid of water for an important base. Could the location have been dictated by special considerations? The Šumerian name *City of Supreme Place* suggests control functions; so do the Hebrew names of its three hills: Zephim, *Observers*; Moriah, *Seer, Director*; and Zion, *Signal.*

Zecariah Sitchin realized that a southerly line from Baalbek through Jerusalem reaches the most prominent point in the Sinai, a peak standing out clearly from the air, the one dedicated to the *goddess* Ninmah, while a second line starting at the center of the Sinai, the location of the Tilmun base, going through Jerusalem, reaches Ararat, the tallest mountain in the Middle East. In other words, two straight lines cross in Jerusalem, each one connecting a major spaceport with a mountain peak. (Figure 5.3.1) A beacon in Jerusalem could assist pilots landing at the spaceports. With a mountain in view, if they aligned their flight with that peak and with the beacon, they'd be pointed straight at their destination.[2]

In Jerusalem, the Hebrews encountered the Mesopotamian roots of their culture.[3] Kingship was central to the societies of Mesopotamia. The most esteemed rulers there had been called *enši, righteous shepherds*, and as the prophet Samuel was about to anoint David, he heard:

take the youth David son of Jesse from herding of sheep to be the shepherd of Israel

The Jews began adopting the style of rule their Šumerian ancestors had known, but they didn't do so all at once. David was a transitional figure. Though he was a fearsome warrior and a crafty politician, he kept a court that was rather modest. It took another generation for

Mesopotamian kingship to be fully revived. Like the rulers of Šumer, David's son and successor loved gold, hoarded treasure, kept a magnificent court, and enjoyed an immense harem. Solomon traded with distant lands and, through negotiation and marriage, further expanded the kingdom. And just as the rulers of Mesopotamia had been pleased to do, he built and supported a temple to his God. A site that was once used by the *gods* became the principal site in the service of the one God.[4]

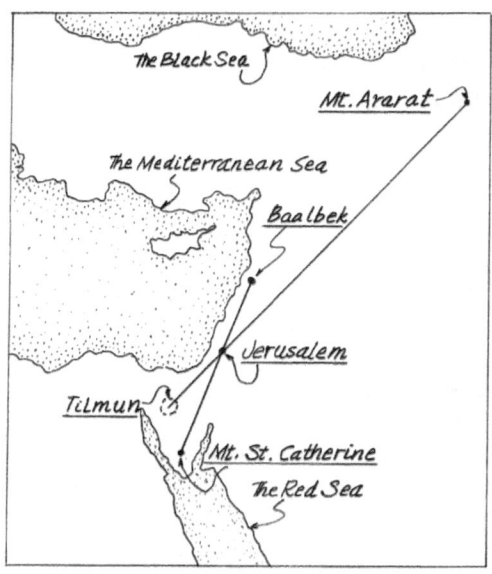

Figure 5.3.1. A line from Baalbek to Ninmaḫ's mountain passes through Jerusalem, as does a line from Tilmun to Mt. Ararat. (Tilmun has not been located with precision.)

The historic Abraham left Ḥarran, outpost of Ur, in a time of turmoil, in service to the chief *god* of Earth, Enlil. Several generations later, the Hebrews were enslaved in Egypt, while the chief *god* of the land, Ra/Marduk, was away pursuing dreams of glory in Babylonia, in what remained of Mesopotamian culture after the devastation caused by the nuclear attack in the Sinai and southern Caanan. The Jews escaped their bondage. In Jerusalem they came upon a great work in stone and earth that had been abandoned by the olden *gods*.

For some time, as they developed their scriptural narrative, the Jews had been incorporating altered tales of the *gods* of Mesopotamia. Now, on Mount Moriah, they incorporated a massive construction of those fading *gods* into the ceremonial focus of their religion. Eventually two Jewish nations, Israel and Judah, became full-fledged states in the Šumerian mold, with governance involving intrigue, alliance, betrayal, civil war, assassination, and all the rest. Like the cities of Mesopotamia, Jerusalem had a king, army, treasure trove, and priestly class.

On the Temple Mount, the religious traditions of Mesopotamia were partly recreated. The Temple itself incorporated the basics of the shrines of the *gods* of Mesopotamia: a sequence of spaces leading to an inner sanctum. In the glorious raiment of the high priest the magnificent clothes of those who served the *lofty ones* were recalled. The devotion with which the olden *gods'* attendants had prepared food for them may have been lost to conscious memory, yet the roasting of sacrificial beasts at the Temple reproduced that vital service, in altered form. There was a great difference, of course: rather than the *god* of the city, the Jews had the God of the Universe. The activities on the elevated enclosed platform, originally built by the *lofty ones*, melded the Jews' awe of the One with the reverence once felt by their ancestors for the olden *gods*. The city and temple were innovations for a culture that had been nomadic and pastoral , and yet they were also throw-backs to the culture's origins in the cities of Šumer.

Centuries after the political power of the Jews was crushed by the Romans, as Islam was expanding, the Arabs conquered Jerusalem. They felt the pull of Mount Moriah just as the Hebrews had. Their oral tradition told them that the hilltop was sacred. Though the original reason for its holiness was lost to their memory, the Jews had confirmed its sanctity. The Muslims dedicated to *Allah* the place that had belonged to the *ilu*, the *lofty ones*, long before it belonged to the Jews' *El Elelyon*. The historical reality of the *anunnaki* ascending from there in rockets, no longer clearly recalled, was reflected in their experiencing the hill as a place of communion with Heaven and in their thinking of it as the site of Moḥammed's ascent.[5]

If the Muslims and Jews ever come to terms with what actually drew their ancestors to the hill they both revere, the way would be open for them to respect each other's claims. If they accept that the departed false *gods* against whom the founders of their faiths railed, flesh and blood giants whose rule on Earth failed, then the fear will start to fade that their religions are under threat, which long ago they actually were because of humanity's lasting attachments to the departed olden *gods*.

They will then see that Mount Moriah and the entire Old City have been rendered holy from having been the focus of devotion for so many hearts. They would feel supported, not challenged, to know that other faiths align with them in awe of the place. Their adversaries would then be their spiritual allies, and they would know that they both can be as one in worshipping the One, despite the differences in their forms of devotion.

Next we shall consider what else The Mesopotamian Tale can tell us about how Judaism, Islam, and Christianity relate to each other.

[1] Some consider the Hebrew Bible to be historically accurate and others see it as the origin myth of the Jews, mostly fictional, written *de novo* centuries after the events it reports. The emerging consensus is that the reality lies between those two extremes, fact and invention being intertwined in its books. Regarding the Bible's accounts of matters like kingship and construction, while exaggeration and error may have intruded, the canonical texts seem to be essentially factual. As archaeology in Palestine and Sinai proceeds, it has provided confirmation and interpolation for many biblical passages.

[2] There's a passage in the Epic of Gilgameš suggesting that the northern and southern spaceports were connected in some way. Having failed to enter the site in the cedar forest, Gilgameš appeals to the *god* of rockets to help him enter the one in the Sinai:

o Šamaš the land I wish to enter…
the land which with the cool cedars is aligned
I wish to enter, be thou my ally

In what sense could bases hundreds of miles apart, in vastly different terrains, have been *aligned* with each other? Two sight lines, each going from a spaceport to a prominent landmark and passing through a navigational facility in Jerusalem, would constitute alignment of a sort.

[3] It's assumed that Hebron was important to David because it is the site of the cave said to be the final resting places of the Hebrew patriarchs and matriarchs. Yet it may be that what first made Hebron, like Jerusalem, a holy site to the Hebrews was the earlier presence of the *anunnaki*. The entrance to the cave revered as the site of the ancestral tombs is within a building whose base contains giant stones twenty feet long.

[4] How much Solomon's construction was an act of spiritual devotion and how much it was one of political calculation is unclear. The psalms make David's reverence evident, but Solomon's lifestyle hardly seems to be that of a *man of God*. In fact, later in life he embraced the religion of the olden *gods*.

[5] The most holy site in Islam was also originally devoted to the olden *gods*. In the center of the Sacred Mosque in Mecca stands the Ka'aba, the focus of the pilgrimage every Muslim is obliged to make at least once in his lifetime. Before the city was taken by Moḥammed's forces and the Ka'aba was dedicated to Allah and to Abraham's family, the shrine (rebuilt more than once) held idols and was holy to the followers of the *lofty ones*.

God, Savior, Prophet

Christianity and Islam, religions whose adherents together outnumber those of all other faiths combined, both sprang from the religion of the Jews, a people who, though at times numerous and respected, never had more than local power. The Mesopotamian Tale helps us understand how their faith had such influence.

From the time of our birth we were enthralled with the *anunnaki* nobles who brought us into existence and told us they were deities. When present in the cities, the highest *gods* were venerated in public ceremonies and tended in chambers atop the towering ziggurats. Worshipping, tending, and loving the *lofty ones* was central to our identity.

The Greeks and Romans, never having experienced flesh and blood *gods*, placed magnificent statues of deities in hilltop temples, in emulation of the way the Mesopotamians had always tended the *lofty ones*. Through prayers and offerings, they experienced connection with divine entities who existed solely in their feelings, thoughts, and art. A life centered on devotion to the community's *gods* was all that civilized humanity had ever known; living without such a focus was inconceivable.

The nomadic tribes of Canaan and Arabia knew about the national and international *gods* in the cities of Mesopotamia, but the *lofty ones* who ruled them were local figures, lesser *anunnaki* nobles. Just as the great *anunnaki* made war on rival cities, these minor *lofty ones* led their people in battle against other tribes. There are episodes in the Bible in which God seems to be a deity of just that kind. Those passages suggest that the tribes that embraced Judaism had earlier been followers of local *gods*.[1]

When the influence of the *lofty ones* was fading, the nomads, like the populations of the cities, had to adapt to life without them. For the Canaanites who became Jews, their adaptation involved the presence of a newcomer, a man who was making his personal journey from the old religion toward a new one. Abraham, a person of means, son of a priest of the *god* of Ur, sojourned in their land with his sizable retinue. Genesis says that in Canaan he conversed with God. The accounts of those encounters are open to interpretation, for we've reasoned that the historical Abraham was sent on his mission by Enlil.

The roots of Hebrew culture were in Šumer, where each city's life centered on its *god*. In Egypt the Jews were subservient to a culture focused on the same *gods*, known there by different names. Leaving Egypt, they were surrounded by tribes who revered the *lofty ones*. In Babylonian exile, Jews again lived in the world of those *gods*. When they returned to Jerusalem, the powers ruling the city, first Persians, then Greeks, then Romans, all prayed to their versions of the same divinities.

On their long journey the Jews strived to remain devoted to the unseen Creator of All. Their leaders implored them not to return to the form of worship from which their culture had emerged, the religion of every civilized society there had ever been. Somehow the Hebrews managed to sustain the concept of a non-incarnate unitary divinity. But how had they originally come to their knowledge of the One?

Most likely from the priests of the *gods*. When the Bible says that the One is the *God of the gods*, it hints that the *anunnaki* were aware of the Maker of All. It appears that they knew about non-manifest Source ... yet it wouldn't do for their followers to worship the One. That would have rendered humanity less awe-struck and obedient. There would have been no way, however, for the *lofty ones* to keep awareness of the Prime Maker from their priests. Leaving behind the cities of the *gods*, Abraham carried a most precious gift, the knowledge of the One, received from his priestly father. Abraham's conversations with God in Genesis can be read as a fictionalization of his spiritual awakening to the One.[2]

By whatever means the Jews came to know that which gives shape and movement to the universe, and however they maintained and developed their devotion, by the time the Hebrew Bible was organized in final form, their concept of God had evolved far from what it had been for a collection of tribes in Canaan a thousand years earlier. It was a layered, complex concept, blending together the diverse elements of their experience. Some Bible passages are just like the accounts of a *god* smiting the the warriors of a rival *god* in Mesopotamia. Some present God as lawgiver, one of the roles of the *gods* of the cities. Some have God sounding like that righteous moralist, Enlil. Others echo Šumerian accounts of the planetary *god* Nibiru appearing in the sky and wreaking havoc. Other passages laud the generative principle of the universe. The Hebrews grasped that an invisible power and intelligence creates and maintains the world, but didn't totally dismiss their ancestors' attachment to diverse, lesser concepts of divinity. Systems, both biological and cultural, evolve that way, the old not discarded, but contained within the new.[3,4]

Liberating themselves from the worship of the *anunnaki* pantheon, the Hebrews emphasized their awareness of the infinite intelligence that manifests in all things. The *anunnaki* had interfered with the innate human sense of the One by claiming: *We are your makers and gods*. What they said was true regarding their role in our birth. But by claiming divinity, they obstructed humanity's connection with God. The Hebrews blazed a trail to knowledge of the One; the two other monotheisms followed.[5]

Yet it was a mighty struggle for the Jews to devote themselves exclusively to the One and erase all allegiance to the *gods* of their Šumerian and Canaanite ancestors. The Arabs also had to deal with the departure of the *gods*. Some Arab tribes continued to worship the *lofty ones* through idols,

5.4 God, Savior, Prophet

as the Greeks, Babylonians, and Egyptians were doing, but many Arabs were Jewish and faced the same dilemma as the Hebrews. In the peoples forbidden to worship *graven images*, the hunger for an immediate, palpable connection with the divine was intense. It drove what happened next.

Deep feelings for the *lofty ones*, rooted in humanity's birth, were still pulsing in the Jews. They could be challenged by priests and prophets, but not eradicated. The memories of the *anunnaki* living in their midst had faded; the emotions connected with them had not. There was ferment and sectarianism within Judaism, with mounting cravings for an embodied godly presence. That hunger was magnified by reminders of the *gods*; all the cultures the Hebrews were in contact with worshipped them. Even the Jews' Temple priests were drawn to them. As noted earlier, in outward form the rituals on the sacred mount closely replicated the worship of the olden *gods* who'd once possessed the site.

Prophetic texts written before the time of Jesus told of a Savior. The hope was blossoming that humanity could again have palpable divine sustenance.[6] After Jesus appeared among the Children of Israel, many were taken with the idea that He was sent to them by God. Later, when the Gospels were taking form, they incorporated themes from the then ancient traditions of Mesopotamia.

- In the immaculate conception of Jesus there is an echo of the texts that tell that the first humans were conceived through *in vitro* fertilization and born from the ova of *anunnaki* surrogate mothers.[7]
- The Gospel of Matthew contains the paternal lineage of Jesus from Adam through Noaḫ, David, and Joseph. The lengthy account seems barely relevant to us, yet it was meaningful in its time. The lawful ancestry of Joseph, the legal father of Jesus, was proclaimed in the same way in which the lineages of the *demigod* kings of Šumer were lauded.
- The birth of Jesus in the context of the marriage of Mary and Joseph echoes the collaboration of the great *gods* Ninmaḫ and Enki in bringing the first humans into existence. It may be no coincidence that Ninmaḫ's astrologic sign was Virgo, the virgin.

Some of the Arab neighbors of the Hebrews worshipped the *olden gods*. Others embraced Judaism, practicing the faith in their own style. Still others became monotheists when the Persians brought Zoroastrianism into northern Arabia. The mix was varied and fluid. Islam began as a heterodox trend within Arabic Judaism, just as Christianity began within Israelite Judaism. (See Figure 5.4.1) Moḥammed destroyed the idols worshipped by the polytheistic Arabs and coerced them into devotion to the one God. By so doing he induced in those Arabs the yearning that was already felt

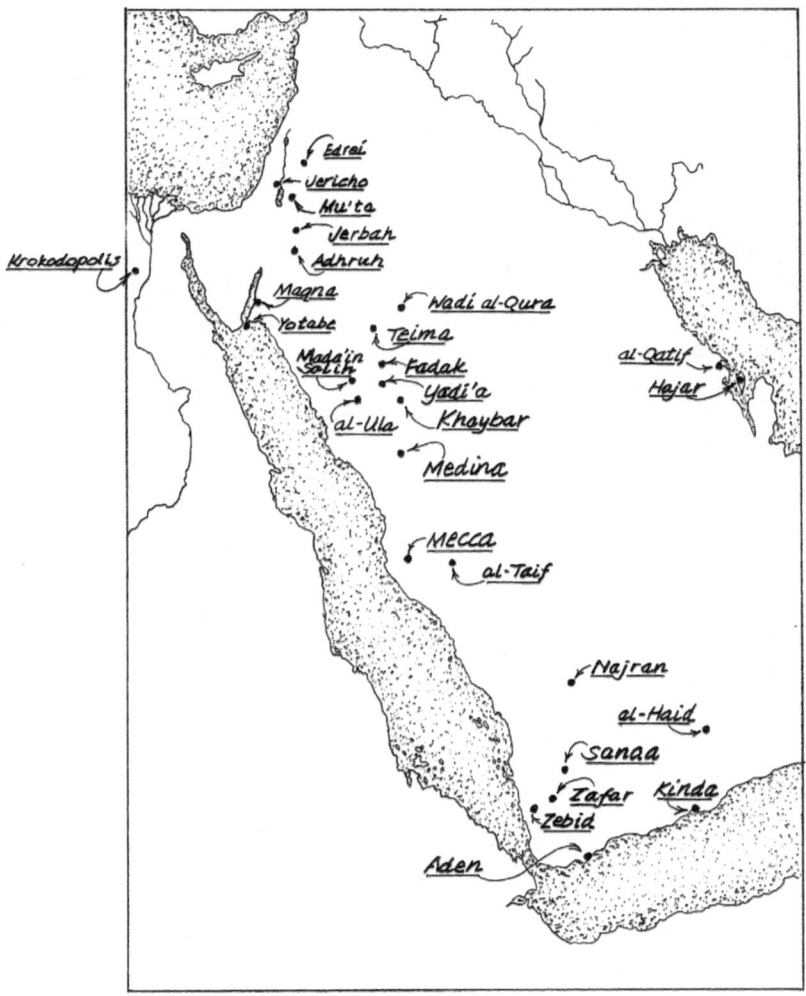

Figure 5.5.1. Jewish Arab towns in the time of Moḥammed.

by the Hebrews and by the Jewish Arabs. Eventually, the Arabs found relief from that hunger by embracing a charismatic man who brought them new teachings from God. In time, the Arabs elevated Moḥammed from one of several proselytizers of the One, to virtually *demigod* status as the greatest, infallible, final prophet sent to humankind.

The second of the monotheisms springing from Judaism shared with the first the belief that Spirit had manifested on Earth in a teacher for all humanity. Both Christianity and Islam answered cravings resulting from strict obedience to the first Commandment *I am the Lord thy God - Thou shalt have no other gods before me.* Jesus and Mohammed had very different relationships with God in the two theologies, yet the emerging religions were more alike than their adherents now care to admit. Early Muslim leaders taught that Jesus was the second most important prophet, that the day of his birth should be celebrated, and that Mary should be honored above all women. They held that Islam was simply correcting Christianity's imperfect revision of Judaism. The two religions offered fresh beliefs that the Maker of All had revealed Himself through a human teacher, filling a void left by the fading of the olden *gods*.

The two faiths spread by different means, Christianity by the conversion of political rulers who remained in place, Islam by military conquest, conversion coming later. When the two faiths turned on each other in Byzantium, Spain, and Palestine, and when they turned on the one that gave them birth, the wars of the olden *gods* found new life in reenactment. The endless conflicts between the followers of competing *anunnaki* lords, inherent in civilization's first belief system, have been reenacted since the departure of the *gods* in the mutual intolerance and hostility infecting the monotheisms. The wars of the *annunaki* lords are the source of an insidious tendency borne by Judaism, Christianity, and Islam, an inheritance utterly opposed to their professed values.

We next explore the development of civic governance after the *lofty ones* no longer ruled.

---

[1] As we've noted, YHWH, transliterated *Yahweh*, the personal name of the Hebrew God, had been the name of the *god* of a group of Canaanite tribes.

[2] Nibiru, Lord of Heaven, prepared humanity for the worship of an unseen God. Between its awesome passages, Nibiru was unseen for more than three millennia.

³ Retaining the name of their local deity made it easier to guide the Canaanite tribes to the new focus of devotion, but doing so eventually presented a problem. Since the living Yahweh had been a lesser, violent *god*, his name was not an entirely fitting one for the Creator of the Universe. The martial role of the *anunnaki* Yahweh of the Canaanite tribes is recalled when the God of the Hebrews is referred to as *Yahweh of Battalions* and *Yahweh of Armies*, phrases ordinarily translated as *God of Hosts*. The problem of having the name of a minor self-deified noble used as the name of the Maker of All was solved with a taboo: the personal name of God was never to be spoken or written. An abbreviated form of YHWH is clearly indicated in Hebrew prayer books, yet instead of saying the name they see with their eyes, Jews perform a mental trick and pronounce, out loud or in their minds, the word *adonai*, Hebrew for *Lord*.

⁴ Over and over, the God of Leviticus sounds like a bloodthirsty Mesopotamian deity. The rituals He prescribes greatly resemble what we know of Mesopotamian rites and customs. Likewise, the exchanges between Moses and God in Numbers reflect what it must have been like for a Mesopotamian priest to deal with his *anunnaki* lord...an overpowering, demanding, selfish, formalistic, self-centered, heartless being. How could the Hebrews have imagined such a deity, had not that experience been carved into their ancestral memory?

The Book of Joshua reveals how much the religion of the Israelites was derived from that of their ancestors in Mesopotamia. For example, serving elaborate prepared food to the many *lofty ones* morphed into meticulously specified sacrifices to the One. Since the Jewish God was non-incarnate, He was offered not the deliciously cooked meats the *anunnaki* nobles ate, but instead the fragrant smoke of burnt flesh. Also, the Jewish people were to love and obey their God, follow his laws, and wage warfare at his command. In return, He would fulfill His promise and grant them land in Canaan cleared of the tribes dwelling there. The olden *gods* of Mesopotamia had done much the same for their faithful followers. A then ancient transactional tradition was updated to conform to the new theology.

⁵ There was a revolution in the same direction in Egypt 60 years following the Hebrews' escape. Pharaoh Amenhotep IV replaced the worship of the many *gods* with a faith focused on one god, in the form of the Sun. He could do this because the influence of the many *gods* was weakening. His religion was imposed by royal decree, though, and after his death the priests of Amon-Ra/Marduk, a *god* who was still influential, re-established the original faith.

⁶ The concept of a divine savior was not totally new to the Jews. In the Hebrew Bible, God repeatedly identifies Himself as the savior of the Israelites in Egypt.

⁷ According to the tablets the very first humans came from the ova of Enki's wife, genetically modified and fertilized *in vitro*. Sex was not involved. Recent Christian theologians, such as Hans Kung, conclude on the basis of textual analysis that the story of the virgin birth was adopted from older stories.

How We Are Ruled

The ruling *gods* of Mesopotamia lived in ease and glory, splendidly clothed and fed, tended by priests, venerated by the populace in festivals. The kings under them were in charge of civic affairs, public ceremonies, and war. A monarch's authority was granted jointly by his city's *god* and by Enlil. The institution of kingship had been personally awarded to humanity by Nibiru's ruler, An. Tablets proclaimed the *anunnaki* lineage of the *men of renown* who ascended to the throne. The people had immense loyalty, respect, and love for the *lofty ones*. To benefit from those feelings, the kings copied their behavior and clothing. (Figure 5.5.1)

Figure 5.5.1. A king, operating under the authority of Nannar (whose symbol, the Moon, appears in the sky) bestowing governorship on a man presented to him by two *goddesses*. From a cylinder seal c. 2000 BCE.

Deference must have been a strong trait in our celestial parent species, judging from how the noble *lofty ones* were obsessed with rank, and from how long the commoners suffered in the mines before rebelling. Deference for the group's dominant leader must also have helped keep the peace for *Homo erectus*, our terrestrial parent species, as it does for all the living great apes. Born with a dual inheritance of deference, we were well-prepared to obey our leaders. The *gods* established laws and customs elaborating and codifying our instinctually mandated deference, sealing our obedience to them and to the kings who served them.

When the *lofty ones* were gone, the authority of the kings could not have been quite so firm as before. In Egyptian, Greek, and Roman societies, the kings and priests formed alliances. The kings became the supreme legal authorities. The priests provided society's connection with the now invisible deities. With statues of the gods in temples, the clergy maintained their standing through ritual; by funding religious sculpture and architecture, the royals confirmed their legitimacy. Civic and religious leaders thrived in mutual cooperation. Some kings, with the support of the priests, even proclaimed themselves to be gods.[1]

Priests and kings were not always friendly, though. Whenever there was tension between the institutions of church and state, the never fully settled division of power between Enlil and Enki was reenacted. Enlil had had supreme authority in law; the tradition of political and military power resting with the king derives from Enlil's authority. Enki had had supreme authority in learning. His retinue of priests were distinct from those attending the other *gods*; they were the main human repository of scientific, technical, and scholarly knowledge. The power of knowledge resting with prelates derives from Enki's authority. With that power, priests could condemn Socrates to death and the Pope could censor Galileo. (It was within that tradition that the universities evolved in Europe as extensions of the Roman Catholic Church.)

In general, church and state have been more often in alliance than in conflict. When national churches were founded in Europe, royal taxes sustained them. Priests anointed kings at their coronations. *The divine right of kings* gained universal credence: once a ruler was enthroned, his authority was said to come from God. That *gods* had once appointed kings was mostly lost to memory ... but not totally. When nobles chose one of their own to elevate to the throne, they claimed they'd been divinely inspired. The elaborate system of rank and lineage among the *anunnaki* was the precursor to the attention paid to royal bloodlines. In the faces and body language of crowds at royal events in London, murals and carvings from antiquity come to life, as homage paid to the *gods* is re-created.[2]

Humans transposed beliefs, feelings, and customs once connected with the *gods* onto royalty, and later onto others. Any type of political leader can now be an object of adulation, as can a celebrity. In the magazines at kiosks and market check-out lines we see the original fixation with the doings of the *lofty ones* morphed into an addiction to the beautiful, famous, and powerful. Celebrity can even be a route to political power, as was demonstrated in the electoral success of Donald Trump in 2016. After all, the *gods* were the original celebrities. The TV show *Downton Abbey* was remarkably popular because it was so reminiscent of Earth's first social order, ordinary folk in service to lords. Through the lens of England in the early 20th century, the show's fans reconnected with Mesopotamia.[3]

The Greeks of classical times invented governance by councils drawn from society's upper strata and by representative assemblies. They experimented with many arrangements, most of them dispensing with royal authority. The Romans adopted those practices, as they did with many things Greek, and they, too, tried a variety of schemes. Centuries of bloody power struggles in Rome demonstrated how unprepared civilized humanity was for anything other than monarchial rule. Representative government went into a long sleep. In its next appearance, in the form of the House of Commons in Great Britain, it was a success in part because it operated under the authority of a king enthroned by divine right. We don't know much about the legislatures of Šumer, yet they could only have operated under the authority of the *gods* of the cities.

Rule in the hands of the representatives of the populace works well when it answers to an unquestioned authority ... which may reside in a well-respected foundational document instead of a king. Though superior to direct rule by a supreme leader in efficiency, fairness, and stability, representative governance seems always at risk from an insidious craving for a powerful leader and a highly stratified society.[4]

Rule not from above, but from within the group, thrived outside civilization. The people who left the domains of the *lofty ones* in order to live in nature freed themselves from the cities' inequality, subservience, and inherited authority. The indigenous and pastoral folk of the world, the descendants of those escapees, discovered natural principles of communal self-regulation and developed societies with equality, respect for all the tribe's members, and earned authority. Chiefs were chosen (and dismissed) by consensus on the basis of their personal qualities and proven abilities, and they still are. Ancestry can be a selection factor in some of these native cultures, but it is never the determining issue.[5]

The radical political philosophy put into practice in the former North American British colonies in the 18th century, embracing personal freedom, an elected executive, and representative councils, did so in proximity to indigenous societies that had personal freedom, chiefs appointed by consensus, and tribal councils. Though the Americans might fear and despise the natives, they had to take notice of the freedom inherent in their lives.[6] Some of the men developing the new federation, while drawing inspiration from Europe, knew about the Great Law of Peace, the *de facto* constitution of the Iroquois federation that for centuries had maintained harmony among diverse nations spread over a huge territory.[7]

In the colonies, freedom from imposed rule in both religion and governance was a widespread goal. Immigrants came, believing that once they arrived they'd be able to worship as they wished. Repression by government-backed churches sent waves of people to North America: Puritans, Quakers, Mennonites, Huguenots, and Jews. In a society developing political freedom greater than had ever before known, true religious freedom was developing in parallel.

The political philosophy of the American patriots drew on the writings of the British and French Enlightenment and on the customs of the Dutch, who brought to New Amsterdam, later named New York, the lessons learned in establishing the first modern government without a king. Nowhere in Europe was there an artistic and scientific flowering to match Amsterdam's, and no other nation was free of monarchy. It was no coincidence. The Dutchmen brought their capital city's cultural diversity, religious tolerance, intellectual freedom, and social mobility to the southern tip of the island the natives called Mannahatta. They could be rigid in religious practice, but its place in their lives was restricted to person and family. The Dutch form of governance, minimally restricted by religious doctrine and unhindered by royal dictate, helped lead the way to the world's first laws separating church and state.[8]

Several of the nation's founders were deeply spiritual men, repulsed by the history of sectarian hostility in the colonies and the mother country. They knew that religion, education, and morality, forming an organic whole, would be important for a self-governing society, yet they also knew that religious doctrine could be complicating and destructive. Some represented states where religion and government were already legally separated. They meant to establish a nation whose legislators and judges would be free of ties to church institutions, theology, and canon law.

The men who gathered in the summer of 1787 in Philadelphia, *City of Brotherly Love*, to create a new nation, absorbed the spirit of a town founded by Quakers, people who worshipped without ceremony, creed, or minister. They also were affected by the spirituality of the natives living outside their settlements, with whom William Penn, the colony's founder, had been intimate. The references and appeals to God during the proceedings of the constitutional convention were not so different from the invocations of the Great Spirit by the natives in the nearby forests. It was a defining moment for humankind, civic leaders directly seeking guidance from the One, in parallel with their unacknowledged brothers in the wilds.[9]

The Constitution's separation of Church and State was relatively easy to achieve because it was drafted during a secular phase, between periodic waves of religiosity. The dominant attitude toward organized religion at the time was indifference; less than 20% of the population attended services. A rejection of religious faith, a capital offense early in the life of the Massachusetts Bay Colony, had become, one hundred fifty years later, a tolerated, even respected, point of view.

The separation of religion and government in the United States was not meant to be absolute, and later surges of religious enthusiasm weakened it. It felt fitting to all but the atheists that the motto *In God We Trust* began appearing on the nation's coins in the mid 19th century. In 1954 the Pledge of Allegiance, by then firmly embedded in the culture, was revised, *one nation* becoming *one nation under God*, a phrase that would have been understood in the cities of Mesopotamia. *In God We Trust* was made the nation's motto in 1956.[10] Some American politicians seek advantage by

5.5 How We Are Ruled

speaking as if God is more on their side than on their opponent's and by proclaiming policies, however irrational they may be, they know will gain them the support of orthodox religious voters.[11]

In the West, state institutions generally have more influence than religious ones. In contrast, in the Middle East, the tendency is often for religion to dominate politics and to control the course of events. When political and religious authority are undifferentiated, the most forceful and cruel versions of rule from above develop.[12] This is evident in the lands where obedience to the olden *gods* began, for in the Middle East dangerous re-enactments of the *wars of the gods* are taking place. A repeat of the disaster caused by the *gods* Nergal and Ninurta when they dropped nuclear bombs in and near the Sinai peninsula is not difficult to imagine.

When conditions are promising, as they were at fortunate moments in Athens, Amsterdam, and British North America, civilized humankind can use reason and good will to craft successful systems of self-governance, as indigenous peoples have done through the ages. In systems of rule from within the populace, authority is awarded provisionally by the whole community, spiritual awareness is a common resource, and stratification in society is moderate and fluid. Sadly, the pull is ever-present to revert to governance with political authority imposed from above, rigid and pronounced social stratification, and religion serving to control the populace ... as if we are fated to return, over and over, to being subjects of the *anunnaki* lords of Mesopotamia and the *demigods* serving them.

Next, we consider one of the most horrific explosions of violence in history, largely a consequence of what was imposed on us by the *gods* of Mesopotamia.

¹ That seems odd to those in the modern world, but it wasn't to those with actual memories of flesh and blood *gods*. In the Pacific theatre of World War II, the power of a belief in the divinity of a sovereign was demonstrated. Absolute devotion to their god-emperor was the source of the otherwise inexplicable ferocity and self-sacrifice of the Japanese warriors.

² The emotions displayed in the presence of the sovereign in England are not entirely transient ones. Nearly a third of Britons have dreams involving quite pleasant encounters with living royalty. Queen Elizabeth II coming to tea and enjoying the visit has been a common one.

³ At the turn of the century, the division between servants and served in England was so complete that English society actually resembled Šumer's. Those in service plus those they served numbered over half the population; more people were in domestic service than were in any other occupation.

⁴ Some nations have moderated this craving by having a titular king, the respect and affection once given the olden *gods* safely directed toward a politically powerless ruler. In Great Britain the arrangement is seriously called into question only when the royals behave in ways that impede the good feelings for them that the people are anxious to maintain.

⁵ There have been nations, such as those in the Congo and on the Hawaiian islands, with hereditary kings but few other features of civilization. How that could have come about in an essentially indigenous culture is not clear.

⁶ Thomas Paine, an architect of democracy in America, and a critic of western civilization, wrote that the natives promoted the natural rights of man in societies that were free of poverty and accumulated wealth. The virtues of the indigenous culture were evident to many whites. Benjamin Franklin, concerned about the substantial numbers of frontiersmen who joined Indian tribes, noted that when American settlers were captured and later liberated, even when treated on their return *with all imaginable tenderness*, nevertheless they would *take the first good opportunity of escaping again into the woods*.

⁷ Having encountered natives on the frontier, George Washington must have known of the Great Law. Benjamin Franklin certainly did. In 1742 a convocation was held in Lancaster, Pennsylvania between representatives of the Iroquois Confederacy and delegations from three colonies. A treaty concerning land rights was signed. Franklin published it in a report on the convocation. He included an address on the issue of disunity in the colonies by the most prominent of the sachems taking part, who stated: *We heartily recommend Union and a Good Agreement between you our Brethren. Never disagree, but preserve a strict Friendship for one another, and thereby you as well as we will become the Stronger. Our wise Forefathers established Union and Amity between the Five Nations; this has made us formidable, this has given us great weight and Authority with our Neighboring Nations. We are a Powerful confederacy, and by*

your observing the same Methods our wise Forefathers have taken, you will acquire fresh Strength and Power; therefore, whatever befalls you, never fall out with one another.

In 1754, when war with France was threatening, there was in Albany, New York another gathering of colonial representatives with the chiefs of the Iroquois Nations. Plans for a national government were presented; the one offered by Franklin, inspired by the native example of a foundational law, was adopted. The Albany Plan didn't lead to immediate action, yet it prepared the way for the Articles of Confederation, which in turn led to the Constitution.

There is an even deeper connection between the traditional self-rule of the Native American peoples and the novel self-rule embodied in the Constitution of the United States. Over countless generations, and over all the inhabited Earth, having separated themselves from the domains of the *Anunnaki* lords, the forbears of the Indians evolved the practice of self-governance. Starting around 1760, Americans began doing the same, though at vastly different pace and scope. Exploring the elements of self-rule, the colonists rediscovered its basic principles, preparing to separate themselves from the domains of the old-world kings.

The ancient indigenous tradition of consensus development reached through extensive conversation re-emerged. Political discussion was constant and intense over the thousand linear miles of settlement, in a manner that had never happened in civilization. Conversation took place at all levels and in every possible venue: in newspapers, pamphlets, books, proposals, and plans; in town councils, courts, assemblies, taverns, and coffee houses. In 1787 the Constitution began with "We, the People" because, in essence, it had been written by the entire populace over the course of several decades. The national political conversation continued to be intense over several more decades. In time, though, the advice of the Iroquois wise men was forgotten, the conversation broke down, and the unity it nurtured was lost.

[8] When New Amsterdam's governor moved to expel a group of Jews recently arrived from Brazil, his superiors in Holland overruled him. Their goal was to support the development of the colony's commerce. They started the city on its course to become the commercial capital of the nation to be.

[9] The Iroquois stated firmly that the Great Law of Peace was divinely inspired.

[10] Some Americans now have no choice but to display it on their cars; it's on the license plates issued by several states known for conservative religiosity.

[11] This aberration is as old as the republic. Thomas Jefferson's beliefs on matters of faith were considered idiosyncratic. His inclusion of the phrase *nature's God* in the Declaration of Independence was, to orthodox theologians, highly offensive. When he was seeking election to the presidency, a slogan voiced for John Adams, his opponent, was *God and a religious president, or ... Jefferson and no God.*

[12] The harsh secular governments of Germany under Hitler, the Soviet Union under Stalin, and China under Mao may appear to be counterexamples, but in those regimes the states operated like religions; the people regarded their supreme leaders much as humans once regarded the *gods*.

Civil War in America

When the *gods* found they needed workers in their gold mines they employed genetic manipulation and crafted the human race. For eons, slavery was the only condition of life humans knew. It did not have to be enforced. Physical and intellectual inferiority, shame-based emotions, and material dependence combined to insure subservience; they also determined the base layer human identity.

With the wars of the *gods*, defeated survivors embodied a second human identity: the slave ruled by the whip. Carvings of slumped captives roped together show what life was like for the vanquished, headed for service to a *god* and king not their own (See Figure 7.3.6 on page 320).

Later still, *anunnaki* commoners took human women as mates; their offspring added a third identity to the human spectrum. Through that unplanned second level of hybridization, *men of renown* were born, more like the *lofty ones* than humans had ever been. They were not, though, a secure privileged class, for they bore within themselves the sense of inferiority that characterized the basic human identity.

After the flood a fourth identity developed; some humans gained in status as scribes, priests, merchants, artisans, even kings. The core identity of the lowly slave stayed in place in them, nonetheless.

Near-constant warring produced plentiful human booty and made enforced slavery commonplace; the Book of Exodus doesn't suggest that the Israelites' harsh existence in Egypt was in any way unusual or unnatural. From the Mediterranean basin, Arabs introduced slavery to Africa; Greeks and Romans spread it into Europe. Europeans took slaves from Africa to their colonies in the Americas, starting early in the 17th century. From the horrors of the sugar plantations of the Caribbean, mass slavery entered British North America through Charleston, South Carolina. It grew rapidly in the southern United States in the 19th century, leading to debate, political maneuver, and bloodshed in the decades preceding the outbreak of civil war in 1861.

Three factors dramatically increased the need for slaves in the South. Vast stretches of land were opened for planting. Technical advances in processing magnified the demand for raw cotton. And by 1803 the importation of slaves was outlawed. As a consequence, the mid-century prices for slaves were up to two hundred times what they'd been.

A tragic restaging of humanity's origin resulted. The plantations of Virginia, the Carolinas, and Georgia were not so well suited for large-scale crops as were the newer ones of Alabama, Mississippi, and Louisiana and couldn't compete with them. Instead, the older plantations began producing the growing work force for the newly opened lands; they turned to breeding slaves as their main source of income. That enterprise replayed how humankind came into existence, for we had been bred for inescapable toil. The birthrate among slaves in the older plantations increased to nearly four times the previous norm. By 1860, the old South had sent a million souls westward, adding an increased rending of family ties to all that the enslaved population was already enduring.[1]

A second reenactment was also in progress. Masters were engaging in sex with slaves. This became well known; by 1830 the term *fancy girl* was appearing shamelessly in commercial notices of the slave trade. White men interbreeding with their female *property* reenacted what had once gone on between *anunnaki* commoners and human women.[2]

All organized warfare is horrific because it reignites the love of war we fell into through our service in the wars of the *gods*. Civil war is the most vicious kind of war because it reenacts the eternal rivalry of the clans of the chief *gods* Enlil and Enki. The American Civil War was by far the most destructive of all civil wars because with it emotions were unmasked whose source was the slavery into which humankind was born.

In the United States, where there was more personal freedom than the civilized world had ever known, a conflict-laden revival of humanity's original bondage took place. Liberty could not tolerate being so compromised; slavery could not be sustained in a free nation.

The cause of the war was slavery. The other factors that have been cited, states' rights vs. federal power, low tariffs vs. high, and agrarianism vs. industrialization, all revolved around slavery and cotton. Ulysses Grant knew war was coming as soon as he heard that Lincoln had been elected because of how strongly, years before, Lincoln had condemned slavery.

In the South the Civil War is often called the War Between the States. That's interesting, because it was the product of warring states of mind. A slave identity resides within humanity's Collective Unconscious. With a mindset of *freedom for all*, the Unionists confronted their inner slave identity by aiming to do away with the institution. With a mindset of *liberty for the elite*, the Confederates developed a more complex engagement with their inner slave identity; they meant to bury it even deeper by reconfirming their master identity. The social ideal for the North was democratic; for the South it was aristocratic. The conflict was driven by starkly opposing ways of dealing with humanity's original condition and, as we are about to discuss, of conceptualizing the nation.[3]

Colin Woodard explains in *American Nations* that from the time of first settlement, three cultures formed in the North, allied in assigning the highest value to freedom, holding it to be the universal right of mankind.[4] That view had been passed on to them by British farmers, traders, and parliamentarians, and by Dutch merchants. Its source was in the self-reliant Anglo-Saxon and Norse strains of British culture, and in the libertarian leanings of the Dutch. Their forbears were familiar with freedom and self-rule ... a spiritual gift from the humans who left the settlements of the *anunnaki* lords and ventured out on their own.

First in this regard were the New Englanders. The Yankees, the ones who had triggered the American Revolution, became the most ardent defenders of the Union. Slavery violated their ethic of self-sufficiency, its cruelty disgusted them, and they determined to end it once and for all. In them the suffering inherent in humanity's birth into slavery was rising fast toward consciousness. It called many of them to Abolitionism.

The Abolitionists drew strength from the second Great Awakening, a wave of religious enthusiasm that swept the country in the early 19th century. The first Great Awakening in the 18th century had spiritually prepared the colonies to do away with British rule; the second assisted in readying the North to do away with slavery. Inspired groups of *Wide Awakes* began forming in the North and West, starting in 1860. These were companies of young men ferociously opposed to slavery. Dressed in military-style hats and homemade capes, they marched through towns at night, unarmed or lightly armed, in ominous torch-lit silence. By the fall of that year, there were half a million of them, from Maine to California. The name of their movement suggests deep forces coming into awareness.

At the start of the war, political realities ruled out proclaiming emancipation as its goal, yet the hatred of slavery was always its driving force for the Yankees. The sentiment was strong. In 1854 a runaway slave was captured in Boston. Federal law required that he be returned to his southern owner. It took hundreds of soldiers with loaded rifles, backed by artillery, to deter a mob from freeing him.

Except in the Appalachians, the people of the South had never been passionate in the cause of personal freedom and broad democracy. Woodward's book explains how the two main cultures of the South were allied in the principle that true liberty was granted to very few.[5] Their tradition was one in which an elite stratum governed a mass of obedient citizenry. It came to them through the Royalists and Cavaliers in England, having flowed from the Norman strain of British culture. The spiritual ancestors of these people were of two kinds: the noble elite who served the living *gods* and the obedient enthralled masses.[6]

As humankind's original plight bubbled toward consciousness in the nation, the South's response was the opposite of the North's. The typical southerner aimed to defend himself against his buried slave identity by solidifying his role as lord and master, or at least the master's ally. The oligarchs of the Deep South thought of their society as a towering human achievement. They claimed that it was modeled after the republics of Rome and Athens, where the elites could follow higher pursuits only because of the labor provided by their slaves.[7]

William Harper, Chancellor of South Carolina, said that ordinary humans were ... *born to subjection [and that it was] the order of nature and of God that the beings of superior faculties and knowledge, and superior power, should control and dispose of those who are inferior.* James Hammond, former governor of the state, said that slavery was the ... *foundation of every well designed and durable [republic]* and that enslaving the white working class would be a *glorious act of emancipation.* George Fitzhugh, an influential writer from the Virginia aristocracy, declared to the North that he was ... *quite as intent on abolishing Free Society as you are on abolishing slavery.* He and others argued that slavery's preservation wasn't the main issue; it was defeating democracy. Without knowing it, these men were reaching even further back than the Roman and Greek slave-states. They yearned for a society like the one ruled by the *gods*, with themselves as modern *demigods*.[8]

The southerners' feelings about slavery were not entirely what they seemed. Overt proslavery attitudes masked deeper antislavery ones, whose ultimate sources were in humankind's earliest suffering. Mary Chestnut, wife of a former U.S. senator from South Carolina, and a clear-eyed observer of the South, wrote in her diary as war was breaking out that two-thirds of the slaveholders in the Confederate army disliked slavery as much as the Abolitionists, yet were going to offer their lives for it.

The southerners' secret hatred of the institution helps explain something that's little known: they themselves brought about its end. Given the compromise built into the Constitution, slavery could never be outlawed through due process, no matter how the Abolitionists fumed and threatened. The matter was clear to Lincoln; he believed that the South would never have to resort to war over slavery.

By firing on Fort Sumter, the Charleston artillery men opened the way for slavery's abolition. When the Emancipation Proclamation was issued a few years later, Secretary of State Seward wrote that it had been...*uttered in the first gun fired at Sumter, and we have been the last to hear it.* The close connection was common knowledge in the North. A watchmaker was repairing Lincoln's timepiece when he learned of the bombardment. He inscribed on a hidden inside surface within the case, *The first gun is fired. Slavery is dead, Thank God.*

By firing on the flag, sacred symbol of the United States of America, the hotheads in Charleston awakened patriotism on both sides. While the South was now freed to despise the banner, the North rallied to it. Literally overnight northerners began organizing regiments. As psychologically wedded as the southerners were at the surface to the identity of slave-master, and as dependent as they were on slave labor, nothing short of a war could separate them from the way of life that, in their depths, they hated ... so they began that war.

5.6 Civil War in America

In *A History of the American People* historian Paul Johnson states: *there are many irrational and ... inexplicable aspects to the whole controversy over slavery ... which baffle historians, as they baffled ... people in the middle at the time.* The Abolitionist Frederick Douglass wrote that powers beyond human understanding were at work: *we have fallen into the mighty current of eternal principles – invisible forces – which are shaping and fashioning events as they wish, using us only as instruments to work out their own results...*

From The Mesopotamian Tale we learn what those forces were: our early traumatizing and humiliating servitude surging into awareness, producing two opposite responses to long-buried memories. Both sides took up arms in the cause of freedom as they saw it. One fought as if none were free unless all were free; the other fought as if for some to have freedom, others had to be deprived of it.

Their fervent cries combined into a perfect formula for disaster:

We will finally feel free! Soon there will be no more slavery in this land!

We will finally feel free! Soon we will be confirmed as the masters of this land!

---

[1] When profit margins were high, traders could pay to transport their human *property* by water for a portion of the journey. The most unfortunate of the slaves, though, made the entire journey on their bare feet. Men (in shackles) and women trekked the dirt roads from northern Virginia to the flesh markets of Natchez and New Orleans, twenty miles a day for a thousand miles, with small children in the supply wagons and overseers on horseback.

[2] The black Presbyterian minister Henry Highland Garnet asked the participants at a black convention in Buffalo, New York in 1843 to *think of your wretched sisters, loving virtue and purity, as they are driven into concubinage and are exposed to the unbridled lusts of incarnate devils.*

[3] Naturally, many people on both sides held mixed and intermediate positions. Most Unionists in the South knew to keep quiet. A quarter of a million southern Appalachian men, though, enlisted in regiments fighting for the Union. It wasn't so much that the mountain people objected to slavery; it was that they hated the rich slaveholders. They sensed that in the eyes of the southern oligarchs, they were barely a step above the enslaved blacks.

[4] He calls these nations within the nation, extending from Maine to eastern Pennsylvania: Yankeedom, New Netherlands, and Midlands.

[5] He calls these nations within the nation Tidelands (the eastern parts of Maryland, Virginia, and North Carolina) and Deep South.

[6] The southern oligarchs were also reenacting another theme from Mesopotamia: brother-favored-over-brother. Many of the wealthy men settling the Deep South were the younger sons of the British gentry. They had substantial riches, but were forced to leave the grand households in which they were raised. British law, with roots reaching back to Šumerian culture, dictated that inherited land was to be granted intact to the eldest brother.

[7] Charleston's British consul sent messages to London (where the need for cotton required cooperation with the Confederacy) commenting bitterly on the oligarchs' delusions. He said in one communication: *It is rather hard that we are to dance to the fiddle of this dirty little abortion of an imperium.*

[8] Lincoln knew that this was the broader issue manifested in the Civil War. Could people be free and self-governing, or would civilized humanity forever be ruled by those who had gained power through inheritance or manipulation? Civilization had always tended toward rule by elites who had status and wealth. Slavery in America was the cutting edge of the blade that separated humanity from freedom: subjugation to power. Lincoln had spoken of the world-wide importance of the principles in the Declaration of Independence when, heading to his first inauguration, he personally raised the flag at Independence Hall in Philadelphia, saying, *[there was] something in [the Declaration] giving liberty, not alone to the people of this country, but hope to the world for all future time.*

In his address at Gettysburg he said that the war was testing the principles of governance through self-rule. The United States was *a new nation conceived in liberty and dedicated to the proposition that all men are created equal,* and the war was testing *whether that nation or any nation so conceived and so dedicated can long endure.* Could self-rule succeed as the basis for a nation state? When it had been tried in the past, as in Athens and Rome, it had required slave labor. In the late 18th century, the Dutch experiment had begun to totter, and in the first half of the 19th, the revolutions for liberty in Europe had all failed. The revived monarchies of the Continent were hoping for the collapse of the American experiment at the very moment Lincoln was speaking. He saw that government *of the people, by the people, for the people* was at risk and could indeed *perish from the Earth.*

A Few Other Things

<u>Verbal Time Capsules</u>

When we call an attractive woman a goddess, we tap into buried memories of the *anunnaki goddesses*. We believe we're comparing the woman to sculptures of Greek and Roman deities; those perfect female forms, however, were based on idealized memories of the female *lofty ones*. The *lofty ones* were quite tall. That may be why a woman who is exceptionally alluring but short is never called a *goddess*.

When we say someone is *a big man* or *a man of stature*, we're meaning to cite his influence, wealth, or wisdom. The analogy to physical size is apt because it draws on our memories of the *gods*, who in addition to being skillful and powerful, were incredibly tall.

When we call ourselves *children of God*, we mean that our relationship with the One parallels the relationship of child to parent. Yet there's a hidden meaning below the metaphor. The *anunnaki* were one of our parent species, so it's literally true that we were *born of the gods*.

In a well-established tradition, monarchs use the *majestic plural* to refer to themselves. With this practice they perpetuate the practice of the kings of Mesopotamia who spoke not only for themselves, but also for the *gods*, the sources of their authority.

We speak with nostalgia of *golden ages*, such as that of chivalry, sailing ships, railroads, and jazz. When we do, our words connect us with the people of classical Greece and Rome, who looked back with longing toward a *golden age*. They glimpsed that age through the subsequent ages of iron, bronze, and silver. The golden age of their imagination was the best of all ages, when everything was wondrous and gold was plentiful.[1]

<u>Raise Your Right Hand</u>

Gestures, too, can serve as time capsules. As we swear an oath, we reproduce the universal sign of recognition and adoration made to a high *god*; we raise the right hand, palm forward. In many Mesopotamian carvings the gesture is made by humans and by lesser *gods* facing supreme *divinities* ... a moment of truth, then as now, (See Figures 3.5.1.a, 3.5.4, 3.6.1.a and b, 3.6.8.b, 3.9.4.b, and 3.9.8) Humanity has adopted and modified the gesture with good intentions, as in a vow and a priestly blessing, and with horrid purpose, as in the Nazi salute. (Figure 5.7.1)[2]

Figure 5.7.1. a. From Jan Van Eyck's "Arnolfini Wedding" (1434).
b. A neo-Nazi mass murderer in a Norwegian courtroom (2016).
c. Men being sworn-in for a hearing in the U.S. Congress (2016).

Being Big

The height of the *anunnaki* still affects us. For thousands of years, when we were near the *lofty ones*, we inclined our faces upward and *looked up to them*. The buried memory of having done so makes us keen to do the same with leaders today. Historical records and photographs show that political and military leaders are often taller than most of their countrymen.

The Word of God

Fundamentalists say that the humans who penned the books of the Bible were instruments of the divine ... in effect channeling God. The Mesopotamian texts incorporated into the Hebrew Bible in reworked versions included Šumerian originals that had been dictated by the *lofty ones* to their scribes. That means that there actually are *words of the gods* buried within many biblical passages, and that there's a factual nugget in the mystical claim that Scripture is the *word of God*.

Deference

Deference is an instinctual trait in many mammals. When a member of a group gains physical dominance, deference maintains social order. There's no need for frequent, costly testing of the alpha animal; the others defer to his posture and manner. However, in humans deference can be induced without dominance having first been established. Psychological studies show that if someone acts as if he expects to dominate, those around him subordinate themselves, even after it's clear that it makes no sense to obey just because he acts as if they should.[3]

There's a high cost in resources and lives when dominance is achieved without being earned, be it in business, government, or the military. This uniquely human trait is far too dysfunctional to have evolved naturally on this planet. The Mesopotamian Tale teaches that we were made to serve *gods* who wanted total power over us. What could have been more convenient for the *anunnaki* than to have humans automatically defer to anyone who *lorded* over them? Our aberrant deference response can only be the result of the *anunnaki's* genetic manipulation of *Homo erectus*. That modification may not have been difficult for Enki and Ninmač achieve if automatic deference was inherent in their species, as seems quite possible.

The Lust for Gold

Beginning with Adam Smith, economists have argued that basing monetary systems on national stores of gold, continuing a connection going back to the royal hordes of antiquity, makes no sense. In the United States the link wasn't broken until the 1970's.

We are closing down the trade in new furs and ivory on humanitarian grounds. When it comes to gold, however, we pay no attention to the suffering of miners in the world's open-pit hells, or to the killing and crippling of deep-mine workers, from breathing dust that could easily be eliminated through proper ventilation. Over 5,000,000 slaves died in the gold mines of Brazil, according to colonial records. Only a powerful lust for the glistening substance could keep us unaware of one of history's worst genocides. The actions of prospectors in the gold rushes of the 19th century led Native Americans to call gold *the yellow metal that makes white people crazy*. A craving for gold can raise its market value well above what its scarcity and utility warrant.[4]

To the *anunnaki* gold was more than a vital commodity to be shipped home. They were adorned with gold bracelets, rings, and crowns. They ate and drank from golden dinnerware. They wielded gold implements in rituals. They loved the glistening substance. It was the metal of the *gods*; later it became the metal of the kings. Within our hunger for gold is emulation: to have gold is to be a bit like a *god* or a king.

Also within our craving for gold is a wish for feelings of fulfillment. Finding gold was our original reason for being. Because it made us valuable to our *gods*, it brings us a deep, inexplicable feeling of satisfaction.

These two aspects of our early history help us understand why gold yields a sense of status and a feeling of fulfillment that other precious substances do not quite provide.

Half-Breeds

Persons of mixed race are often derided by members of both their parent races. There are well documented factors in the psychology of groups that account for much of the hostility toward them, yet a factor of another kind is also involved. We are all *half-breeds*, a mix of *anunnaki* and *Homo erectus*. People who are obvious mixtures begin to remind us of that. Biracial persons are punished for threatening to release buried memories from mass amnesia. Their intermediate features stir the memory of what has always been too painful for us to be aware of.[5]

Hating the Jews

Discussing the several sources of Anti-Semitism would be off-subject, yet our radical reading of the Mesopotamian tablets uncovers another possible cause of the hatred the Jews have suffered. The subtle nature of this potential cause will make assessing the extent of its impact difficult.

It's ironic, but The Book that has sustained the Jews may have been an insidious source of antipathy toward them. The Hebrew Bible has kept open a channel to the injurious conditions of life under the *lofty ones*, with passages that reflect the Šumerian accounts of humanity's origins and early times. Covert within many biblical tales are the confusing, shaming, and traumatizing circumstances of our beginnings. Jewish scripture kept rousing the Collective Unconscious. Had it not done that, the anguish of our origins would have stayed more deeply buried. Memories of events like the Flood would have been better sealed in mass amnesia. In other words, one of the forces driving the hatred of the Jews may have been an unconscious impulse to kill the messenger bringing bad tidings.

Twelve

Twelve sons of Išmael, son of Abraham. Twelve sons of Jacob. Twelve sons of Esau. Twelve Hebrew tribes. Other groups of twelve tribes. Twelve Apostles. Twelve tables of Roman law. Twelve months in a year. Twelve inches in a foot. Twelve objects in a dozen; twelve dozens in a gross. Twelve members of a criminal jury. Twelve hours AM and PM. Twelve double-hours in the Taoist day. The number twelve has a unique place in human affairs. What is its allure?

The *anunnaki* believed that twelve was the ruling number of the Solar System, with twelve major members surrounded by three stacked circles of

5.7 A Few Other Things

twelve constellations each.⁶ So that life on Earth would be in accord with the celestial order, they established another circle of twelve: the supreme council of twelve *gods*, six male, six female. The number in that circle was always twelve; a successor was named when one stepped down. Twelve divinities continued to rule after the olden *gods* were no longer present. Six males and six females ruled over the rest of the Greek gods; six male-female pairs were the most powerful of the gods of Rome.

The number twelve became precious to humanity not because it was represented in the heavens, but because Earth had once been ruled by twelve supreme divinities. Contemplating twelve of anything, those *gods* came to mind, perhaps vaguely, yet strongly enough. As civilization developed, it felt proper and comforting whenever the number twelve appeared in the framework of the culture. Somehow, it still does.

---

[1] The Golden Age was conceived of as the time of humankind's origin, when life was free of all difficulty and scarcity. The passage of time had transformed memories. As The Mesopotamian Tale reveals, life did have those qualities in humanity's first age ... but for the *gods*, not their human servants.

[2] As the *Star Trek* series was first being developed, Leonard Nimoy suggested that his character, when offering a blessing upon parting, use a particular gesture. It involved holding the fingers of the raised right hand in a certain way. As a boy, Nimoy had seen the gesture as he peeked at the hereditary priests blessing the congregation of his orthodox synagogue. (They had held the fingers in a way that replicated the first letter of the Hebrew word for *Almighty God*.) The Christian prelates' hand raised in blessing derives from the Israelite practice, which in turn derived from the way the high *gods* of Mesopotamia were greeted.

[3] The trait of unearned deference in response to verbal and bodily posturing was clearly one of the factors contributing to the phenomenon of Trumpism in the United States, which made its astounding appearance in 2016.

[4] Virtually all economists agree that the market value of gold is augmented.

[5] It was clear that the vituperation endured by President Barack Obama was largely fueled by racist sentiments, conscious and unconscious. It was less evident that those sentiments had an accelerant: he was not just *black* ... he was *half white*.

[6] The twelve members of the Solar System were the nine planets (including Pluto) known to us plus the Sun, Moon, and Nibiru. There are circles of twelve constellations located above and below the circle of the twelve signs of the Zodiac.

Part Six

Conclusion

What I've learned from The Mesopotamian Tale, can it help me improve my life, solve my problems, find more peace ... right now?

As more and more people learn about The Mesopotamian Tale, can the information really help achieve the radical transformation humanity needs?

Part Six addresses questions of this nature.

What Now?

We cannot solve our problems unless we know ourselves, and we can't know ourselves unless we know where we came from. This is as true collectively as it is individually. The Mesopotamian Tale, therefore, leads to a vital question: if we are beings made from two different beings, who are we?

I'm a member of the species *Homo sapiens*, but what does that really mean? I have discovered how two species were genetically combined to make the first of my kind, and that our lives today are still affected by our earliest human ancestors' confusing, traumatizing, and humiliating conditions of life. Within myself I sense my two parent species.

I already knew about one of them from the study of his fossils and by extrapolating from his living relatives, the great apes. I call him *Homo erectus*. A small furry creature of Earth, at home in the wild, he held his place on the developing homonin line until events caught up with him. When my *Homo sapiens* ancestor appeared, he couldn't compete with him and he died out ... except for how he lives on within me, genetically and spiritually. A child of the planet he loves, he is curious, social, and innocent. I sense him, distinct, inside.

I've recently learned about the other being within me from the words and images left by my ancestors in Mesopotamia who knew him when he walked the Earth. They called his kind the *lofty ones*. He is a tall smooth-skinned humanoid from a planet that was once much like Earth, but became an artificially sustained world in deep space. He brought his planet's skill to this one; also, its strife. He is accomplished, proud, learned, and violent. He eventually returned home ... but lives on in me, genetically and spiritually. I also sense him, distinct, inside.

The first humans were in awe of the *gods*, painfully aware of how inadequate they were in comparison. Living with the *gods*, similar to them in many ways, my first human ancestors were challenged to grasp who they were. I sense them also, distinct, inside, a third presence.

When I'm quiet, I can hear those three distinct voices from the past.

• I hear the being who'd evolved naturally, and who wanted no more than to move freely over the face of Earth, drinking in her beauty, enhancing her vitality, and living in harmony with the diversity of life to which she gives birth.[1]

• I hear the being from the *Planet of the Crossing*, trapped in this lesser body with its short life span. He came to Earth to extract mineral riches; he dominated, exploited, and waged war. Now he is marooned here within struggling humankind. Faster and faster, he is bringing forth the advanced technology that he misses. And still makes war.

• I hear the hybrid child of two worlds and two heritages, born into confusion about his identity, traumatized, and shamed.

From time to time, we find ourselves longing for life to be simple, desiring to just *be*, to cease all our striving to *do*. Those authentic wishes come from memories recorded long ago by *H. erectus*. There's nothing wrong with those desires, though the scripts driving them stand in need of overwriting with positive ones.[2]

From time to time we tell ourselves we don't belong. The ultimate source of that message is the voice of the *lofty ones*. Unpleasant as it is, it's not to be squelched, for it too has authenticity: the *lofty ones* didn't belong here.[3] The memories that drive that voice's emotions are also due for overwriting with new ones, for the *gods* have much to gain through their merger with *H. erectus*. Among other things, they can connect with their own roots; our extraterrestrial forebears evolved from lower primates millions of years ago on Nibiru. By honoring *H. erectus* living along with them inside *H. sapiens*, they acknowledge their genetic ancestry.

From time to time we tell ourselves we're inadequate. The ultimate source of that message is the voice of the first *Homo sapiens*. It's not to be squelched or resisted, for it has authentic origin. The scripts of inferiority that drive it, though, can be be overwritten with new ones, as humankind, through learning about our forgotten origins, emerges from the dual curse of subservience and dominance.

From time to time we ask, *Who are we? What's our purpose?* As troubling as those questions can be, they also are authentic and not to be suppressed. They were voiced by the first *H. sapiens*, confused about their nature and place. We've tried to relieve our confusion through religion, philosophy, and therapy, but amnesia for our origins has limited what we've been able to achieve. Until we recover what's blocked from memory, the deep uncertainty and questing will persist.

How is it possible for three entities of consciousness, that of *H. erectus*, that of the *lofty ones*, and that of earliest *H. sapiens*, to remain distinct within that of modern *H. sapiens*? Addressing that complex issue involves discussions beyond the scope of this work, in the field of consciousness studies. Yet familiar circumstances illuminate the matter to some extent. Those born to parents of different races know what it's like to feel at times like a member of one race, at other times like a member of the other, and sometimes as if they belong to neither. In fact, having distinct parental parts is a universal experience. In addition to expressing one's own identity, each of us thinks and acts to a degree like our father and to a degree like our mother, through the process of identification.[4]

My earthly *H. erectus* self says, *This is not the way I am meant to be,* while my celestial *anunnaki* self says, *I don't belong here, I'm trapped,* and my earliest *H. sapiens* self asks, *Who am I? What's my purpose?* These troubled states of mind will begin to reconcile and find relief as the modern *H. sapiens* consciousness remembers what's been long buried in mass amnesia. It can soothe the three voices from the past, telling them that their beliefs are based in scripts that once made great sense, but that can now be overwritten with ones more timely and positive, such as: *We've learned that we're elements of a partitioned entity, two original beings dwelling within a third. In mutual respect, let us unite in an alliance more potent than we've ever known.*

As I learn about the two distinct genetic sources of my existence and open up to the three ancestral voices within me, not only do I more fully understand who I am, but many feelings and perceptions spontaneously begin to change. For everyone who develops it, this awareness facilitates healing and makes contentment easier to achieve.

• • •

Can we use The Mesopotamian Tale to transform our way of life?

In the chapter The Human Condition we dealt with the sources of our tragic state. We said that new hope will arise when we realize that the reason we haven't been able to ameliorate our plight is that until now we've been blinded by amnesia and hobbled by trauma and shame. Spurred by a new infusion of optimism, we'll move beyond trying to bring relief to our suffering and begin to engage its original sources.

We know that healing can succeed for suffering rooted in traumatization and shame. The work relies on understanding the psychologies of trauma and affect, and on combining a variety of interactions: of sufferer and healer, aware of their relationship; of thought and imagery; of sensation with cognition; of right hemisphere with left; of visceral phenomena with mental functions. Drawing on what The Mesopotamian Tale teaches, the skills that have been developed in one-on-one healing processes of this sort can be scaled up to address the conditions of large groups. An illustration:

We've been hostile to our neighboring nations for as long as we can remember. We've been certain that we had sound reasons, old and new, great and small, to feel as we did ... until we came to see that they are enemies mostly because we believe they are, and because they believe we are theirs. If we didn't have those beliefs, we might be in competition instead of hostilities.

We were startled to learn how it all began: early humans lived in awe of powerful, superior beings who claimed to be gods. Those great ones manipulated their followers into hating the followers of other self-deified lords, who ruled other states. That made our forebears eager to fight and die in the wars their gods waged for power and riches. We have learned that in time the gods were replaced by kings who, also lusting for power and riches, used their people's loyalty to perpetuate hatred for neighboring folk. Not only that, allying with priests and bishops, the kings manipulated religious sentiments to intensify their subjects' hostility toward others.

That's how we came to call upon God to grant us victory. We believe our faith justifies our asking for His favor, and hope our enemies will be proved wrong to have the same expectation. We now see we are both wrong; in asking for divine intervention, we are unwittingly updating beliefs imposed on us by selfish, warring, self-proclaimed gods who often decided our fate in battle with their powerful weapons.

Everything shifted as we realized that our feelings toward our neighbors result from entrapment in scenarios that began in falsehoods ages ago. After we saw that each generation has taught the next to think of their neighbors as enemies, we knew we had to halt the transmission of hatred.

We woke up to the fact that we've been guided by thoughts based in fabrications. We've been living in a very bad dream. Our anger should be directed not at our traditional foes, but at those in the past who got us to believe lies and who manipulated us, and at those who right now aim to do the same ... for they must be confronted if we are to emerge from the trap of our deeply engrained patterns.

If we align our feelings with the love that's the essence of the One, we will be able to develop a bond with our neighbors and enjoy happy relations with them. We won't be saying God wishes us to live in peace; that's almost as wrong as saying God supports our urge to dominate through violence. From our life under the gods, we came away with the concept of a personified supreme being wanting us to do this or that. We're working at leaving those ideas behind.

We are learning how belief patterns with origins in the distant past trigger fight and flight threat responses and angry emotions, overcoming our reasoning abilities. We are learning to pause whenever we have those all-too-familiar thoughts and feelings about our neighbors. We wait, giving ourselves a chance to distinguish what's actually going on from what was implanted in our ancestors and transmitted down the generations. We are becoming conscious of our personal and group processes, and as a result, are growing more rational.

This has not come easily. We've needed reconciliation commissions; exchange programs for children; international schools and works projects; revised curriculums, including experiential programs in affect and trauma psychology; conferences; workshops; food fairs; interdenominational services; and attention to discord within each of our nations, since personal problems keep some people invested in communal hatred and divisiveness. Those folk, who hold to their obnoxious nationalism, need to be engaged with kindness while their harsh behavior is compassionately restricted by their communities.

6.1 What Now?

Leading large groups into self-awareness is obviously easier said than done, yet there's no reason to think it impossible. At the level of small groups, the psychology of the affects and scripts is being applied in the Restorative Practices movement;[5] programs for groups are finding success using principles developed in individual trauma treatment.[6] The principles are known. Creativity in scaling up the efforts is what's needed. The arts have always had a place in these efforts; informed by The Mesopotamian Tale, their role can become more vital than ever.

Transformative healing processes have proven themselves at the individual and small group levels. As they incorporate the teachings of The Mesopotamian Tale they can be successfully increased in scale.

• • •

How can The Mesopotamian Tale aid in tackling the problem of excessive, persistent shame?

Learning to identify and manage shame, a neural reflex, is central to the healing processes we've just discussed. When poorly handled, shame leads to many dysfunctional feelings and behaviors: rage, vengeance, honor killing, suicide, addictions, arrogance, greed, machismo, vanity surgery, massive body building, bullying, bragging, gambling, and overspending. These all have their ultimate source in shame. They function as defenses when its feelings become unbearable. They do their job so well that the shame they cover is often difficult to identify.

As a consequence, the mental health and legal professions rarely grasp that shame is the root of much psychopathology and criminality. Many professionals, furthermore, are limited by blindness for their own shame emotions; to prevent their personal feelings from being evoked, they insulate themselves against appreciating shame felt by the people they encounter in their work. Poets, novelists, playwrights, and film makers, often more adept at dealing with their inner selves than lawyers and (sadly) therapists, have offered countless illustrations of how shame contributes to the human condition.

Mesopotamian and Egyptian carvings and murals depicting small naked humans bowing low as they bring offerings to *gods* and kings, make it evident that the people were meant to feel shame and to accept that it was their fate. Shame's transient neuronal response (involving the diminished muscle tone and averted eyes we see in those images) became linked with scripts of inferiority, inadequacy, and dependency, keeping the *lofty ones* and the kings securely dominant. Those scripts, embedded in the

Collective Unconscious, make us feel shame more strongly, and keep us caught in it longer, than we would if we'd had a kinder early existence.

Better management of shame is important, complex, and challenging. We don't see shame as a beneficial evolved response, because the pain it can generate is much more obvious than its benefits. Rational management of shame becomes a less daunting task when we learn that it's an evolved reflex with survival value *and* that through no fault of our own we are prone to feel it with an intensity that's unnatural and injurious.

We all have our work to do in managing our day-to-day shame emotions. The Mesopotamian Tale can be a strong support for the learning that's needed to better deal with these feelings.

• • •

Religion has at times magnified the tragedy of the human condition. Can The Mesopotamian Tale help bring about changes in belief and practice so that in the future religion will never increase suffering, only reduce it?

The way the first humans were treated by the powerful beings they took to be *gods* closed the trap of the human condition. Religion has had a major role in keeping us in it ... and can have a role in our escape.

Religious wars, sectarian genocides, and pogroms count among humanity's worst excesses. The Mesopotamian Tale reveals the original source of the enmity between people of different faiths: the emotions the *gods* roused in their followers, making them keen to battle the worshippers of other *gods*. Killing the devotees of a foreign deity was a legacy easily adapted to later social orders; in the wars between nations, religion has partnered all too well with politics.[7]

Phrases and images of martial violence permeate the literatures of Christianity and Islam. Both have long embraced war, rationalizing bloodshed as if unaware that in so doing they were violating their own principles of peace and love. For hundreds of years Jews knew violence only as victims; now the Israelis have revived the ferocity of their biblical forbears. The three monotheisms allow their core values, founded in the love that is the essence of the One, to be tainted with mankind's lasting attachment to the jealous bloodthirsty *lofty ones*.

The creed of the warrior involves devotion unto death to something greater than self. The object of devotion may be incomparably good or hideously evil; it can inspire actions that are noble or depraved. To understand the creed, and to have hope of rationally guiding it, we need to acknowledge its origin: civilized humanity's enthralled obedience to power-hungry, self-proclaimed *gods*.

The monotheisms serve to perpetuate the warrior creed, primarily through their tendency to personify infinite eternal Source. Other faiths, while holding lesser deities to be divine, are clear about the diffuse, non-personal, nature of the One. The theologies of the three monotheisms, though they contain concepts of formless Spirit, are strongly inclined to render Source as a being. They were born in the lands once dominated by the flesh and blood *lofty ones*; the memory of those *gods* keeps pulling the monotheisms into the error of personifying the One.

The main trouble with that pull is that the *gods* were wedded to violence. As devotion shifted from the *lofty ones* to the One, memories of the violence of the *gods* were imprinted on the concept of God. Civilized humanity had been led to believe that the powerful war-loving lords from Nibiru were deities, and that to be devoted to them involved killing. After the supposedly divine beings departed, the emerging monotheisms understandably formulated a Supreme Being accepting and encouraging violence. In the Hebrew Bible, the foundational document of the three faiths, God has contradictory attributes, many of them involving violence: accepting but vengeful; compassionate yet cruel; loving and jealous; beneficent but angry; forgiving yet judgmental. How are the faithful to be less vengeful, cruel, jealous, angry, and judgmental than their God?

The United States is the most violent of the fully developed nations and the most religious. No coincidence. Until quite recently around 75% of adults said they were affiliated in some way with a religious institution. Sectarian sentiment intrudes into the nation's political process, despite the statutory separation of church and state. The country's high rate of religious observance corresponds with its propensity for war.[8]

America's violence is also directed toward itself. In the 20th century, the number of people killed by guns on the nation's streets was greater than the number of soldiers killed on its battlefields in all its wars. The United States has a per capita rate of violent crime several times that of developed countries and is in a class by itself in mass murder. No sport comes close to American football in causing severe injury.[9]

To be the religions of peace they wish to be, the monotheisms need to see that their tendency to think of the One as a being perpetuates the self-serving manipulations of humanity by the *lofty ones*. Until the monotheisms cease personifying the divine, there will be no permanent reduction in mass violence in the cultures they dominate, only pauses. Knowledge of the Mesopotamian Tale can facilitate that fundamental change.

Christians could release their fixation on Father and Son, and focus on Holy Spirit.[10] Their faith's practices could become more like its Quaker and Unitarian Universalist offshoots.[11] Jews could give *ruach* (the holy wind) the attention that *Yahweh* has always received, radically revise a liturgy centered on glorifying Him, and become more open to their spiritual tradition of *Kaballah*. Muslims could encapsulate and retire the violent precepts within Islam and move from the faith's harsher formulations toward its gentler forms, such as Sufism. The monotheisms would thus strengthen currents they already possess, ones that are at the cores of Taoism, Buddhism, and the faiths of indigenous peoples.[12]

Small religious movements in the United States are proceeding in this direction, supporting people in reconsidering their ideas about a personified, demanding deity. Pastors and congregants in recovery, to use their term, from fundamentalist upbringings, have organized a slow-growing network. Harvard's Humanist Community Project supports the development of groups of freethinkers, humanists, and agnostics throughout the nation. In a society permeated with a religiosity that easily endorses war, these developments are encouraging.

The monotheistic hierarchies will dig in their heels to keep the tales from Mesopotamia from being accepted as the true early history of mankind. They will insist that the Hebrew Bible is the word of God, refusing to see the obvious: that the poets and scholars who wrote and edited that great work adapted accounts and themes left by the Šumerians to fit a new theology.[13] The establishments will seek to maintain power through their orthodox position on scripture, which people will support as long as they feel a need to remain in amnesia.

It may turn out that the most important interventions serving to liberate humanity from our tragic condition will be the ones that undo the way Judaism, Christianity, and Islam keep our devotion to the olden *gods* alive through the personification of the Divine ... our original devotion having demanded and rewarded service in war to violent deities.

When the Dalai Lama says "My religion is kindness," he reminds us that the usual trappings of faith can be replaced with practices flowing directly from love, our primary subjective experience of the Divine. Though our concept of the One was distorted by those who misled us, our inherent awareness of Source was not lost. When the false concept of divinity once imposed upon us is seen as the distortion that it was, it will be easier than ever to rid ourselves of all it has produced.

• • •

How can The Mesopotamian Tale helps to overcome the obstacles conventional science and scholarship present to transforming humanity's status quo?

Just as religious authorities will oppose anyone's taking the tablets about the Mesopotamian *gods* as factual accounts, scientific and scholarly authorities will refuse to consider that solid data and rigorous thinking give support to the idea that extraterrestrial humanoids crafted us using laboratory genetics.[14] In the religious and scientific orthodoxies we have an example of dialectical process: mutually antagonistic systems of thought allied in a common purpose. They will both oppose the idea that we are hybrids and that we had a horrific early history.[15]

In the professions, mindset and career will form bulwarks against open-minded approaches to The Mesopotamian Tale, but thinkers not committed to the orthodoxies will begin to undermine the obstructionism. The mood in the disciplines will begin to shift toward serious consideration of The Mesopotamian Tale; brave scientists and scholars will propose testing the hypotheses of this book and others like it with honest rigor.

Reputations, academic positions, and research funding will be at stake. Sincere investigators will find themselves facing peers who claim to be examining theses objectively when they are only seeking to discredit them. The discussion around The Mesopotamian Tale will be polluted by derision, misrepresentation, character assassination, and threat. It's helpful to recall that revolutions in science have often followed fierce initial rejection of work that's ahead of its time. In our fast-paced world, the obstacles may crumble quickly once they are weakened.

Thoughtful people have always sought to understand the universe, make sense of humanity's path, and find their place in the scheme of things. If The Mesopotamian Tale is accepted as an introduction to the true history of our species, many books will then have to be reconsidered. No masterworks will need to be discarded, yet the task of integrating the truths they convey into a new world view will be huge.

Sweeping change can take place in scholarship and science once an opening is created. The Mesopotamian Tale provides such an opening as well as a map for investigators to follow. Courage and patience will establish the validity of The Tale and will cleanse the air around the enterprise when it's been fouled by hostile reaction. Then The Mesopotamian Tale, manifesting in the work of the scientists and scholars it inspires, will be a potent agent for social and individual transformation.

• • •

What are the personal dimensions of the societal changes that are necessary if we are to escape our trap?

When astronomers locate Nibiru, we'll have confirmation that The Mesopotamian Tale has basis in reality.[16] About 900 years from now, as the golden orb draws near, we may have even contact with our former *gods*.

Hopefully, long before then we'll be using The Mesopotamian Tale as a catalyst to transform our culture. Otherwise, in nine more centuries our descendants will probably be living in one of our apocalyptic movies.

As individuals and as a species, we hold tightly to what's familiar, and what's most *familiar*, we receive through our *families*. We all need healing in our relationships with our parents analogous to what humanity needs in our relationship with our celestial parent species.

As individuals, we carry hurt and anger from childhood, having been neglected, wounded, misunderstood, or abused to a greater or lesser extent. Efforts to recover from what we went through growing up must incorporate an understanding that our parents gave us a lot beyond physical existence and material support, and that they did the best they could, considering what they had to deal with in themselves and their world. Our parents are within us; and if we don't have compassion for them, we won't have it for ourselves.

Personally addressing the way in which we've been affected by how we were wronged early in life would help each of us to move beyond denial, anger, blame, and reenactment. This is as true for our species as it is for us individually. The *lofty ones* did us great harm, yet given who the traumatized beings from Nibiru had become before arriving on Earth, could they have done any better? We need to forgive the *lofty ones*.[17]

Our societal and personal tasks are inseparable. There's risk if someone confronts humanity's destructiveness without first confronting one's own ... one's shadow side. Self-work builds the humility and fortitude needed to responsibly take on a role in changing society. We've already seen enough injury by preachers, therapists, and politicians *talking the talk* without having *walked the walk*. Communities of seekers, generalizing from their inner work, are coming together to focus on the great questions, including the mystery of the human condition. All power to them.

Personal healing is a requirement for having a role in humanity's healing. There's a reciprocal relationship between the two. The truth can set your free ... and some freedom is needed to accept and apply the truth.

• • •

What models do we have for bringing about broad, swift change?

In the thirteen British colonies in North America a new awareness began developing around 1730, led by itinerant preachers. Called the Great Awakening, it was a spontaneous, non-doctrinal movement lasting more than two decades. It created a national consciousness in spirit, binding people in a common, elevated view of human nature and societal purpose. People had come from many different lands, had developed distinct cultures in the different colonies, and had organized diverse forms of governance; the Great Awakening emerged in response to the strains of fragmentation. Its leaders proposed to meet the social and spiritual needs they sensed and did so in a manner that prepared the populace for the political and military upheaval that would bring about a new kind of nation, one in which the government derived its authority solely from the people, a government meant to release its citizens from the pattern established by the *gods* and the kings who had served them.

Nothing like the Great Awakening had ever happened. It was as if it sprung from the very ground. Those courageous pastors of a nation that was yet to be did not bow to engrained theologies or existing conventions. Their efforts were coordinated in spirit, not organized by agreements. They knew that the theological disputes that for a hundred years had caused moral and physical violence in the colonies had to end. They bore the hostility of the established institutions with equanimity, focusing people on what was universal and eternal for all humankind.

Their methods were flexible and creative. They held large meetings. They printed essays and sermons in pamphlets and made them available at minimal cost. Liberation from the restrictive traditions of the established denominations fortified the desire for liberation from the restrictive application of British law. The preachers' voices were in synchrony with those of inspired secular writers such as Thomas Paine.

Without the Great Awakening, the forces of divisiveness might have overcome those of unity, the war might have been lost, and the Constitution not ratified. Those unlikely successes in war and politics depended on the spiritual unity the Great Awakening had produced.[18]

In the early 19th century, a second Great Awakening took place, another spontaneous movement of spiritual renewal led by preachers, rising in response to a critical need. Mass meetings and printed material again stirred the nation, preparing it for another time of war and reorganization ... the one that would release it from the curse of slavery. The voices of these preachers were in harmony with those of the inspired secular writers of their time, such as Thoreau, Emerson, and Whitman.

Will there be a Great Awakening to stir humanity, as the two Great Awakenings did in the United States? Will brave leaders come forward to inspire hearts and minds, as American preachers and secular scholars did in the 18th and 19th centuries? If it happened before, it can happen again.

• • •

When might such an awakening start?

Maybe it already has, in a development that's been in process for several years. As this author sees it, science fiction and fantasy films have been presenting The Mesopotamian Tale in a form that avoids traumatization and disbelief: in small bits and as make-believe. Themes and story lines read as if lifted from the tablets of Šumer.

In one film, humans are enslaved by the minions of a tall living being who is considered divine. In another, aliens come to Earth to mine gold. In another, a superior human is created by gene splicing with an advanced alien humanoid. In one of the most famous of these films, the path of early homonin evolution is altered by an alien intervention. In some of these movies, beings with superior powers walk (and fly) amongst us.

One story element at a time, the cinema is introducing many of the events of our early times without overwhelming the audience, preparing the way for conscious engagement with The Mesopotamian Tale and with the hypotheses of this book. (See Appendix / The Movies.)

Through popular cinema genres the memory of our origin and early times is emerging from the Collective Unconscious. Popular culture may be better equipped than our scientists, scholars, philosophers, and priests to take the lead in developing a world view in which The Mesopotamian Tale is central.

---

[1] The literatures of the monotheisms, grounded in the Hebrew Bible, when telling of the fall of humanity from an original state of grace, speaks of that state as one of harmony, love, innocence, and balance with nature. What they are describing, through the fog of partial amnesia, is the existence of *Homo erectus*.

[2] The groups who left civilization and became the world's indigenous and pastoral peoples nurtured the *H. erectus* voice within themselves and made it central to their identities. Native cultures can teach the world's dominant cultures to honor that voice; some native people in North America are sharing their wisdom, with incredible generosity, intending to support the healing of our world.

³ In Saul Bellow's novel *Humboldt's Gift*, the title character, a poet, wrote of a perennial human belief that there's a lost home world and that we are castaways on an insufficiently civilized imitation of that world. Bellow had heard the voice of the *lofty ones* inside himself. In addition, he'd glimpsed the unusual aspects of our origin; he had Humboldt write that we are not entirely natural beings.

⁴ Another example of non-pathologic partitioned consciousness deserves mention. We've discussed how our brains integrate three neural structures developed at three points in evolution: reptilian, mammalian, and advanced primate. Within each of the three parts there's a system dedicated to assuring survival. Since we respond to imminent threat *like* a lizard, *like* a lion, and *like* a thinking person, often simultaneously, do we not have access to all three levels of consciousness?

⁵ As of this writing, the modality is making promising beginnings, especially in Australia and the United States.

⁶ The retreats for veterans and their families sponsored by several organizations in the United States are good examples.

⁷ Karen Armstrong claims in *Fields of Blood* that religion has been unfairly viewed as a force driving nations to war. She argues that the driving energy is political, and that the state uses religion for its purposes, but she fails to explain why religion lends itself so well to those purposes. In The Mesopotamian Tale we learn that the functions of kings and priests were paired under their ruling *gods* in a way that intertwined their authorities. Military success, political dominion, plunder, and religious subjugation, the four linked goals of Mesopotamian warfare, were powerful in combination. The formula has been repeated countless times throughout history, each of the components essential to the overall effort.

⁸ The term *superpower* is well-deserved. The United States Navy is more powerful than all the other navies on Earth combined. The nation's military budget is greater than the sum total of those of the ten next largest military establishments. War is a fixation in America. Tens of thousands are involved in battle reenactments annually. In one recreation of the Battle of Gettysburg, 20,000 men and women took part. It's estimated that 100,000 hobbyists fight battles with elaborate displays of miniature soldiers in their homes and at conventions. Books, movies, and games about war are enormously popular.

⁹ Another form of violence in America deserves mentioning, though it's an issue outside the scope of this book. No other country any longer practices the routine nonreligious circumcision of its newborn boys. Its incidence in the U.S.A. is less than it was, but it is still a common custom. To those who approach the matter objectively, it's evident that the procedure involves significant risks and losses, physiologically and psychologically, while providing no medical benefit whatsoever ... a socially sanctioned form of violence against the most vulnerable.

¹⁰ The religion based on the teachings of Jesus was thriving before His role as the son of God became doctrine. The Christian faith could continue to thrive if that

doctrine were widely rescinded and replaced with a theology emphasizing the manifestation of the Divine in all humans.

[11] The Quakers relate to God as Inner Light and oppose war on spiritual grounds. In a 1930 pamphlet, the Quaker philosopher Rufus Jones said, *[Quakers] have gone far towards taking [the principal teaching of Jesus] seriously, i.e., towards actually trying it. Insofar as they have accepted his ideals and appreciated his spirit, they have seen that war and the method of hate and vengeance are impossible ... A new way must be found ... We have seen ... peace-laden text[s] in the New Testament quoted from the pulpits of war defenders and interpreted so as to justify or hallow participation in the battle line ...*

[12] Aldous Huxley called the innate awareness of the One *the perennial philosophy*. His book by that title shows that many cultures have had such awareness.

[13] We've discussed the biblical revisions of Šumerian texts such as those dealing with: the way Earth was formed and humanity crafted; the interbreeding of humans and *anunnaki*; the global deluge; Marduk's attempt to build a launch platform in Babylon; and the destruction of the *cities of the plain* near the Dead Sea.

[14] Unorthodox scientists, also working within egoic limitations, may not be all that open-minded about The Mesopotamian Tale, either.

[15] Mainline religion and mainline science have tended to be covert allies. They have both rejected the idea that natural processes are manifestations in matter and energy of a real, intelligent, primordial Source that's more basic than any presently understood form of matter and energy. What they have both ignored has gone by many names: the One, Chi, Prana, Great Spirit, Vital Force, Animal Magnetism, Orgone, and Morphogenetic Field. Religious and scientific cultures tend to look away from primordial Source in opposite directions, religion, toward mystical concepts, and science, toward mechanistic ones. (See Appendix B.)

[16] The orbit and color of Planet X will match the orbit and color of the Planet of the Crossing in the Mesopotamian tablets. That will be impossible to ignore.

[17] Traumatization in the *anunnaki* is discussed in the next chapter. There are no indications that the *gods* ever aimed to harm the human race (except in the case of Enlil before the global flood). Our suffering in their wars appears to have been to them unavoidable collateral damage.

[18] Edward G. Burrows and Mike Wallace, using developments in the city of New York as examples, explain in *Gotham* that religious orthodoxy, which retreated further in the 1760's, always supported the social order; that pluralism, individualism, and anti-authoritarianism were habits of mind both religious and secular; and that the challenges to the religious establishment led to an organizational sophistication that facilitated the emergence of new political forms.

More Questions

Are humanity's current struggles really reenactments of conditions on Earth when it was ruled by the anunnaki?

Some are. As an example: the extreme disparities of wealth and power in many nations. The first humans dwelled at the bottom of the social order. All-powerful, alien lords possessing great wealth were at its top. It is painful to acknowledge that it is much the same today.

When humans and *anunnaki* interbred, elite humans were born, superior to the common people in abilities and power. Yet they weren't secure in their superiority. In the new elite the original lowly human self was submerged but not erased, making their elevated status tenuous.

In the chapter on the American Civil War we discussed how a tenuous sense of superiority led the Southern elite to violently confirm their role as slave-masters. In whites who were lower in the social order, the buried servant identity was closer to consciousness. They strengthened their sense of security in society through alliance with the elite.

The same sort of insecurity is a factor in American society today. It drives some extremely wealthy persons to seek ever-greater riches. They are compelled to distance their privileged real-world selves from the identity secretly carried inside, the one that's been basic to the human identity from the beginning: a powerless lowly being. Compelled by an unconscious need, they become socially toxic wealth addicts.

The same dynamic is at work when a more empowered majority group manifests hostility toward a less empowered minority. Sometimes the dominant group has a fear of their underlings that is absurd in its intensity. It's the repugnance they feel for their own repressed identity of lowly, powerless being that drives their attitudes and behavior, especially when they are facing any degree of actual challenge to their power and wealth. The dynamic can operate even when the suppressed group isn't a minority, e.g., the women of a patriarchal society.

Another reenactment of life under the *anunnaki* is the authoritarian nationalism that began surging in the second decade of the 21st century, in countries where democratic rule had been long established, as well as in ones where it only recently had been adopted. Several versions of power hungry demagoguery gained momentum. Populations were once again drawn to relive humanity's original attachment to domineering *lofty ones*, the tendency spreading from nation to nation by contagion.[1]

Could the creation of humans have been just a collateral event in the anunnaki's acquisition of gold? Similarly, could the development of an elite breed of humans have been a collateral event, the result of loneliness in anunnaki commoners? Or was something deeper being manifested that the lofty ones didn't reveal because they were unaware of it?[2]

Maybe something else was indeed going on. Consider the possibility that the need for gold on Nibiru, and the difficulty of obtaining it on Earth, gave the infinite intelligence of the universe a rare opportunity to know itself in a new way ... through hybridizing two homonin lines at vastly different stages of development. In *The Republic*, Plato presented the idea that humans were created by the gods because the task was too lowly to be performed by the One. Was Plato informed of the Mesopotamian accounts of the crafting of humanity by the *gods*? Was he intuiting that the One had assigned to the *anunnaki* the mechanics of making a new species?[3] If we were made not so much *by* the *anunnaki* as *through* them, in a trial of a new sort of evolution, a pair of complementary processes would seem to be involved, as if in a cosmic experiment. One of the processes is obvious: a young species has its development accelerated. The other is not so evident, as reflected in our next question.

The line of Homo erectus could clearly gain by being combined with the genes of a more developed humanoid, but what benefit would accrue to the line of the anunnaki through hybridization with a primitive hominin?

The culture of the *gods* existed under a golden globe for millions of years; the lives of *lofty ones* spanned tens of thousands of years. Could their culture have reached a plateau, and life on their world become dull? If so, *Homo erectus* could bring rejuvenation.

Nothing about the culture of the *gods* changed in their half a million years on Earth; at the end of their stay, everything was as it had been when it began. What they put energy into was self-glorification, destruction, and reconstruction. As a result, they got nowhere and produced nothing.

A static colony suggests a static home world.[4] While we can't really know what it means to live for thousands of years, it's likely that one of the things making us such seekers and explorers is our short lifespan. Let us imagine an experiment in evolution of the sort contemplated above coming to a successful end:

A primitive hominin species on Earth, at peace with itself and with its environment, is fused through biotechnology with a much older, more advanced one from another planet, a species that is static and warlike. The newly crafted creatures becomes violent as a result of what they inherit from, and how they are treated by, the extraterrestrial race. In time, the extraterrestrials depart. After centuries on their own, through suffering and turmoil, the new beings rid themselves of their violent tendencies and shake off the trauma, shame, and confusion they've been suffering. They develop a new way of life, combining the innocence of their less evolved parents with the abilities and knowledge of their far more evolved ones.

Do the Mesopotamian texts establish a clear time line for the crafting of Homo sapiens from Homo erectus?

They do not. There's an enormous span of time between An's granting permission to Enki and Ninmaḫ, and the date of the oldest fossils of *H. sapiens sapiens*. Perhaps fossils will one day fill the gap. Perhaps the creation epics, reporting on laboratory processes, condense what was a lengthy enterprise, one that involved *in vivo* steps in addition to the *in vitro* ones. Hopefully, geneticists will clarify the picture.

Could factors other than the ones we've discussed be contributing to the tragic human condition?

For some, the following is obvious; for others, it is speculative at best. The root *geo* comes from the Šumerian word for Earth, *ki*, meaning *carved out* or *hollowed*, referring to the worst of the impact wounds our planet endured, the collision with Nibiru's moon, whose scar is the Pacific basin. Our *hollowed out* world carries memories in its vibrational Field of the extreme violence it suffered. It has also received other massive impact wounds. The Field of our wounded species resonates with the Field of our wounded planet. That magnifies the effects of our suffering under the *anunnaki*. (Appendix B discusses the Field.)

Did our trauma come in part by direct transmission from the anunnaki?

Yes, trauma is contagious and the *lofty ones* were living in trauma. It seems they had no desire to live in peace. In not one of the texts unearthed from the ruins of Mesopotamia is there a word of opposition to war, a lamentation over bloodshed, or an expression of longing for a harmonious world. That's remarkable. In their endless warfare, the *lofty ones* felt at home, caught in reenactments of their traumatic experiences. Prime among those experiences was Nibiru's ejection from the inner Solar System, a terrifying ordeal. In addition, they must have been re-traumatized each time their planet passed through the Asteroid Belt.

Why did the Mesopotamian cultures write only on clay tablets?

The Egyptians, like the Šumerians, didn't have trees that could serve as a source paper, yet they made sheets to write on from the papyrus plant. The reeds in the marshes of southern Šumer might have been used in a similar way, and paper could have been made from fabric, yet for thousands of years the *gods* kept the scribes incising in clay. Could it be that the *lofty ones* meant to leave behind a trove of records in a medium resistant to deterioration ... so that humans could one day rediscover what they were fated to forget?

When is Nibiru going to return?

If the unexpected solar eclipse of the 6th century BCE was caused by Nibiru's passage, as seems likely, its last visit to the inner Solar System was in 556 BCE. The *šar*, the interval between its visits, is 3,600 years. If that has not changed, then Nibiru will return in the year 3044.

[1] At places in Isaiah Berlin's writings, he sounds as if he learned of the link between authoritarian rule and violence from the tablets about the wars of Mesopotamia. He observed in *The Crooked Timber of Humanity* that the methodically crafted machinery of balanced self-rule does not lend itself to *a passionate battle-cry to inspire men to sacrifice and martyrdom and heroic feats*. His words could easily serve to describe how the *lofty ones* used their followers' devotion to maintain power.

[2] The answers to this question and the next one are based in this author's personal point of view in matters spiritual and scientific.

[3] When the *gods* who crafted us were fading out, the Hebrews took them out of the creation narrative. The Mesopotamian Tale presents the crafting of humanity as the *anunnaki* had reported it to the scribes. Perhaps both Genesis and The Republic reflect awareness of the ultimate source of material reality, knowledge that the *lofty ones* were loathe to bestow on humanity.

[4] This is illustrated in human history. The remarkable pace of development in the European settlements in North America was merely an accelerated version of the robust currents of change already flowing in the Old World when migration to the New World began. The static Greek colonies around the Mediterranean, in contrast, reproduced the relatively stable cultures of their mother states.

May It Come to Pass

These are some of the principal lessons of The Mesopotamian Tale: How Earth achieved its present form and orbit. Who the lofty ones were and where they came from. What brought them here. What led them to fashion humankind. How the circumstances of our early existence led to our tragic condition. The deluge. The origin of civilization. The end of the rule of the gods.

May The Mesopotamian Tale be disseminated in every possible way: books, films, the arts, school curricula, the Internet, and social media.

•

May groups engaged in spiritual, humanistic, and environmental initiatives see that this book and others like it give support to their agendas ... and as a result fruitful liaisons develop.

•

May religious leaders who understand that the source of all that's manifest is not to be personified be available as guides for those wishing to emerge from mass amnesia.

•

May intentional communities form around this book's lessons, showing by example how a new world view can be put into practice.

•

May scientists and scholars be inspired to test the conclusions we've drawn from our study of the texts and carvings from Mesopotamia. May their academic departments support new interdisciplinary efforts. May seasoned researchers bravely put their reputations at risk. May courageous young scholars be willing to risk their futures for the sake of humanity's.

•

May *Evolution Diverted* motivate the healing disciplines to give the psychologies of trauma and affect the attention they deserve.

•

May astronomers soon discover Nibiru, The Planet of the Crossing.

Part Seven

Appendices

Appendix

The Psychologies of Trauma & Emotion

Ours is called a *triune* brain. It has three component divisions that developed in three distinct phases of evolution. In each of the components there's a system that specifically supports the survival of our species.

- As the reptiles emerged, the *threat response system* developed in their nervous systems, with the hard-wired reaction patterns of *fight*, *flight*, and *freeze*. The anatomic component of the brain governing those responses is the *brain stem*. The first portion of the brain to appear in the course of vertebrate evolution, it is referred to as the *reptilian brain*.

- A second protective system appeared with the mammals, the *emotions*, at the core of which are the *affects*, nine response patterns, also hard-wired. The anatomic portion of the human nervous system governing the experience and expression of emotion is the *limbic system*. This component of the brain, the next to evolve, is called the *mammalian brain*.

- Additional life-protective functions appeared with the advanced primates; they involve *thinking*. The nerve centers that govern our thinking are located in the *neo-cortex*. This third and final anatomic component of the brain to appear is referred to as the *human brain*.

This appendix serves as a primer for the first and second of these protective systems; they are not widely understood, and many practitioners are unfamiliar with the treatments that are rooted in their workings. We won't be discussing the third system because its scholarly and popular literatures are vast and because it's well known to psychotherapists.[1]

The Psychology of Trauma

The neural centers in the brain stem that regulate the body's organs, along with the nerves connecting the organs with those centers, constitute the Autonomic Nervous System, the ANS. It is organized in two divisions. For each organ, the two divisions of the ANS affect it in opposite ways. As an example, one branch expands the pupils and the other contracts them.

Normally, the ANS is a pendulum, its two divisions dominating neural output in alternation. The organs work around functional midlines: constantly sped up, then slowed down; tensed, then relaxed; infused with more blood, then with less. For instance, with mild activity a person's pulse may measure 74 beats per minute, yet it will be at that exact rate only a fraction of the time. Under the alternating influences of the two ANS branches, the pulse will constantly vary from, say, 70 to 78.

While the ANS exercises control over the physiologic functioning of the organs, it also supports complex behaviors that protect us and enhance our lives. One branch of the system offers protection by supporting aggression and defense. It sharpens alertness, speeds pulse, strengthens cardiac contractions, opens arteries to skeletal muscles, and slows functions that aren't critical at the moment, such as digestion. In this way, the ANS helps the animal to escape, protect itself, or attack.

The other ANS branch enhances our lives by assisting nutrition, group cohesion, and procreation. It generates a sense of ease, empowers digestive activity, slows the pulse, eases cardiac contractions, narrows the arteries to skeletal muscles, and contributes significantly to sexual arousal. The animal is then better enabled to eat, socialize, and mate.

When danger is detected, the alarm branch dominates, producing the *threat responses*, characterized by pounding heart, muscles readied for action, and more vigilance. These responses restrict cognitive functioning somewhat, so we can act reflexively, without having to think. There are three ANS alarm patterns. *Flight* gets us away from danger. *Fight* comes up if we can't or shouldn't escape. *Freeze* takes over if neither *flight* nor *fight* is possible, or if we are unable to choose between them.

In nature, after the flight, fight, or freeze response achieves its aim, the animal that has survived the threat returns to a neutral state by discharging any remaining ANS activation with physical activity, such as shaking or jumping. A human can complete his emergence from an activated state by trembling, screaming, crying, or shaking; by sitting quietly and tapping into inner resources; or by finding a compassionate listener. Social convention, though, often rules out these spontaneous restorative maneuvers, turning ANS activation, a set of transient responses that evolved to sustain life, into a static life-impairing condition.

This state of body and mind is called *trauma*. (We'll use the term to mean the state one can get stuck in after a critical event, rather than the overwhelming experience.) In trauma the alarm branch stays active, while the relaxation branch is suppressed. Trauma takes hold when (1) one of the threat responses is triggered by intense sensation and emotion and (2) social context or learned inhibition prevents the person from processing the resulting emotions, feelings, and images.

Overwhelming experiences are common: injuries, losses, assaults, natural disasters, accidents, and major illnesses. A series of lesser events can also become overwhelming, such as repeated emotional wounding. Since our culture often prevents a spontaneous release from ANS alarm, persisting trauma is not uncommon. Unless recovery from trauma is achieved, it becomes a fixed condition. When serious, trauma can produce nightmares, insomnia, flashbacks, irritability, explosiveness, hyper-vigilance, panics, depression, numbness, addictions, and suicide. When less severe, trauma is a component of many psychological conditions.[2]

We sometimes limit the devastation trauma causes through total or partial amnesia for the circumstances that produced it. Blocking an experience from consciousness makes it less likely that similar events later on will trigger trauma's physical and mental symptoms. The protection provided by amnesia is imperfect, yet as a coping strategy it has value.

We also deal with trauma by reenacting the initial overwhelming event, whether or not it's well remembered. The re-creation is an unconscious attempt to replace the outcome of the traumatizing event with a more successful one, the second time around. Often the strategy backfires, but when it works, ANS alarms are no longer so easily recruited. The potential benefit in re-living overwhelming events has been known to shamans for ages; in sacred ritual they lead the sufferer on a healing journey through his troubled past. Mental health clinicians are learning to use structured approaches to the same end. Here's how someone having a successful course of such treatment might summarize his experience:

I've learned that events that seriously upended me left me prone to having visceral nervous system reactions that strongly influence my feelings and actions. Through experiential therapies I've reduced the ease with which those responses are triggered. In EMDR sessions beliefs making me vulnerable to triggering are overwritten by more positive ones,[3] and in SE sessions my ANS regains its natural balancing oscillations, as memories are detoxified.[4]

The Mesopotamian Tale teaches that early in the life of civilized humankind, frequent warfare traumatized successive generations of warriors. The trauma state can diffuse outward from traumatized persons through direct contact. Soldiers with combat Post-Traumatic Stress Disorder, if they aren't helped to heal upon returning home, seed trauma into their communities. Throughout history trauma has spread from the warriors to their families, and from the families to the rest of society. An especially pernicious type of transmission takes place between generations, through parenting skills deformed by trauma. Trauma is now being spread through television and the Internet. News staffs, traumatized through repeated exposure to the worst manifestations of the human condition, spread trauma via contagion.

Civilized humankind is a traumatized super-organism, living in a shared state of ANS alarm. Our species' behavior closely parallels the symptoms of a person with PTSD. We're out of touch with ourselves, over-reactive, self-destructive, prone to addictions, challenged to learn from experience, and we fall repeatedly into violent reenactment. Clinicians are learning to treat trauma in individuals and small groups. Learning how to scale up their methods to bring healing to trauma at the mass level is one of the healing professions' pressing challenges ... and golden opportunities.

The Psychology of Emotion [5]

As mammals developed, they acquired emotions, internal states that provided their lives with additional protections and new enhancements. Emotions sharpen a mammal's understanding of its surroundings and of its own condition, and facilitate communication with others of its kind. When danger appears, emotions heighten the animal's awareness of what's occurring and assist in alerting its group. When external and internal conditions are sufficiently positive, emotions support the connectedness needed for nurture, cooperation, and procreation.

Mammalian emotions are more complex than reptilian ANS responses. At their physiologic core are nine neurologically patterned reflexes called *affects*. The affects are critically involved in the processing of sensation. The flood of inbound impulses in the sensory nerves, if unranked, would overwhelm the brain's ability to make use of them. Affects serve to augment the ones that are the most relevant at the moment. The circuitry of an affect elevates selected sensory information over the mass of inbound data, produces bodily feelings, and raises the highlighted information to the level of consciousness. A few examples:

The affect *fear* accentuates the glimpse of a tiger at the edge of a clearing. The affect *distress* augments the pain in one's foot as one steps on a thorn. The affect *surprise* facilitates rapid response as a car starts to skid. The affect *interest* focuses attention on an effective advertisement.[6]

The emotions' highest priority is alerting us to danger; accordingly, the majority of affects are unpleasant: *anger, fear, distress, shame, disgust* and *dissmell*.[7] There are two pleasant ones, *interest* and *enjoyment*; they're the cores of all positive emotion. One affect is neutral, *surprise*; it clears the consciousness, readying the brain to use other affects to deal with what just occurred. This is a small number of neural responses, given the wide range of emotions, yet the delineation has held up.[8]

An affect's constellation of behavior, facial expression, and posture is seen in its purest form in babies. As a child develops, emotional life gets more complex. Since an affect is energized in a social and physical context, associations form between the affect and aspects of the environment at the moment it was activated. Those associations coalesce into *scripts*, narratives and images that fuse a person's internal and external events. A script remains linked with the affect around which it was organized. Other scripts are likely to also be linked to that single affect.

An emotion combines three things: an affect, that by itself quickly passes; the affect's bodily feelings, that last a bit longer; and a script, a long-lasting mental construct. Scripts provide speedy evaluation of a situation; with scripts we needn't assess events afresh every time.[9]

Trouble follows when a script that's been recruited by an affect assigns a meaning to a situation that doesn't match reality. For example, if you say something with enthusiasm to your spouse who's standing at the kitchen sink, but you're not heard over the running water, you'll experience a brief, automatic, negative affect: shame. If that scene is similar to ones in which you as a child were repeatedly ignored by your mother, you are likely to recruit scripts formed in those early events, such as *she really doesn't care about me* or *I'm not important at all*. It will feel as if you've just had it demonstrated that the central person in your current life doesn't care about insignificant you. What would have been a quick, mildly unpleasant experience becomes a persisting painful emotion ... when the reality is that your mate simply couldn't hear you.

An affect can recruit more than one script. Also, a second affect may be activated along with the first; anger often arises when distress persists. One's internal response to external cirumstances, therefore, can be complex; an event that initially invokes just one affect can produce a complex mix of ideas and emotions.

Let's take as an example a child suffering pain for a prolonged period. He will create scripts that remain linked with the the affects of distress and fear. Later in life, when in pain, any of the scripts he formulated as a hurting child may be called forth. They may include:

> *The world is not safe. People aren't dependable. When I'm in trouble, I'm on my own. No one really cares about me. If I were loved, I'd be better cared for. I'll be punished for making a fuss. They don't believe me. I'll get even with them some day. Big boys don't cry. I'm not worthy of attention. I deserve this. I wish I were dead.*

By themselves, affects are short-lived. It would take just seconds for the brain to emerge from the sensations of an affect, were a script not recruited. If the looping of script and affect is not recognized for what it is, the resulting emotion persists. Cognition and sensation can then combine to create a mood, a state that has a life of its own.

To stay in the positive affects as much as possible, one must learn to ride the ascending energy of interest and the descending energy of enjoyment, in alternation. Those whose upbringing did not support enjoyment will overly depend on interest to sustain a positive state, leaving them prone to fall into negativity, since the rising energy profile of interest cannot be maintained indefinitely. (It can lead to manic states and to intellectualism.) Similarly, exclusive reliance on enjoyment, with its descending energy profile, is problematic. (It can lead to lassitude.) A balance of the two positive affects is much to be desired.

The positive affects are rewarding; the emotions they produce have momentum. We want them to continue, and therein lies a problem. The setting in which a positive affect is initiated may change, making the pleasant ideation and feelings no longer appropriate. If the change involves the onset of danger, were the positive affect to continue, there could be trouble. For the emotions to best serve the cause of survival, the positive affects need to be shut down quickly when no longer warranted. Tomkins concluded that the affect of shame evolved to do just that.

Shame is an auxiliary affect. It is activated only if a positive affect is suddenly impeded despite a wish for it to continue. Shame's aversive feelings end one's pleasant sensations, emotions, and cognitions … swiftly and decisively. By doing so, the affect shame (often in tandem with fear) allows a faster response to a potential threat. It can also aid in keeping life pleasant. By replacing good sensation with bad as well as it does, shame tends to motivate a person to quickly reestablish enjoyment or interest.[10]

When shame is experienced in more than minimal intensity, its feelings are markedly unpleasant. They include generalized malaise, a sense of collapsing or cringing, a deep stab of pain, a loss of muscle tone, and a dulling of vision. Still, the experience would be forgotten if felt only briefly. In animals and well cared for young children the state quickly fades because no script is involved. It's uncommon in our culture, though, for anyone past early childhood to have shame activated without a negative script being recruited. The emotions that can be generated when shame is activated are as varied as the types of scripts that the affect can be linked with: *embarrassed, ashamed, abandoned, rejected, hurt, lonely, exposed, disappointed, helpless, disrespected, rejected, weak, stupid, ugly, incompetent, unattractive, defective, humiliated, mortified.* Quite a list!

Affects are contagious, transmitted through eyes, facial expression, tone of voice, skin color, and the bio-energetic field. This has survival value when an external challenge is involved. But when shame is triggered by a negative script that's not fully justified by circumstances, it broadcasts an affective state unwarranted by reality. Society's woes are to a great extent the result of shared toxic scripts that cause shame to be magnified and disseminated through emotions and moods.

We have four basic maneuvers that provide some relief from shame-based emotions; they have become the sources of a plethora of troubles. These four escapes don't involve positive states; they just feel less bad than the shame emotions … at least at first. One of these is *withdrawal*, with which one disengages emotionally, and often physically, from the person or situation that led to the shame emotion. *I don't have to put up with this! I'm out of here.* Another is *avoidance*, a mental maneuver with which one evades the importance, or even the reality, of what just occurred. *Who cares? It was no big deal.* A third is *attack self*, through which one assigns blame to himself, possibly leading to depression. *I'm so stupid! I should know better by now.* The fourth is *attack other*, which involves many forms of hostility and violence. *That jerk cut me off! Those damned immigrants!*

These behaviors aren't effective escapes from shame. They are cul-de-sacs a person can enter when he can't identify, tolerate, and find a positive way beyond a shame emotion. Among the four maneuvers of *avoidance, withdrawal, attack self,* and *attack other,* people tend to favor one over the other three, though in an especially bad shame episode, one may cycle rapidly through all of them. Some people live in one defensive state all the time. Most of us know someone who constantly manifests *attack other*.

Shame emotions and the maneuvers that are used to evade them are the unrecognized generators of much human dysfunction. *Withdrawal* is a factor in dissociation and sociopathy. *Avoidance* is the at the root of addictions, all of which serve to blunt and evade shame emotions. *Attack other* is a factor in violence, racism, and road rage. *Attack self* is active in masochism and suicide. To more effectively deal with crime and psychopathology, authorities and clinicians need to learn how easily we experience the affect of shame and how automatically we maneuver to escape the shame emotions via the four defenses against them.

A fictional report from someone in affect-oriented therapy:

I thought I was living in reality. I've been learning, though, that my perceptions, feelings, and actions are often shaped by scripts formed so long ago that I can't remember ever having lived any differently. Scenarios from earlier in life intrude and distort the present to make it fit my unconscious expectations. What I think is objective truth has actually been filtered through internal stories. As I learn to step out of my scenarios and perceive the world as it is, I can find my way more easily, no longer bringing pain from long ago into the present. I'm learning this one old, hurtful story at a time. Also, I'm becoming progressively better able to identify my most common defense against shame-based emotions when that defense takes over … realizing that behind it lurks the affect shame, and that the shame results from the interruption of a good feeling I'd been having. That good experience was always forgotten when my defense took over. Now I pause (focusing on something of interest or a mantra that's soothing in order to reestablish positivity) and then search my memory for that recently lost positive experience. These are skills I'm developing with the help of my therapist and the support of my loving partner, both of whom have witnessed many episodes of shame-driven behavior.

● ● ●

To solidify our grasp of the way affects and scripts operate, let's apply what we've discussed to the development of the religions of the Greeks and the Hebrews after the departure of the *lofty ones*. To quickly review: impediments to *interest* and *enjoyment* can produce *shame* based emotions, and to defend against them we are habituated to engage one or more of four attitudes: *attack other, attack self, withdrawal,* and *avoidance*.

When Earth was ruled by the *anunnaki*, they were the source of *interest* and *enjoyment* for human worshippers, yet the realities of humanity's subjugation repeatedly interfered with those positive states, resulting in countless experiences of *shame*-based emotions. Scripts of weakness, inferiority, and dependence led to those emotions' becoming prevalent, helping to create the human condition. When the *gods* left, the positive feelings for them were interrupted in yet another way: a new category of *shame* emotions emerged, linked to scripts of abandonment.

To ward off *shame* emotions related to the abandonment by the *gods*, the Greeks turned primarily to the defense of *avoidance*. The religion they developed held that a pantheon continued to oversee humankind. It was simply that knowing about the dieties had become more challenging. In Mesopotamia the people had witnessed the *lofty ones* in magnificent ceremonies, and when the living *gods* were in residence, the populace knew that their *gods* were being privately tended to by priests and royals. After Šumer was devastated, almost all the *gods* disappeared; by the middle of the 6th century BCE, they were no more to be seen or heard.

The Greeks chose a path that involved avoiding and denying a painful, humiliating reality. The unstated assumption of their religion was that it was unnecessary for their deities to be physically present. With oracles, rituals, divination, heavenly signs, prayers, and sacrifices, contact with the gods would be maintained. From that point of view, humanity had suffered no loss; nothing bad had happened. *Avoidance* let Greeks hide from the *shame* of humanity's abandonment by the *lofty ones*.

The Hebrews, meanwhile, used a combination of *withdrawal* and *attack other* to ward off their *shame*-based feelings. First, *withdrawal*. It involved dismissing the *gods* as if they'd never been real. Priests and prophets preached that the *anunnaki* didn't matter. The Hebrew Bible documents a long, contorted process of pulling away from the *lofty ones* – an extended effort at *withdrawal* – anchored by the First Commandment. While its authors preserved much of the literary heritage of Mesopotamia, they did so in a way that removed the *anunnaki* from the narrative, leaving only traces we can discern by peering through the screen of Jewish theology.

A person in *withdrawal* from someone with whom they've had a shame-inducing interaction may think something like *I'm not going to have anything to do with him any more*. That's how the Jewish people were told to deal with the *gods* their ancestors had loved. *Forget about them*. The Jews also used exclusive practices, such as dietary laws, to enact *withdrawal* from the wider world, which was still devoted to those *gods*. Jewish *withdrawal* was most pronounced in the communities of ascetics, who lived apart from everyone who was to them insufficiently devoted to the One.

The Bible also resonates with the Jews' *attack other* behavior, their endless religious and military conflicts with the cultures with whom they came in contact, all of whom continued to worship the olden *gods*. The prime source of the hostility toward the Hebrews in antiquity, which even before the advent of Christianity and Islam was considerable, was the Jews' denigration of the religious beliefs of everyone else.

The *shame* produced by the abandonment of the *gods* quickly dissolved in those Jews who acknowledged Jesus as the Messiah; they could dispense with the defenses of *withdrawal* and *attack other*, just as Jesus's Greek followers could dispense with the defense of *avoidance*. No longer suffering a painful abandonment, they enjoyed a saving embrace.

As we mentioned, severe *shame* can recruit all four defensive attitudes in succession ... as it did for the Jews in the tumultuous times before and after the life of Jesus. We've just discussed their use of *withdrawal* and *attack other*. Now for the remaining two defenses. The Jewish ascetics utilized *attack self* with their restrictive lifestyles, the extreme sects even practicing self-flagellation. The worst manifestation of *attack self* occurred in the mass suicide of the Essenes, as Roman legions were about to deprive them of the *withdrawal* in which they were living at Masada. They couldn't imagine enduring the inescapable *shame* of slavery.

In the practices of the Sadducees on the Temple Mount, the defense of *avoidance* operated through their replication of Mesopotamian traditions. It looked for all the world as if nothing had changed. As in Šumer, there were hereditary priests supported by the populace, elaborate ceremonies, a sanctified precinct, and a rich treasury. The priests' practices paralleled what their nomadic ancestors had left behind in Mesopotamia. While their ideation separated them from the religion of the past (their God was the God of the Universe, not the *god* of the city, and was the only deity, not one of many), their actions replicated the form of Šumerian devotion to the olden *gods*. Much as the priests of Mesopotamia had roasted meats for their *gods* to eat, the priests of Jerusalem offered the smoke of *burnt sacrifices* to their God. The words were quite different; the aromas were much the same.

[1] How the three protective systems act in unison is poorly understood. Learning how they do that may greatly advance neuroscience and psychotherapy.

[2] The first clinician to incorporate the neurophysiology of trauma in diagnosis and treatment was Wilhelm Reich. In the 1930's he proposed that chronic over-activation of the alarm branch of the ANS occurs in many psychological conditions. The restoration of healthy ANS alternation was both a goal and an objective measure of healing in the body-oriented psychotherapy he pioneered.

[3] Francine Shapiro's Eye Movement Desensitization/Reprocessing method.

[4] Peter Levine's Somatic Experiencing method.

[5] Scientists and clinicians have been advancing the understanding of emotion ever since Charles Darwin's publication of *The Expression of the Emotions in Man and Animals* in 1872. Our discussion is primarily informed by the mid-20th century work of Silvan Tomkins, PhD, who developed Affect Script Psychology.

[6] The affect of interest allows you, while reading this note, to focus attention on its content, over the plethora of concurrent stimuli flowing into your brain.

[7] The affect *shame* will soon be discussed. To avoid confusion at this point: *shame* designates a specific neurophysiologic response, an affect, not the state of being ashamed about something, one of many emotions that derive from the affect. *Dissmell* is to aroma and inhalation as *disgust* is to taste and ingestion.

[8] Since affects can be energized at different levels of intensity, Silvan Tomkins said it would be more accurate to refer to them in a way that reflects their range from low to high, that is: anger/rage, fear/terror, distress/anguish, shame/humiliation, interest/excitement, enjoyment/joy, and surprise/startle. For the sake of simplicity we'll refer to each affect with just the first word of each of the pairs.

[9] The affects are simple biological phenomena. The emotions are, in addition, biographical ones, involving scripts, time-bound cognitions that bring the past into the present. Psychotherapy focusing primarily on scripts can be effective for certain conditions. Cognitive Behavioral Therapy, Rational Emotive Therapy, and Eye Movement Desensitization/Reprocessing are among the clinical approaches that involve the methodical identification and management of scripts.

[10] Shame stalks love. In a couple's life together there are inevitable sudden interruptions to enjoying the feeling of connectedness. The greater the level of intimacy in the relationship, the more intense the shame caused when it's impeded. The degree of success a couple has in learning to master shame (and the defenses against it) largely determines the fate of their relationship.

Appendix

The Field

Around the turn of the 20th century the vitalists were finally defeated. They were the scientists who were convinced of the existence an infinitely fine medium, motionless, mass-free, filling all space and permeating all matter ... the specific life force. They called it the Ether. They were outmaneuvered by the mechanists, the scientists who said that no such life force or medium exists, and that interstellar space is absolutely void except for sparse atoms. The two opposing ways of understanding physical and biological reality can be traced back to the pre-Socratic philosophers of Greece. Victory was achieved by informal majority vote, not fact.

The results of late 19th century experiments with light were said to have proved that there is no Ether. The arguments for and against Ether's existence are outside this book's scope, yet the fact is that an experimental demonstration of its nonexistence never took place; those who ran the experiments never claimed their findings disproved Ether's existence.[1]

The continuum that western physics called the Ether was central to humanity's early sciences. In antiquity it was conceptualized as Prana in India, as Qi in China, and as Pneuma in Greece. More recently it's been called Animal Magnetism, Vital Spirit, Od, Morphogenetic Field, Orgone, and Field of Life. We will refer to it as the Field. It is manifest in a remarkably wide range of well-documented phenomena.[2]

Healing with Prayer Praying can speed recovery from illness even across long distances and without the patient knowing of the effort.

Energy Healing Hands-on methods involving focused intention can relieve pain and significantly alter the course of an illness.

Shamanic Healing Appealing to ancestral and communal spirits in ritual can resolve physical and mental conditions, both acute and chronic.

Psycho-kinesis Small objects can be moved and shaped by intention.

Electronic Anomalies Computer applications that generate strings of random digits can be influenced by thought to increase or decrease how often a selected digit appears.

Biological Anomalies The electrical resistance along the surface of a leaf can be affected by the thoughts of a person who is near the plant.

Clairvoyance People can know about distant events in real time.

Precognition Persons can have knowledge of events yet to occur.

Localization Dowsers can find missing objects (and people) on maps. Pets can cross expanses of unfamiliar terrain to reach their owners.

Extra-sensory Perception People can identify things blocked from view and sense when someone out of sight is looking at them.

Animal Communication Slime molds, masses of thousands of undifferentiated cells, efficiently navigate mazes in search of food. Large flocks of birds and schools of fish move as a single organism, with coordination too perfect to be provided by sensory information alone.

The conclusions of those who have studied the Field include the following. It provides the most fundamental means of communication between organisms. Transmission through the Field is instantaneous. Animals sense the Field in parallel with bodily sensation; this accounts for some of the speed and accuracy of the specific senses. The Field unites individual human minds within the species' collective mind, bringing all of us into connection. Since lifetimes overlap, the Field contains a record of all that humanity has experienced. Carl Jung called this aspect of the Field the *collective unconscious*, a phenomenon supporting this book's argument.

We've discussed how the human condition is perpetuated because the trauma, shame, and confusion of humanity's life under the *anunnaki* are transmitted between persons, groups, and generations. It's likely that our verbal and nonverbal means of transmission, well-studied by psychologist, are supplemented by transmission through the Field, a function that conventional psychology remains stubbornly unaware of.

The Field has different names, in keeping with its different aspects: in physics, the *ether*; in psychology, the *collective unconscious* and *ESP*; in biology, *animal magnetism* and *morphogenetic field*; in Eastern traditions, *qi* and *prana*; in philosophy, *the One*; and in religion, *holy spirit*, *Source*, and *God*. Grasping the unity behind these several aspects can be challenging.

In addition, there's an aspect of the Field about which we know practically nothing: its capacity to produce electrical and mechanical energy.[3] Two geniuses of the 20th century, Nikola Tesla and Wilhelm Reich, independently pursued the application of this capacity. If we tentatively assume that the Field can actually serve as a power source, we may be able to glimpse a solution to a newly discovered puzzle.

The *gods'* principal mines and smelters were in southern Africa; their petroleum resources were far away, in Šumer. The Mesopotamian tablets

7.2 The Field

don't reveal how energy was provided for their African enterprise. The puzzling findings just mentioned are located in Botswana, Zimbabwe, and the Republic of South Africa: ruins of fieldstone structures covering thousands of square miles. Archaeologists hypothesize that they are the remains of houses, corrals, and roads. That idea doesn't hold up. But what about a possible relationship to *Anunnaki* industry?

The structures are of two kinds. One consists of circles defined by low stone walls. The circles are arranged together, some bunched, some nested. Except where they have collapsed, the circles are complete and lack the openings that would have been needed for the movement in and out of people and livestock. Clearly, they could not have been enclosures meant to contain or shelter people or beasts

Furthermore, the territory they cover is vast; one system is nearly as big as Los Angeles. If the circles were enclosures serving as houses and corrals, the population would have been immense ... yet these enclosures covered so much of the area over which they are spread, there wouldn't have been sufficient land left over to produce the needed food.

The second type of fieldstone structure consists of parallel walls, many forming branching networks. Some of them connect to the round enclosures. These walls are 4 to 9 feet high, containing passages 6 to 8 feet wide. These can't be roads. Their walls are too close together and some of them go straight up slopes that are too steep for animals drawing carts. They are more like channels than roads. (Figures 7.2.1 & 7.2.2)

Admittedly, it would be highly speculative to extrapolate from what little we know of the work of Tesla and Reich regarding the Field as a practical energy source, and posit an industrial function for these structures. Yet it would not be an illogical theory. Perhaps we are seeing the ruins of a system that somehow used stone circles to gather energy from the Field of the planet and then caused the energy to flow to the *gods'* smelters through stone-walled troughs. Such a process is well beyond our present physics, but not beyond our imagining.

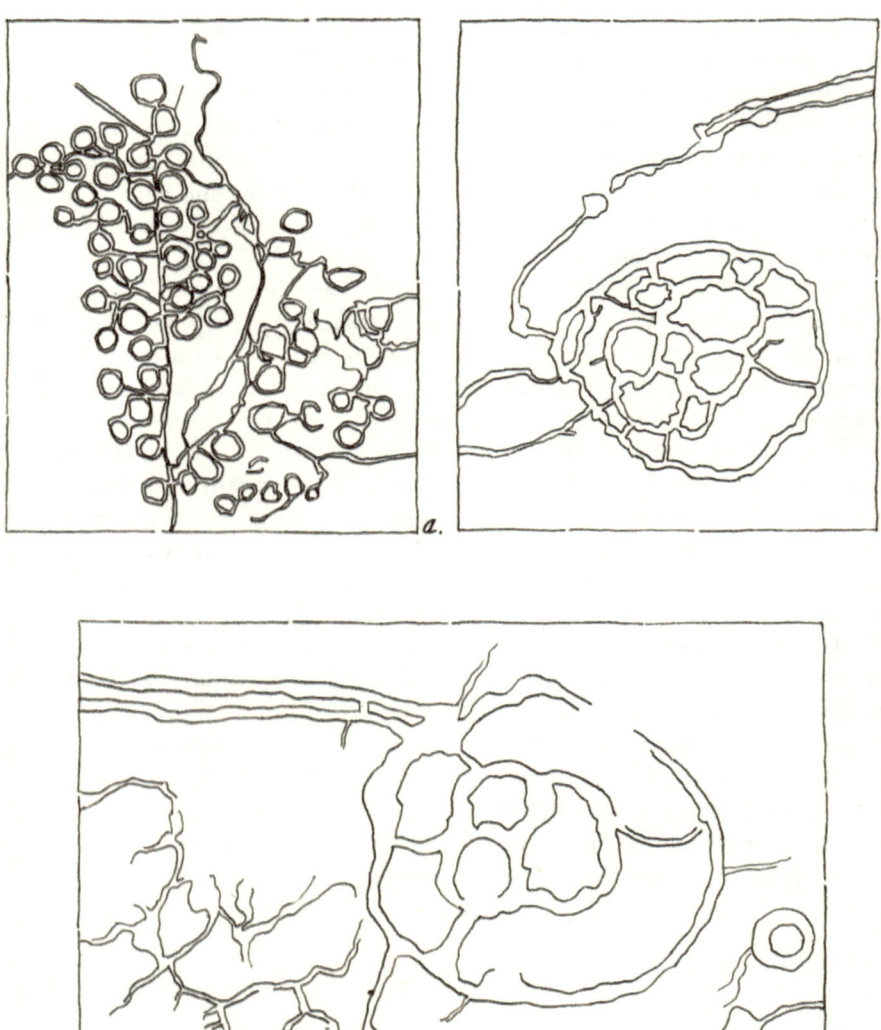

Figure 7.2.1. The ruins of stone enclosures and channels in southern Africa. From aerial photographs taken by Michael Tellinger.

7.2 The Field

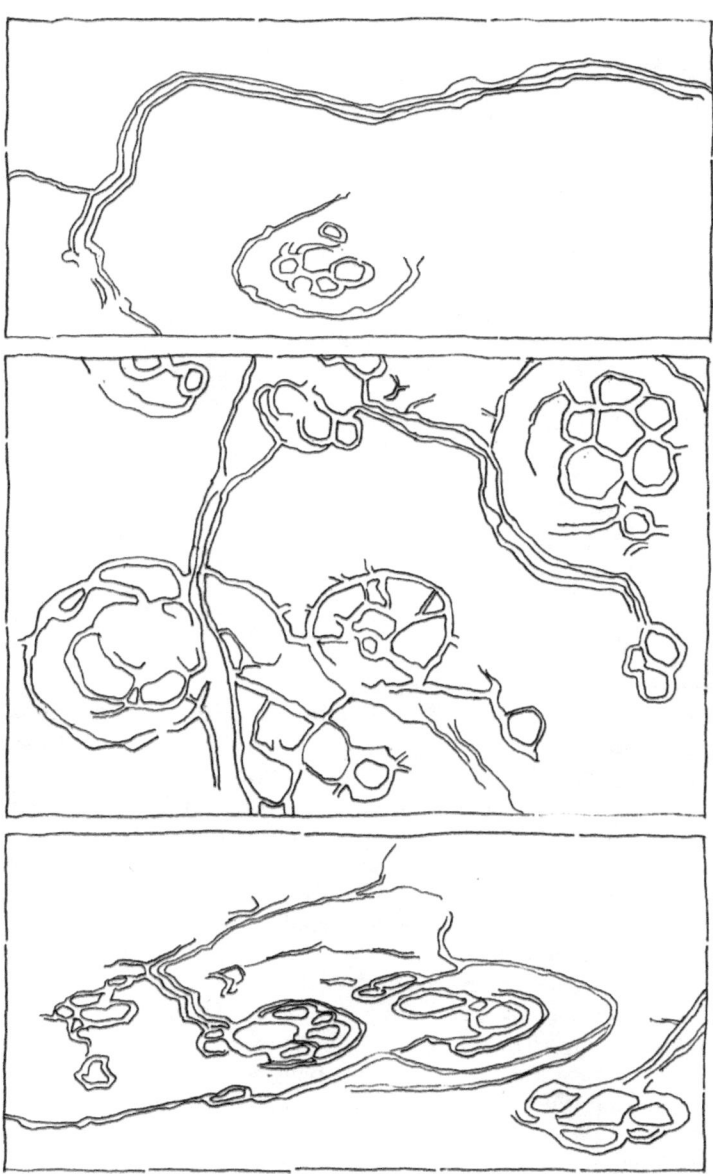

Figure 7.2.2. Other views of the enclosures and channels. How could these have been roadways, houses, or corrals?

[1] The experiments were performed in 1887 by Michelson and Morley, a physicist and a chemist. Not only did their studies leave open the question of the existence of the Ether, 20 years of experiments by the esteemed physicist Dayton Miller, published through the mid 1930's in peer-reviewed journals, some in collaboration with Morley, consistently yielded positive results for the existence of the Ether. Miller's studies were so convincing that Albert Einstein wrote in private letters that if Miller's work were free of fundamental errors, his own theories of Relativity would collapse. Yet the earlier studies, less precise and elegant than Miller's, were misrepresented in later journal articles by physicists intent on proving that the space of the Universe is empty and dead. The issue has implications for cosmology. The supposed non-existence of the Ether leads directly to the Big Bang Theory. Were mainstream science to accept the existence of the primordial cosmic medium, the Big Bang would be discarded, along with another counterintuitive idea, that the cosmos contains vast quantities of undetected *dark matter*. This will take time, though. When a band of prominent astronomers offered alternatives to the Big Bang, their arguments were dismissed.

[2] These phenomena are routinely dismissed by pseudo-rational debunkers.

[3] Some advanced Eastern martial arts practitioners claim that this aspect of the Field has a use in combat ... a use that's caricatured in the *Star Wars* films.

Appendix

Endless Conflict

Between the completion of Šumer's post-deluge rebuilding and the catastrophe of the Sinai war, there was a span of over three millennia. It was a time during which *gods* and kings and the cities they ruled repeatedly rose and fell, one of shifting alliances, intrigues, and wars. Destruction and reconstruction cycled, over and over. This appendix covers the first two of those millennia ... *gods* fighting each other for the acquisition of power, wealth, and prestige at a cost beyond measure in human suffering.

Standard histories of this period are in agreement with the content of this appendix, except in one regard. In those accounts the kings and priests maneuvered for power and riches using mythical deities to validate their rule over gullible populations. That's understandable. Until now, this period has been seen through the lens of events that had their start after the *lofty ones* were gone: civic and religious authorities using unseen gods to help maintain obedience and cohesion and to obscure their own selfish purposes. Scholars have as yet no way of knowing that in the period we are considering the *gods* were totally real and were firmly in charge. As far as we can tell the events that follow fall between 3,760 BCE and 2,024 BCE.[1] (See pp. 8 & 9 for geography and p. 24 for genealogy.)

• As the major settlements are rebuilt, Kiš is made Šumer's first capital.[2]

• Babylon, *Babilli, Gateway of the Lofty Ones*, is the next city to dominate all the others. Marduk, Enki's oldest son, claims the right to rule it. He leaves Egypt, where he is known as Ra, and launches a coup in Babylon c. 3,500 BCE. Without authorization, he prepares to build an elevated platform in the city with which to launch spacecraft. For that effrontery, he is expelled from Mesopotamia and returns to Egypt.[3]

• In Egypt, Marduk encounters his younger brother Dumuzi, whose marriage to Inanna Marduk had opposed, because it linked his father's clan with that of Enlil, Inanna's grandfather. The tension between these two sons of Enki ignites when Inanna campaigns for admission to the pantheon of the twelve high *gods*. War breaks out between their armies.

• A conflict with Marduk causes Ningišzidda, another of his five brothers, to leave his African domain.[4] (There is evidence that he settled in Mexico.)

• Dumuzi wants to have a son who'd inherit his rank and wealth, but his marriage to Inanna has failed to produce an heir. Under the *anunnaki* rules of marriage and inheritance, he could accomplish his wish by fathering a son with his wife's sister. When his sister-in-law refuses his advances, he forces himself on her ... with Inanna's foreknowledge.

• Dumuzi is seized; he is to be put on trial. He escapes with the aid of Inanna's twin brother, Šamaš. Dumuzi's rape of his sister-in-law gives Marduk an excuse to move against him once more. Again Dumuzi is seized; again he escapes. In the ensuing melee, he is killed, though his death was not intended. Inanna vows revenge against Marduk.[5]

• Marduk goes into hiding. He is caught. Inanna attacks the structure in which Marduk is confined, intending to kill him. (Texts hint that his prison is the Great Pyramid of Giza.) Inanna's great-grandfather, king of Nibiru, convinces Inanna to desist and to have Marduk put on trial.

• Marduk is sentenced to remain entrapped ... so that he'd eventually die. His son arrives and appeals to Inanna. Dumuzi's killer is found. Ninmaḫ negotiates an agreement: Nergal replaces Marduk as Enki's rightful heir and Marduk accepts another exile. His condition for agreeing is that his precinct in Babylon remain hallowed ground.[6]

• Inanna, now widowed, journeys to Africa, intending to use the *anunnaki* code of inheritance much as her late husband tried to do; she plans to conceive an heir for Dumuzi's rank and wealth by union with his brother Nergal. This enrages her sister Ereškigal, Nergal's wife. She has Inanna seized and executed. Her body is hung on a stake. To bring her back to life Enki sends android emissaries who are immune to the death rays guarding her body. They bring Inanna to Enki's residence in Eridu.

• Inanna appeals to An and is proclaimed *goddess* of the third region, which includes the valley of the Indus with its main city, Aratta. She is also given authority in the new capital of Šumer, Uruk, where a shrine to An is built. Her travels between the two capitals provoke disputes over issues that include her sexual life.[7] (Figures 7.3.1 through 7.3.4)

• Replacing Ninmaḫ, Inanna is brought into the pantheon of twelve. She is assigned Ninmaḫ's zodiacal sign, Virgo, and Ninmaḫ's planet, Venus. The rituals of Inanna's worship in Uruk include male temple geishas and an annual sacred union of the king with the *goddess*.

• Inanna charms Enki into giving her the keys to several processes and fields of learning. He comes to his senses and retrieves them.

• Uruk falls; Ur becomes the new capital. In a period of rapid transfers of power, kingship switches among Ur, Kiš, Uruk, and five other cities. Enlil expresses disgust with the doings of *gods* and humans.

7.3 Endless Conflict

Figure 7.3.1. A cylinder seal showing Inanna lifting her skirt, a gesture of hers that appears many times.

Figure 7.3.2. A cylinder seal illustrating an episode in the Epic of Gilgameš in which Inanna attempts to seduce the hero. He is seeking the *long life* of the *lofty ones*, and complains that she'd not won it for any of her human lovers over the ages.

Figure 7.3.3. Inanna — on a large clay plaque. No image from Mesopotamia has been found with one of the *lofty ones* less than fully clothed — other than Inanna. Here she has a bird's wings and feet, befitting her renown as a pilot. The piece conveys a fusion of power and eroticism ... as the tablets say Inanna did in life.

Figure 7.3.4. Inanna's sexuality explicit in a stone carving.

- Inanna falls in love with a human and with his help ends the turmoil in Šumer; together they build the first Mesopotamian empire, Akkad. He reigns as Šarrukin (Sargon) the Great, starting c. 2,400 BCE. Their realm will eventually stretch from the Mediterranean to the far shore of the Persian Gulf. Its capital, Akkad, is an exalted city. Šarrukin is given many honorific titles. (Figure 7.3.5) The *Era of Ištar*, Inanna's Akkadian name, is proclaimed. She appoints her daughter high priestess in Ur.[8]

7.3 Endless Conflict

Figure 7.3.5. Sarrukin the Great. A carved portrait from Akkadia.

- Šarrukin conquers the *first region* of the *gods*, the domain of the three sons of Enlil, but avoids Babylon, city of Marduk, which lies within it. He respects the neutrality of the *fourth region*, Tilmun, in the Sinai.

- Šarrukin enters Babylon to gather soil from Marduk's sacred precinct, to use in building a launch platform outside Akkad. Marduk is enraged by the intrusion and sacrilege and by Inanna's plan to increase her power with a spaceport. He returns from Egypt and makes war on their empire. Some of its cities rebel. Inanna enters the fight; much blood is shed. Other *gods* join her. They are unable to defeat Marduk. Šarrukin dies.

- The *gods* hope Nergal can persuade his brother Marduk to give up his assault on Akkad. He journeys from Africa and promises Marduk that if he returns to Egypt, he'll protect his interests in Babylon, where devices are located that control the region's vital functions, such as water distribution. Marduk's return to Egypt would enable him to obtain certain objects of power, so he accepts Nergal's offer. But Nergal doesn't live up to his pledge; the control systems are neglected and havoc results. The nobles, enraged, blame Marduk. They destroy his palace in Babylon.

- Nergal and Inanna, granddaughter of Enlil, form an alliance, creating a new link between their two clans. Inanna reinvigorates her rule in Akkad. Leading brutal battles with the assistance of Naram-Sin, grandson of Šarrukin, she re-expands the Akkadian empire. (Figure 7.3.6) Hers is not the usual sort of campaign, one *god* aiming to conquer the city of another. Inanna now aims to rule over all the *gods*. She seizes the spaceport in Lebanon and conquers cities in Canaan, including Jerusalem (with its spaceflight center) and Jericho (dedicated to her father, Nannar).

Figure 7.3.6. A stone plaque with Inanna presenting Naram-Sin with a victory wreath. She is sometimes, as here, depicted carrying weapons on her back.

- With Nergal's support, Inanna invades Egypt, passing through Tilmun, violating its neutrality. In keeping with Inanna's grandiosity, Naram-Sin, proclaims himself *King of the Four Regions*. He loots and defiles Enlil's holy precinct in Nippur. During this campaign Innana's power and influence grow immense. (Figure 7.3.7) In a text exalting her:

With An she takes her seat upon the great throne
With Enlil she determines the fates in her land

- Having watched the progress of Inanna's ambition with dismay, the high *gods* call a council and decree her arrest. They strip Inanna's temple in Akkad of her symbols and weapons. She evades capture and hides for seven years, most likely under the protection of Nergal, ally and brother in law.

Figure 7.3.7. Inanna receiving gifts. No other goddess was ever depicted wielding such authority. In the sky, her celestial symbol and her father's.

7.3 Endless Conflict

- Inanna resumes her efforts to overthrow the existing order. She aims to become the *queen of queens*. She seizes the *House of An* in Uruk and destroys the symbols of her great-grandfather's authority. She desecrates the sanctuary of Enlil, her grandfather, in Nippur. Enlil and Ninurta gather an army in the mountains and counterattack. They flatten the center of Inanna's worship and power, Akkad, and lay a curse on it. Inanna is sheltered in Ur by her parents Nannar and Ningal.[9]

- Enlil's forces overrun the Akkadian empire, despoiling all its cities except Lagaš and Nippur. He proclaims Ninurta as his successor and grants him rule over Lagaš, c. 2,200 BCE. Ninurta's rule is graced by his widely adored wife Bau. At the decree of the council of great *gods*, the king, Gudea, builds the Girsu, an elaborate temple, to mark Ninurta's ascension. This project deepens a sibling rift since Ningišzidda, son of Enki and rival of Marduk, directs its construction. Lagaš has long been a stable and important city. In this period, it develops further, with new codes of justice and morals, enhanced military skills, a more delicate sculptural style, and a further refinement of Šumer's language and script.[10] Ninurta gains the allegiance of the rugged tribes in the mountains northeast of Lagaš and provides them with horses for battle, consolidating the power of his clan.

- Inanna, taking advantage of Ninurta's absence, returns to Uruk and seizes power. At her direction, the king of the city takes up a weapon that was not to be touched without permission having been granted by the circle of the high *gods* ... and falls dead. Inanna's coup fails.

- Enlil issues a major proclamation. Nannar, born on Earth, not Ninurta, born on Nibiru, is to have the right of succession. In a time when the power of the *gods* over their human subjects is no longer absolute, Enlil's decree may have been meant to counter the allegiance that both Marduk and his son Nabu gained among the population by taking human wives. Nannar makes Ur the capital of Šumer c. 2,100 BCE. The city will dominate Šumer's final period of glory. Its territories grow grain for all of Mesopotamia; its workshops turn out goods famed throughout the Middle East. On Enlil's order Ur-Nammu, the city's king, issues a new legal code, with the intention of initiating a moral revival. Ur's infrastructure, cultural life, trade, and alliances expand greatly.[11]

- Nannar repairs the damage in Nippur remaining from Inanna's attack. His parents, Enlil and Ninlil, return there to live. Nannar restores the edifices of the *gods* in other cities, too. Enlil gives Ur-Nammu, ruler of Ur, a powerful weapon and orders him to wage war on cities in the western portion of the realm, which, as a result of Nabu's diplomacy, have become allied under Marduk. Ur-nammu is killed in a chariot accident. The vessel returning his body to Ur sinks in a storm. Disillusioned, the people feel betrayed. If their great *gods* are all-powerful, how can they allow such things to happen? The authority of the *lofty ones* continues to fade.

• Šulgi, Ur-Nammu's son, ascends to the throne of Ur. He builds a shrine for Ninurta in Nippur. He embarks on a long mission, reaching the southern Sinai, building altars and roads, including a route along the western shore of the Gulf of Aqaba. He returns to Ur, where he succumbs to Inanna's charms. He installs foreign troops in Larsa. Five Canaanite cities loyal to Marduk (including Sodom and Gomorrah) make a thrust that takes them close to the edge of Tilmun c. 2,050 BCE. On orders from Nannar, Šulgi sends mercenaries to suppress the five cities. He also builds a wall at the western edge of Šumer as protection against forces loyal to Marduk. For his licentious existence in Ur and for abandoning the lands west of his wall, An and Enlil decree his death.

• Šulgi is succeeded by his son Amar-Sin, who establishes a residence in Eridu, the original settlement at the head of the Persian Gulf.

• After twenty-four years in Egypt, Marduk enters Harran, the western trading outpost of Ur, gaining an important base. He sends Nabu as his emissary to several Šumerian cities. He wages war on Enlil, sacking his precinct in Nippur. Nabu travels to Canaan, seeking adherents.

• War breaks out c. 2,040 BCE between the five Canaanite kings loyal to Marduk and four Šumerian kings loyal to Enlil and to Inanna, whose ambitions have ended. Marduk, as before, aims to conquer the central part of the Sinai peninsula, *Elparan, Place Glorified by the Gods*, and with it the Tilmun spaceport. His forces are stopped short of their goal. In a punitive response, Nabu's city, Borsippa, south of Babylon, is destroyed. This military campaign was the prelude to the disastrous Sinai war discussed in Chapter 3.9, Conflict and Catastrophe.

• Amar-Sin, leader of the allied kings of Šumer, sets sail from Eridu, intending to round the Arabian peninsula and secure Tilmun. He is bitten by a scorpion and dies. His brother Šu-Sin ascends the throne. He rebuilds Enlil's precinct in Nippur. Enlil and Ninlil return to dwell there; as reward, Ninlil gives Šu-Sin a powerful weapon. He constructs a magnificent touring boat for the couple, but an effigy is found onboard with an evil inscription, and they depart. Forces loyal to Marduk besiege several Šumerian cities. Šu-Sin lengthens the defensive wall in the west.

• Šu-Sin's successor, his brother Ibbi-Sin, withdraws from the western portions of Enlil's domain under continued military pressure from Marduk. He bolsters the defenses of Ur and Nippur. Šu-Sin appoints

7.3 Endless Conflict

himself the high priest of Inanna in Uruk and Ur. Omens of doom and destruction are cited frequently, including a lunar eclipse in 2,031 BCE. Enlil's domain is weakening. Marduk's forces break through the western wall and the cities immediately east of it come under his control. With these defeats, Nannar is discredited in the eyes of the people.

• Marduk's further advance eastward is brutal. Temples are defiled, including even Enlil's *Lofty House* in Nippur. Ninurta accuses Marduk of that high crime. Enlil returns in a rage, calls a council, and demands punishment for Marduk. The culprit actually is Marduk's brother and enemy Nergal, who had formed an alliance with Enlil's son Ninurta. Enki stands up for his firstborn son and makes a claim, based in astrology, that the time has come for Marduk to ascend to ultimate power on Earth.[12]

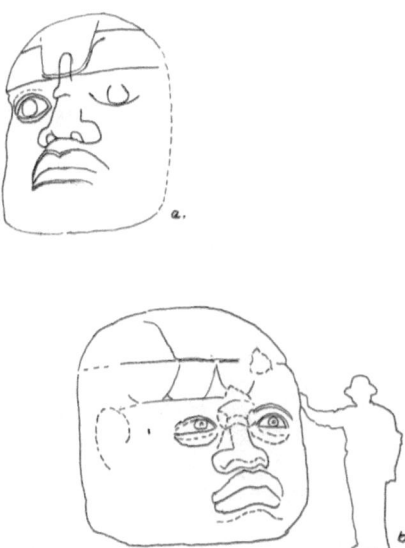

Figure 7.3.8. Giant Olmec heads.

¹ The age from the crafting of *H. sapiens* to the deluge is far longer than the period covered in this appendix. The flood having destroyed much of Mesopotamia, that age is not so well documented, yet the surviving texts reveal that it was much the same as this one. That means that the soil of Mesopotamia has been soaked in human blood for tens of thousands of years. Small wonder that it still is.

² The populations have now largely recovered from the deluge; there are hundreds of thousands of people in Šumer. Some of the cities contain 10,000 souls.

³ Marduk's grandiose plan in *Babilli* is the source of the *Tower of Babel* tale in the Hebrew Bible. Like Marduk's platform, it was built in order to reach the heavens and punishment was administered for the hubris that drove the project.

⁴ There's textual evidence that Ningišzidda was worshipped as a *god* in Mexico. The huge stone heads carved by the Olmecs have prominent African features. They well may be depicting this *lofty one's* retinue. (See Figure 7.3.8)

⁵ The tale of the murdered *god* and his lamenting widow became a popular theme in the Middle East, retold in many versions over the centuries.

⁶ This proclamation deprives Marduk, the firstborn son, of his claim to primacy when his father's rights are reassigned. In Marduk's view, his father, also the firstborn son, was wronged by being denied primacy in the rule of Earth, and now he's being similarly mistreated. The rivalry between Nergal and Marduk is a factor in the disastrous attack on the Sinai spaceport and the five cities.

⁷ The kings of the two cities argue over who would enjoy her favors. In one text the king of Uruk taunts the king of Aratta on the subject. No tablets have survived that speak of Inanna's thousand-year rule in the third region of the *lofty ones*; the Vedas, however, tell of land and air battles between divinities during this period, and a catastrophic ending for the culture is consistent with archaeological findings.

⁸ In the Akkadian language, *akkad* means *united*. Akkad was the first regime to include several widely separated states. The epithet came to designate the empire, as *United States of America*, at first a descriptive phrase, became a compound noun.

⁹ Akkad, capital of the world's first empire, was the only major city that was destroyed but never rebuilt. It has not yet been located by archaeologists.

¹⁰ During the rule of the king Uruinimgina, known as a social reformer, the word for freedom, *amargi*, appears in a political context for the first time.

¹¹ The name Ur, originally meaning *settled place*, came to signify not just one magnificent, rich, and productive center of civilization, but the very concept of city. It is contained in the Šumerian name for Jerusalem, *Ur-Šulim, city of the supreme place*, and is the ultimate source of *urban*.

¹² This pivotal moment in history coincides with the start of the narrative that begins on page 120.

Appendix

The Movies

It seems as if The Mesopotamian Tale has been appearing, in bits and pieces, in the themes and story lines of science fiction and fantasy movies. The Collective Unconscious appears to have found in the cinema a means of reconnecting us with our buried memories. We'll first discuss several film categories and then specific films. The categories ...

Superheroes Superheroes have extraordinary powers and distinctive garb, as did the *lofty ones*; through them we recall the *gods* who once lived among us.[1] Superheroes have cloaking identities as ordinary humans; this is a subtle reminder that we contain elements of the *gods* within our selves.

Invasion When aliens arrive on Earth to eliminate humanity, humans are threatened in a fictional version of what actually took place, for the *anunnaki* did indirectly bring about the end of the planet's most advanced hominin, *H. erectus*, by crafting the vastly superior *H. sapiens*.

Disaster When our planet is threatened by an approaching celestial body, we see ourselves endangered by a movie recreation of the close approach of Nibiru that led to the global deluge. When a force of nature runs amok in a disaster movie, we watch a recasting of the deluge itself.

Immortality Movies in which a character endowed with immortality doesn't age, or magically recovers from what should be a mortal wound, tap into our buried memories of the *long life* of the *anunnaki*.

Possession Alien minds function within human bodies in *Invasion of the Body Snatchers*, *K-Pax*, *Under the Skin*, and *The Host*. When we came into being, an *anunnaki* consciousness became a component of our composite human self, as discussed on pages 275-277.

Next, the films ...

• In *The Day the Earth Stood Still* (1951, remade in 2008) an advanced alien, revolted by our way of life, comes to wipe us out. Enlil, with similar feelings, meant to do the same. In the original film, a boy's compassion leads the agent of doom to relent; this recalls the role of Zisudra's virtue and Enlil's change of attitude toward humanity. In the remake, plant and animal specimens are collected as the cataclysm approaches, recalling Ziusudra's bringing *seeds of life* aboard the vessel of salvation.

- In *2001: A Space Odyssey* (1968) we are shown an intervention by aliens that has an impact on hominid evolution. The workings of the alien monolith don't resemble the *anunnaki's* intervention in our evolution, yet its importance for humankind is made clear.

- A central element in the *Planet of the Apes* movies (nine films, starting in 1968) echoes the Šumerian creation epic: a primitive primate is given enhanced abilities in the lab of a more advanced one.

- In the *Star Wars* movies (starting in 1977) humans are living *in a galaxy far, far away*, depicting what's clearly implied in the Mesopotamian epics: humanoid lines can develop independently on different planets.

- In *Meteor* (1978) a body in a cometary orbit passes through the Asteroid Belt and threatens Earth, just as Nibiru did right before the flood.

- In the world of *Star Trek* (thirteen films from 1979 through 2016, plus five TV series), the *prime directive* for the explorers is articulated from time to time. They are not to alter the destiny of any advanced species, i.e., they are not to do what the *anunnaki* did to *H. erectus*.

- The director of *Blade Runner* (1982) clearly felt that the Epic of Gilgameš was worthy of updating. (Of course, he thought of the epic as a myth, not a factual account of an actual quest by a king of Uruk.) In the retelling, humanoids crafted with genetic engineering are anguished over their short lifespan; they make a dangerous journey seeking a life-extending intervention by the powerful man responsible for their creation; they do not succeed. Neither did Gilgameš, trying to reach An.

- In *Species* (1995) DNA from an advanced alien creature is combined with our own; a humanoid being with enhanced abilities is the result … much as *H. sapiens* was made from *H. erectus* using *anunnaki* DNA.

- *The Man From Earth* (2007) explores how people react when they encounter someone whose self-healing and regenerative powers have enabled him to live for thousands of years without aging.

- In *10,000 BC* (2008) the minions of a tall *god* hold an entire society in servitude. The *god* turns out to be mortal; the enslaved humans take control of their destiny. We did the same after the *gods'* hold on us weakened and we became disillusioned about them.

7.4 The Movies

- *Splice* (2009) has parallels with the doings of Enki, Nimaḫ, and Enlil: a male-female pair of genetic engineers use their own DNA in crafting a new creature. Human-hybrid sex enrages their supervisor. This tale has many parallels with the doings of Enki, Ninmaḫ, and Enlil.

- In *Another Earth* (2011) a planet closely resembling our own enters the Solar System and transfixes humanity ... just as Nibiru used to do.

- In *Melancholia* (2011) a planet heads for a collision with our planet, just as one of Nibiru's moons did when Ki (Earth) was Tiamat.

- In *Thor* (2011) a being possessed of a powerful weapon comes to Earth. A woman opines that when others of his kind appeared ages before, people naïvely thought they were divinities. Her words describe how humans actually viewed the weapon-bearing *gods* of Mesopotamia.

- In *The Avengers* (2012), the brother of the alien in *Thor* comes to Earth and, wielding his own weapon, tells a crowd of cowering people they were born to serve ones such as he, just as humans were made to believe.

- In *Cowboys and Aliens* (2012) aliens come to Earth to extract gold, and treat humanity with great cruelty. The parallels are unmistakable.

- With *Prometheus* (2012) the director of *Blade Runner* returned again to the Epic of Gilgameš. In this movie, it is learned that tall humanoid aliens crafted us using their own DNA. In *Blade Runner*, the role of the powerful man paralleled Enki's in Šumer. In *Prometheus*, the role of the powerful man parallels Gilgameš's: he initiates an expedition to meet the makers and is accompanied by a loyal android.

- In *The Host* (2013) tiny, gentle alien life forms arrive, aiming to optimize life on Earth by entering every human body and supplanting its consciousness with their own. A woman forced to undergo the combination procedure keeps the mind of her alien companion from fully eclipsing her own, and the two engage in a complex relationship.

No Mesopotamian tablet yet unearthed speaks of an inner conflict of this sort; it is unlikely that such a text ever existed. Who would have dared articulate a struggle of minds within the new hybrid species? We surmise, though, that such a conflict was a reality in our early life and that it's still with us, a component of the human condition.

This film does more than reflect on the celestial-terrestrial merger that brought humankind into existence; it looks forward to a resolution of our divided internal state. Toward the end of *The Host*, to the amazement of representatives of both species, a way is found to allow each mind to live in awareness of the other, in harmony and love, within a human body, a discovery that brings joy to those who witness the first such event.

It's then revealed that the conflict in the film's heroine between two minds, human and alien, has been going on covertly in all humans who underwent the combination procedure. This means that every suppressed human mind has been longing for freedom but was unable make its plight known. It becomes clear that all humans can have their freedom without totally dislodging the implanted aliens, a procedure which, when attempted before, had always been fatal to both creatures.

The Host ends with humanity looking ahead to an existence enriched by the presence of an advanced consciousness living in loving symbiosis with its own, and with the alien beings looking forward to true acceptance, no longer needing to dominate. To this author this is more than a story with a happy ending. Through this movie the Collective Unconscious seems to be whispering to us:

Two different forms of consciousness can dwell in peace and love in a composite being, to the benefit of both. It can be done. Take heart. The cosmic leap involved in your diverted evolution, with two beings merged to reside within a third ... that leap can yet produce a glorious result.

---

[1] In one of the later *Superman* films, as the father of the future superhero is about to send his infant son to Earth, he says, *He will be a god to them*. Toward the end of *Wonder Woman* (2017) we learn that the title character is a demigod, offspring of the human Amazon queen and the chief of the deities.

Part Eight

Coda

Summary

Inspired by a fresh reading of humanity's oldest tales, we've journeyed to a place from which we've glimpsed a route of escape from the tragic condition of humankind. We began with a question. Looking first at civilization's horrors, then directing our gaze to the splendor of the natural world, we wondered: how could it be that the most evolved species on Earth is so destructive of itself, other life forms, and the planet ... since nature does not make mistakes of such scale? This wasn't merely a question of philosophy, but of survival, for despite all our efforts to change our ways, the mayhem continues. We've bought some time, that's all. The consensus among scientists is that the outlook is dark.

A second question logically followed. Could our evolution or our early existence have been unnaturally disrupted? We learned that they both were. Neuropsychology clarified our dilemma, revealing that our self-destructive behaviors are perpetuated by systems in the human brain that developed in three phases of evolution, each one, ironically, meant to insure our survival: the threat responses, the emotions, and the cognitive abilities. Over-activation in the three protective brain systems keeps us, respectively, in trauma, emotional imbalance, and confusion. (The process has a parallel in the immune system: when it's swamped by threats to the body, over-reacts, and produces an autoimmune condition.) But how was it that we got so traumatized, imbalanced, and perplexed in the first place?

Over a hundred years ago, archaeologists and linguists began uncovering the ultimate causes of our plight ... literally *uncovering* the vital information, for it was in the form of writings and carvings buried in the ruins of Mesopotamian cities. The accounts contained in the artifacts could have right then revealed the source of our condition, but the discoverers believed that the tales of extraterrestrial deities were the products of our ancestors' imaginations. They couldn't appreciate the true significance of the ancient texts and images.

There was at first just one man, not a recognized scholar, working alone, who viewed the tales from outside the standard frame of reference of our culture, and grasped that they weren't fictional, but basically factual ... history written in pre-scientific, poetic language, a story so startling it's no wonder it could not be taken at face value:

The Mesopotamian texts and carvings tell that we're a hybrid species, developed through genetic manipulation by a humanoid race who came here from a planet that most of the time dwells unseen in deep space ... and that they combined their DNA with that of the most advanced primate on Earth to craft a race to serve them.

The narrative assembled from the world's trove of recovered texts and images, called The Mesopotamian Tale, was read through from beginning to end and then examined in portions. We found it to be supported by scientific and scholarly evidence.

The primary thesis of *Evolution Diverted* is that The Mesopotamian Tale is compiled from sources that are historically accurate in their essentials. At this moment in time the best way to give support to the thesis is to conduct a *thought experiment* and test its utility. Accordingly, we used The Tale to untangle several puzzles that can't be solved within the limits of conventional thinking. Prime among the puzzles was the starting point of our quest, humanity's sad, precarious condition. The Tale allowed us to see how confusion about our nature and purpose resulted from the way we came into existence; how shame-based emotions were induced by the conditions of our life as slaves of our makers; and how traumatization and a fatal love of war became our lot through service in their armies.

Among the other puzzles we resolved in similar fashion were these: our too-early appearance on Earth; linguistic conundrums in the Hebrew Bible; and giant drawings on the floor of a South American desert. Next, we used The Tale to explain several aspects of human life, past and present, in a fuller manner than we've ever before been able to. These included conflict focused in Jerusalem, and the American Civil War.

Using The Mesopotamian Tale to resolve insoluble quandaries and clarify aspects of human life, we felt its credibility bolstered.

Along our way we considered related matters, including fact vs. fiction, believing vs. knowing, and issues in the world of science; four appendices invited further consideration. Nearing the book's conclusion, we addressed questions that motivated our journey:

How can acknowledging the historical accuracies within The Mesopotamian Tale empower us to ameliorate our present condition and save ourselves and our planet from the fate that's looming? Given our aberrant origin, how can we come to know ourselves and our purpose? What's to be done about the obstacles to taking The Mesopotamian Tale seriously presented by conventional religion and science?

We then addressed a few more questions that arose along our way, and finally we offered a prayer.

Bibliography

The World of the Anunnaki

Bauval, Robert & Gilbert, Adrian. *The Orion Mystery*. New York: Three Rivers Press, 1994.

Childress, David Hatcher. *Technology of the Gods*. Kempton, IL: Adventures Unlimited Press, 2000.

Childress, David Hatcher. *Ancient Technology in Peru & Bolivia*. Kempton, IL: Adventures Unlimited Press, 2012.

Christy-Vitale, Joseph. *Watermark*. NY: Paraview Pocket Books, 2004.

Collins, Andrew. *Göbekli Tepe*. Rochester, VT: Bear & Company, 2014.

Cremo, Michael A. & Thompson, Richard L. *The Hidden History of the Human Race*. Badger, CA: Bhaktivedanta Book Publishing, 1996.

Dewhurst, Richard J. *The Ancient Giants Who Ruled America*, Rochester, VT: Bear & Company, 2014.

Dunn, Christopher. *Lost Technologies of Ancient Egypt*. Rochester, VT: Bear & Company, 2010.

Hancock, Graham. *Fingerprints of the Gods*. NY: Three Rivers Press, 1995.

Hardy, Chris H. *DNA of the Gods*. Rochester, VT: Bear & Company, 2014.

Hardy, Chris H. *Wars of the Anunnaki*. Rochester, VT: Bear & Company, 2016.

Joseph, Frank, ed. *Unearthing Ancient America*. Pompton Plains, NJ: Career Books, 2009.

Kenyon, J. Douglas. *Forbidden History*. Rochester, VT: Bear & Co., 2005.

Lynn, Heather. *The Anunnaki Connection*. Newburyport, MA: New Page Books, 2020

Mertz, Henrietta. *The Mystic Symbol*. Gaithersburg, MD: Global Books, 1986.

Sitchin, Zecharia. *The 12th Planet*. NY: Avon Books, 1976.

" " *The Stairway to Heaven*. NY: Avon Books, 1980.

" " *The Wars of Gods and Men*. NY: Avon Books, 1985.

" " *The Lost Realms*. NY: Avon Books, 1990.

" " *Genesis Revisited*. NY: Avon Books, 1990.

" " *When Time Began*. NY: Avon Books, 1993.

" " *Divine Encounters*. NY: Avon Books, 1995.

" " *The Cosmic Code*. NY: Avon Books, 1998.

" " *The Lost Book of Enki*. Rochester, VT: Bear & Co., 2002.

" " *The Earth Chronicles Expeditions*. Rochester, VT: Bear & Company, 2004.

" " *The End of Days*. Rochester, VT: Bear & Company, 2007.

" " *Journeys to the Mythical Past*. Rochester, VT: Bear & Company, 2007.

" " *The Earth Chronicles Handbook*. Rochester, VT: Bear & Company, 2009.

" " *There Were Giants Upon the Earth*, Rochester, VT: Bear & Company, 2010.

Sykes, Brian. *The Seven Daughters of Eve*. NY: W.W. Norton & Co, 2001.

Tellinger, Michael. *Slave Species of the Gods*. Rochester, VT: Bear & Company, 2005.

Tellinger, Michael. *African Temples of the Anunnaki*. Rochester, VT: Bear & Company, 2009.

Temple, Robert. *The Sirius Mystery*. Rochester, VT: Destiny Books, 1998

von Däniken, Erich. *Chariots of the Gods*. NY: G. P. Putnam's Sons, 1970.

von Däniken, Erich. *Evidence of the Gods*. Prompton Plains, NJ: The Career Press, 2003.

Mesopotamian History & Art

Asher-Greve, Julia M. & Westenholz, Joan Goodnick. *Goddesses in Context*. Göttingen, Germany: Vanderhoeck & Ruprecht, 2013.

Azara, Pedro. *Cornerstone: The Birth of the City in Mesopotamia*. Barcelona: Tenov Books, 2015.

Ataç, Mehmet-Ali. *The Mythology of Kingship in Neo-Assyrian Art*. NY: Cambridge University Press, 2010.

Barnett, R. D. *Sumerian Art*. London: The British Museum, 1969.

Benzel, Kim; Graff, Susan B.; Rakic, Yelena; & Watts, Edith W. *Art of the Ancient Near East*. New York: The Metropolitan Museum of Art, 2010

Biggs, R. D., Myers, J., & Roth, M. T., eds. *Proceedings of the 51st Rencontre Assyriologique Internationale*. Chicago: The Oriental Institute, 2008.

Charpin, Dominique. *Gods, Kings, and Merchants in Old Babylonian Mesopotamia*. Leuven, Belgium: Peeters, 2015.

Chi, Jennifer Y. & Azara, Pedro, eds. *From Ancient to Modern*. Princeton: Princeton University Press, 2015.

Crawford, Harriet. *Ur*. London: Bloomsbury Publishing, 2015.

Curatola, Giovanni. *Art & Architecture of Mesopotamia*. NY: Abbeville Press, 2007.

Evans, Jean M. *The Lives of Sumerian Sculpture*. Cambridge: Cambridge University Press, 2012.

Facey, William. *Back to Earth*. Riyadh, Saudi Arabia: Al-Turath, 1997.

Frankfort, Henri. *Cylinder Seals*. Chicago: University of Chicago Press, 1939.

Frankfort, Henri. *Kingship and the Gods*. Chicago: U. of Chicago Press, 1948.

George, Andres. Trans. & Ed. *The Epic of Gilgamesh*. 2nd Ed. NY, NY: Penguin Classics, 2020.

Gunter, Ann C. *Greek Art and the Orient*. Cambridge: Cambridge University Press, 2009.

Harcourt-Smith, Simon. *Babylonian Art*. London: Ernest Benn, Ltd., 1928.

Hodder, Ian. *The Leopard's Tale*. London: Thames & Hudson Ltd., 2006.

Klengel-Brandt, Evelyn & Cholidis, N. *Die Terrakotten von Babylon im Vorderasiatischen Museum in Berlin*. Saarwellingen, Germany: Saarländische Druckerei & Verlag, 2006.

Kovacs, Maureen G. *The Epic of Gilgamesh*. Stanford: Stanford University Press, 1985.

Kramer, Samuel Noah. *History Begins at Sumer*. Philadelphia: University of Pennsylvania Press, 1956.

Malraux, André & Salles, Georges. *Sumerian Art*. London: The British Museum, 1969.

Mango, E., Marzahn, J., & Uelinger, C. *Könige am Tigris*. Zurich: Verlag Neue Zürcher Zeitung, 2008.

Margueron, Jean-Claude. *Mari*. Paris: Edition A. & J. Picard, 2004.

Mitchell, Stephen. *Gilgamesh*. NY: Free Press, 2004.

Parrot, André. *Sumer*. NY: Golden Press, 1961.

Reade, Julian. *Mesopotamia*. London: British Museum Press, 1991.

Spar, Ira, ed. *Tablets, Cones, and Bricks of the Third and Second Millennia B.C.* NY: The Metropolitan Museum of Art, 1988.

Steymans, Hans U. *Gilgamesh*. Göttingen, GE: Vandenhoeck & Ruprecht, 2009.

Suter, Claudia E. *Gudea's Temple Building*. Groningen, Netherlands: Styx Publ., 2000.

Van De Mieroop, Marc. *A History of the Ancient Near East, 3rd Edition*. Chicester, UK: John Wiley & Sons, Inc., 2016.

Wolkstein, Diane & Kramer, Samuel N. *INANNA Queen of Heaven and Earth*, NY: Harper & Row Publishers, 1983.

Wooley, C. L. *The Development of Sumerian Art*. London: Faber & Faber, Limited, 1935.

Zervos, Christian. *L'art de la Mésopotamie*. Paris, France: Editions Cahiers d'Art, 1935.

Zettler, Richard L. & Horne, Lee, eds. *Treasures from the Royal Tombs of Ur*. Seattle: Marquand Books. 1998.

World History

Berman, Sheri. *Democracy and Dictatorship in Europe*. NY: Oxford University Press, 2019

Brennan, Martin. *The Stones of Time*. Rochester, VT: Inner Traditions International, 1994

Cahill, Thomas. *Sailing the Wine-Dark Sea*. NY: Nan A. Talese, 2003.

Hapgood, Charles, H. *Maps of the Ancient Sea Kings*. Kempton, IL: Adventures Unlimited Press, 1966.

Musgrove, John, ed. *Sir Bannister Fletcher's A History of Architecture*, 19th ed. London: Butterworth, 1987.

Stearns, Peter N., ed. *The Encyclopedia of World History*, 6th ed. NY: Houghton Mifflin Company, 2001.

Velikovsky, Immanuel. *Oedipus and Akhnaton*. Garden City: Doubleday & Company, 1960.

American History

Amar, Akhil Reed. *The Words That Made Us*. NY: Basic Books, 2021

Bowen, Catherine D. *Miracle at Philadelphia*. Boston: Little, Brown & Company, 1966.

Burrows, Edwin G. & Wallace, Mike. *Gotham*. Oxford: Oxford University Press, 1999.

Fischer, David Hackett. *Washington's Crossing*. Oxford: Oxford University Press, 2004.

Goodhart, Adam. *1861*. NY: Vintage Books, 2012.

Goodwin, Doris Kearns. *Team of Rivals*. NY: Simon & Schuster, 2005.

Johnson, Paul. *A History of the American People*. NY: HarperCollins, 1997.

Manseau, Peter. *One Nation Under Gods*. NY: Little, Brown & Co., 2015.

Nevins, Alan & Commager, Henry S. *A Pocket History of the United States*. NY: Little, Brown & Co., 1942.

Packer George. *Last Best Hope*. NY: Farrar, Straus and Giroux, 2021

Perret, Geoffrey. *Ulysses S. Grant*. NY: Random House, 1997.

Strauss, W. & Howe, N. *The Fourth Turning*. NY: Broadway Books, 1997.

Woodard, Colin. *American Nations*. NY: Penguin Books, 2012.

Anthropology, Sociology, and Economics

Junger, Sebastian. *Tribe*. NY: Hachette Book Group, 2016.

Malinowski, Bronislaw. *The Sexual Life of Savages*. NY: Harcourt Brace, 1929.

Morgan, Lewis H. *Ancient Society*. Chicago: Charles H. Kerr & Co., 1907.

van der Post, Laurens. *The Heart of the Hunter*. NY: William Morrow & Company, 1961.

Psychology

Baker, Elsworth F. *Man in the Trap*. NY: The Macmillan Co., 1967.

Bekoff, Marc. *The Emotional Lives of Animals*. Novato, CA: New World Library, 2007

Catherall, Don R. *Emotional Safety*. NY: Taylor & Francis Group, 2007.

Darwin, Charles. *The Expression of the Emotions in Man and Animals*. London: D. Appleton & Company, 1872.

Demos, E. Virginia, ed. *Exploring Affect*. Cambridge: Cambridge University Press, 1995.

de Wall, Frans. *Mama's Last Hug*. NY: W. W. Norton & Co., 2019.

Everly, G. S., Jr. & Lating, J. M., eds. *Psychotraumatology*. New York: Plenum, 1995.

Goodall, Jane. *The Chimpanzees of Gombe*. Cambridge: Harvard University Press, 1986.

Goldman, Ronald. *Circumcision The Hidden Trauma*. Boston: Circumcision Resource Center, 1997.

Herman, Judith. *Trauma and Recovery*. NY: Basic Books, 1992.

Hillman, James. *A Terrible Love of War*. NY: Penguin Group, 2004.

Holinger, Paul C. *What Babies Say Before They Can Talk*. New York: Fireside, 2003.

Kelly, Vernon C. *The Art of Intimacy*. Rockland, ME: Tomkins Press, 2012.

Levine, Peter. *Waking the Tiger*. Berkeley: North Atlantic Books, 1997.

Levine, Peter. *In an Unspoken Voice*. Berkeley, CA: N. Atlantic Books, 2010.

Lynch, Brian. *Knowing Your Emotions*. Chicago: Interest Books, 2010.
Masson, Jeffrey M. & McCarthy, Susan. *When Elephants Weep*. NY: Dell Publishing. 1995

Miller, Alice. *Thou Shalt Not Be Aware*. Harrisonburg, VA: Meridian, 1984.

Miller, Alice. *Breaking Down the Wall of Silence*. NY: Dutton, 1991.

Nathanson, Donald L. *Shame and Pride*. NY: W.W. Norton, 1992.

Reddy, Michael, *Health, Happiness, and Family Constellations*. Kimberton, PA: ReddyWorks Press, 2012.

Reich, Wilhelm. *The Mass Psychology of Fascism*. NY: Orgone Institute Press, 1946.

Reich, Wilhelm. *The Function of the Orgasm*. New York: Orgone Institute Press, 1948.

Reich, Wilhelm. *Character Analysis*. NY: Orgone Institute Press, 1949.

Ross, Gina. *Beyond the Trauma Vortex*. Berkeley: No. Atlantic Books, 2003.

Shapiro, Francine. *Eye Movement Desensitization and Reprocessing*. NY: Guilford, 1995.

Scaer, Robert. *The Trauma Spectrum*. New York: W. W. Norton & Company, 2005.

Sedgwick, E. K. & Frank, A. *Shame and its Sisters*. Durham, NC: Duke University Press, 1995

Tick, Edward. *War and the Soul*. Wheaton, IL: Quest Books, 2005.

Tick, Edward. *Warrior's Return*. Boulder, CO: Sounds True, 2014.

Tomkins, S. S. & Izard, C. E. *Affect, Cognition, and Personality*. NY: Springer, 1965.

Tomkins, S. S. *Affect Theory*. in Ekman, P., Friesen, W. V., & Ellsworth, P., eds. *Emotion in the Human Face*, 2nd ed. NY: Springer Publishing Co., 1982 van der Kolk, B., McFarlane, A. C., & Weisaeth, L., eds. *Traumatic Stress*. NY: The Guilford Press, 1996.

Veblen, Thorstein. *The Theory of the Leisure Class*. NY: Oxford U. Press, 2007 (orig. publ. 1899)

de Waal, Frans. *Mama's Last Hug*. NY: W. W. Norton & Co., 2019

Religion & Philosophy

The Holy Bible / King James Version, NY: American Bible Society.

Alter, Robert. *The Hebrew Bible*. NY: W. W. Norton & Co., 2019.

Brenner, Reeve R. *While The Skies Were Falling*. USA: CafePress, 2013.

Burnet, John. *Early Greek Philosophy*. NY: Meridian Books, 1957 (First edition 1892).

Castenada, Carlos. *Journey to Ixtlan*. NY: Simon and Schuster, 1972.

Cahill, Thomas. *The Gifts of the Jews*. NY: Nan A. Talese, 1998.

Cahill, Thomas. *Desire of the Everlasting Hills*. NY: Nan A. Talese, 1999.

Chardin, Pierre Teilhard de. *Hymn of the Universe*. Paris: Eds. Seuil, 1961.

Edwin, Irwin. *The Works of Plato*. NY: Simon & Schuster, 1928

Ehrman, Bart D. *How Jesus Became God*. NY: HarperCollins, 2014.

Ehrman, Bart D. *The Triumph of Christianity*. NY: Simon & Schuster, 2018.

Frazer, James George. *The Golden Bough*. NY: The Macmillan Co., 1922.

Fynn. *Mister God, This is Anna*. NY: Holt, Rinehart and Winston, 1974.

Goodman, Felicitas D. *Where Spirits Ride the Wind*. Bloomington, IN: Indiana University, 1990.

Hamilton, Edith. *Mythology*. NY: Grosset & Dunlap, 1940.

Harner, Michael. *The Way of the Shaman*. NY: Harper & Row, 1980.

Heilbron, John L. *The Sun in the Church*. Cambridge, MA: Harvard, 1999.

Houston, Jean. *The Passion of Isis and Osiris*. NY: Random House, 1995.

Houston, Jean & Rubin, Margaret. *Manual for the Peacemaker*. Wheaton, IL: Quest Books, 1995,

Huxley, Aldous. *The Perennial Philosophy*. NY: Harper & Brothers, 1945.

James, William. *The Varieties of Religious Experience*. NY: Mentor, 1958 (originally published 1902).

Johnson, Paul. *A History of the Jews*. NY: Harper & Row Publishers, 1987.

Kamenetz, Rodger. *The Jew in the Lotus*. NY: HarperCollins, 1994.

Keeney, Bradford. *Shaking Medicine*. Rochester, VT: Destiny Books, 2007.

Keller, Werner. *The Bible as History in Pictures*. bnpublishing.com: BN Publishing, 2009.

Kornfield, Jack. *A Path With Heart*. NY: Bantam Books, 1993.

Miles, Jack. *God in the Qur'an*. NY: Alfred A. Knopf, 2018.

Mindell, Arnold. *Dreambody*, 2nd ed. Portland, OR: Lao Tse Press, 1998.

Ming-Dao, Deng. *The Wandering Taoist*. SF: Harper & Row, 1983.

Ming-Dao, Deng. *The Chronicles of Tao*. NY: HarperCollins, 1993.

Muggeridge, Malcom. *Jesus Rediscovered*. Garden City: Doubleday & Company, 1969.

Oz, Amos & Oz-Salzberger, Fania. *Jews and Words*. New Haven: Yale University Press, 2012.

Rosenberg, David. *A Literary Bible*. Berkeley, CA: Counterpoint, 2009.

Ruiz, Don Miguel. *The Four Agreements*. San Rafael, CA: Amber-Allen Publishing, 1997.

Ruiz, Don Miguel. *Prayers*. San Rafael, CA: Ambler-Allen Publishing, 2001.

Schama, Simon, *The Story of the Jews*. NY: HarperCollins Publishers, 2014.

Somé, Malidoma Patrice. *The Healing Wisdom of Africa*. NY: Tarcher/Putnam, 1998.

Stapleton, Michael. *The Illustrated Dictionary of Greek and Roman Mythology*. NY: Peter Bedrick Books, 1986.

Storm, Hyemeyohsts. *Lightningbolt*. NY: Ballantine Books, 1994.

Vanier, Jean. *Becoming Human*. Toronto, ON: Anansi Press, 1998.

Van Kampenhout, Daan. *Images of the Soul*. Heidelberg: Car-Auer-System Verlag, 1997.

Unconventional Science & Medicine

Arp, Halton. *Quasars, Redshifts and Controversies*. Berkeley, CA: Interstellar Media, 1987.

Béchamp, Antoine. *The Blood*. London: John Ouseley, Ltd., 1912.

Becker, Robert O. & Selden, Gary. *The Body Electric*. NY: Quill, 1985.

Becker, Robert O. & Marino, A. *Electromagnetism & Life*. Albany, NY: State University of New York, 1982.

Brenner, Myron D. *Bions and Cancer: A Review of Reich's Work*. The Journal of Orgonomy, V. 18, N. 2. NY: Orgonomic Publications, 1984.

Brenner, Myron D. *Orgonotic Devices in ... Infectious Conditions*. Pulse of the Planet, N. 3. Ashland, OR: Orgone Biophysical Research Lab, 1991.

Brodeur, Paul. *Currents of Death*. NY: Simon & Schuster, 1989.

Cohen, Kenneth. *The Way of Qi Gong*. NY: Ballantine Books, 1997.

Coulter, Harris L. *Homeopathic Medicine*. Washington: American Foundation for Homeopathy, 1972.

Cowan, Eliot. *Plant Spirit Medicine*. Newberg, OR: Blue Water Publ., 1995.

DeMeo, James. *Saharasia*. Ashland, OR: Orgone Biophysical Research Lab, 1998.

DeMeo, James, ed. *Heretic's Notebook*. Ashland, OR: Orgone Biophysical Research Lab, 2002.

Denniston, George C., Hodges, Frederick M., Milos, Marilyn F., eds. *Male and Female Circumcision*. NY: Kluwer Academic/Plenum Publishers, 1998.

Duesberg, Peter H. *Inventing the AIDS Virus*. Washington, DC: Regnery Publishing, 1996.

Gauquelin, Michel. *How Cosmic and Atmospheric Energies Influence Your Health*. NY: Aurora Press, 1971.

Gerber, Richard. *Vibrational Medicine*. Rochester, VT: Bear & Co., 2001.

Gofman, John W. *Radiation & Human Health*. SF, CA: Sierra Club, 1981.

Grof, S. *When the Impossible Happens*. Boulder, CO: Sounds True, 2006.

Hahneman, Samuel. *The Organon of Medicine*. Calcutta: Roysingh, 1833.

Hasted, John. *The Metal Benders*. London: Routledge & Kagan Paul, 1981.

Hume, Ethel D. *Béchamp or Pasteur?* Saffron Walden, UK: C. W. Daniel Co., 1923.

Katpchuk, Ted. *The Web That Has No Weaver*. Chicago: Contemporary Books, 2000.

Kervan, C. L. *Biological Transmutations*. Woodstock, NY: Beekman, 1966.

Kilner, W. J. *The Aura*. NY: Weiser, 1911.

Lerner, Eric J. *The Big Bang Never Happened*. NY: Vintage Books, 1991.

8.2 Bibliography

Lucas, Charles W. *The Quantization of Gravity* in *Common Sense Science*, Vol. 22, Nos. 1 & 2, Roswell, GA: Common Sense Science, 2019

Lucas, Charles W. *Response* in *Foundations of Science*, Vol. 14, No. 1. Roswell, GA: Common Sense Science, 2011.

Miller, D. C. *The Ether-Drift Experiment and the Determination of the Absolute Motion of the Earth.* in *Physical Review, Vol. 45.* College Park, MD, 1934.

Milton, R. *Alternative Science.* Rochester, VT: Park Street Press, 1994.

Mitchell, W. C. *Bye Bye Big Bang.* Carson, NV: Cosmic Sense Books, 2002.

Motz, Julie. *Hands of Life.* NY: Bantam Books, 2000.

Nordenström, Björn E. W. *Biologically Closed Electric Circuits.* Stockholm: Nordic Medical Publications, 1983.

Ostrander, Sheila & Schroeder, Lynn. *Psychic Discoveries Behind the Iron Curtain.* Englewood Cliffs, NJ: Bantam, 1970.

Ott, J. N. *Light, Radiation, & You.* Old Greenwich, CT: Devin-Adair, 1982.

Piccardi, Giorgia. *The Chemical Basis of Medical Climatology.* Springfield, IL: Charles C. Thomas, 1962.

Reich, Wilhelm. *The Cancer Biopathy.* NY: Orgone Institute Press, 1948.

> " "   *Ether, God and Devil.* Rangeley, ME: Orgone Institute Press, 1949.

> " "   *Cosmic Superimposition.* Rangeley, ME: Orgone Institute Press, 1951.

> " "   *Selected Writings.* NY: Farrar, Straus and Cudahy, 1942.

> " "   *The Bion Experiments.* NY: Farrar Straus Giroux, 1939.

Sheldrake, Rupert. *A New Science of Life.* London: Blond & Briggs, 1981.

Sternglass, Ernest J. *Low-Level Radiation.* NY: Ballantine Books, 1972.

Velikovsky, Immanuel. *Worlds in Collision*. Garden City, NY: Doubleday & Company, 1950.

Villoldo, Alberto. *Shaman, Healer, Sage*. NY: Harmony Books, 2000.

von Pohl, Gustav Freiherr. *Earth Currents*. Munich: Jos. C. Hubers Verlag, 1932.

von Reichenbach, Karl. *Letters on Od and Magnetism*. London: Hutchinson & Company, 1926.

Wilcock, David. *The Source Field Investigations*. NY: Plume, 2011.

Author's Parting Note

Far along in the gestation of this book I had a dream:

I'm on a park bench talking with a friend who is both a physicist and an observant Jew. He asks what my project is about. I hesitate a moment, then say that its message is, God is real.

Given the primary thesis of this work, you'd think I'd have said, *The gods were real*. The dream revealed a deeper purpose for the book. I hadn't realized how much of the book was about the reality of the One.

I go on to say that the intelligent continuum of the universe -the One- as it manifests in matter and energy, gives form and movement to all that exists and occurs; that when the extraterrestrials who crafted us said they were divinities, they interfered with our innate awareness of the invisible Source of everything; and that as a result western civilization developed a pair of misperceptions. Over time, many people came to think of the un-manifest One as a mystical, supernatural, yet all-powerful Entity, and many others came to think of that which is manifest, that is, all natural form and process, as mechanistic and devoid of Spirit.

Those ideas had long been important to me, though my dream-speech couldn't have been quite so articulate. I'd spoken passionately to my friend, a man devoted to conventional religion and conventional science, the two orthodoxies that are caught in the two misperceptions, mystical and mechanistic.

The exchange was so intense that we both became tearful.

A few days after I had the dream, as a locksmith was leaving my house, our conversation turned surprisingly theological ... and his parting words startled me. They were the ones I'd spoken in my dream, *God is real*. I knew immediately I needed to tell you about the dream, and about the connection between the idea *God is real* and the mission of this book.

As the project progressed from one surprising-to-me idea to the next, and as I was mysteriously led from one helpful book, article, or person to the next, I sensed that the book was writing itself, coming through me more than from me. This seemed particularly true whenever I started to put into words an idea that seemed worthy of a paragraph or two, and watched the idea grow to fill several pages.

I realized that the seemingly erratic sequence of occupations and close relationships characterizing the course of my life had prepared me for this assignment. I felt more strongly than ever that my existence is embraced within the One, and that what had seemed like my choices over the years had actually been personal responses to divine currents. Writing the book had deepened my understanding of my existence.

These realizations, in turn, have enhanced my awareness of what it will take to escape the trap of the human condition. If we are to avoid the destruction we're facing, the necessary transformations are huge, involving fortitude and forbearance in a long struggle. I concluded that we'll be able to maintain the requisite strength only if enough of us have full awareness of the One, that which flows within us, the Light inside and out, manifest in everything that exists, and that we subjectively experience as Love.

Every human being who's been blessed to learn that we are each of us *one within the One* has an opportunity to be free of the most insidious of the holds on us that the *lofty ones* achieved when they proclaimed, *we are your gods* ... our enthrallment with the illusion of a personified divine being ruling the Universe and engaged with our lives. The One isn't a being. Source doesn't have a personality. Those who achieve freedom from that misconception will be among the most influential leaders in our struggle to escape from a potentially fatal entrapment.

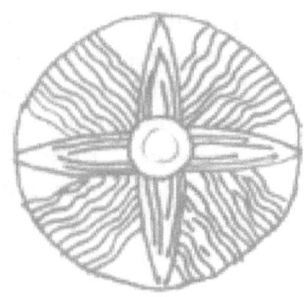

www.ingramcontent.com/pod-product-compliance
Lightning Source LLC
Chambersburg PA
CBHW021352290426
44108CB00010B/210